CW01312185

M. Podworniak
DALEKA DOROHA

A LONG ROAD

Michael Podworniak
Daleka Doroha

M. Podworniak
Warsaw 1944

◆ FriesenPress

One Printers Way
Altona, MB R0G 0B0
Canada

www.friesenpress.com

Copyright © 2023 by Michael Podworniak
First Edition — 2023

All rights reserved.

No part of this publication may be reproduced in any form, or by any means, electronic or mechanical, including photocopying, recording, or any information browsing, storage, or retrieval system, without permission in writing from FriesenPress.

ISBN
978-1-03-919620-9 (Hardcover)
978-1-03-919619-3 (Paperback)
978-1-03-919621-6 (eBook)

1. BIOGRAPHY & AUTOBIOGRAPHY, PERSONAL MEMOIRS

Distributed to the trade by The Ingram Book Company

Michael Podworniak

DALEKA DOROHA
(A LONG ROAD)

Translated from Ukrainian
by Nick Melnyk

MEMOIR

Published by
Doroha Prawdy
Winnipeg - 2023 - Kingston

NOTE FROM THE TRANSLATOR

It has been such an honour to translate Michael Podworniak's book, *Daleka Doroha*. I have had the privilege of knowing M. Podworniak personally and as I read his book, I could again hear his voice and remembered the times when he would preach in church or at some conference.

Michael Podworniak wrote the way he spoke. In my translation I wanted to preserve his style, his character, his voice and some of the expressions that he would often use. When trying to emphasize a point he would often repeat the same word; for example, "the moon rose *high-high* in the sky". His writing is filled with many vivid descriptions; the reader can also experience the colours, sounds and smells that the author experienced. I have tried to translate the text exactly as he wrote it, so that as one reads the words, they can also hear the author who is telling the story. Some expressions were left as they were written in the original languages; their equivalent in English is given in a footnote.

Having researched the various references to historical places and people in the book, I have also added footnotes to the text in order to provide some background to the narrative. Music was an important part of this story. There are many references to songs in the book. I have kept the exact words that the author recorded, usually transliterated into English. Almost each one of these melodies can be found on the internet or have been published in a songbook, especially in *Ridna Pisnya*, published by S. Bychkowski in 1948.

In the **Foreward**, the writer states "Many of us travelled that same road with the author, we had experienced many of the things on that road, but almost two decades since then, much of what we had lived through has been forgotten and erased forever from our memory. But now, with the memoirs of M. Podworniak before us, we can experience again and again in our heart and soul what we had experienced in the past." When the

Ukrainian book was first published in 1963, there were still many readers who could remember many of the events, which they had also experienced personally, but now, in 2023, the majority of them have passed away. In speaking to the next generation, I realized that many of them did not know very much about what their parents or grandparents had to endure. Many were unable to read for themselves what had been written in various Ukrainian books and magazines about those times. One of my goals in translating this book was so that the next generation would become aware and share in these same experiences.

In one of the chapters, M. Podworniak wrote, "Perhaps it is not good to write much about myself…" The book describes the journey of not only the author, but also of more than one hundred believers who left Warsaw with him to go to Germany, as well as several hundred others who were added to that group because of the faithful ministry of the refugees in Germany who shared the Gospel with unbelievers in the camps. Many of them were converted to the Lord and baptized which resulted in hundreds being added to the church. When the war ended most of the refugees eventually emigrated to Canada, USA, South America or Australia and began a new life across the ocean.

Many of those who came to the new land joined an Evangelical congregation where they continued to worship and serve the Lord, raising their families in the faith that sustained them throughout their life. Many of their names are included in the book, but the majority of them are not named.

Therefore I would like to dedicate this translation to the hundreds of children and grandchildren of those parents and grandparents who also traveled a long road, enduring the horrors of the war in Europe and eventually settling in a land of peace and freedom.

Winnipeg, June 2023

Nick Melnyk
Translator

FOREWARD

Our volume of memoiristic evangelical literature is not very large and therefore we sincerely welcome the memoirs of Michael Podworniak, which he gave to our fellowship under the title, *Daleka Doroha*. Many of us travelled that same road with the author, we had experienced many of the things on that road, but almost two decades since then, much of what we had lived through has been forgotten and erased forever from our memory. But now, with the memoirs of M. Podworniak before us, we can experience again and again in our heart and soul what we had experienced in the past. Not only do we see in our imagination the green hills of Westphalia, but we can also hear the noise of the airplanes, cannons, heavy gunfire, and the falling bombs. And beyond all that horror we can see the dawning of a new morning, we can see the freedom we dreamed about; we can experience again those unforgettable moments of our Christian fellowship, those blessings from God which all of us, recent refugees, lived through.

Michael Podworniak's memoirs are written in an interesting manner; the author inserted much of his heart into his writing and therefore the reader will be able to read it with the same heartfelt feelings. In his memoirs *Daleka Doroha* the author has painted in bright colours his personal experiences, his observations, his pain and his joys—all that which he experienced in a foreign land. In 336[1] pages of his interesting book he truly described his long road. And in reading these memoirs, may of us can see our completed journey, our own difficult road. However, the most important thing about remembering the road that we have travelled is that we can again sense how gracious God has been to us.

We trust that future historians, who someday will be writing the history of the Ukrainian Evangelical-Baptist movement outside the borders of

---

[1] The was the number of pages in the original Ukrainian book

Ukraine, will appropriately value M. Podworniak's mémoire and will be able to find much material for their theme. This is indeed the importance of the memoir, *Daleka Doroha*.

It is essential to sincerely thank the author, who in spite of all his other responsibilities was able to find the time to share with his readers all that he had experienced. A sincere thank-you to brother and sister O. and L. Kurka from Saskatoon for their financial help in printing this book.

The Christian Publishers

Doroha Prawdy
1963

INTRODUCTION

Eighteen years have passed since the end of the Second World. During those years many memoirs have been added to Ukrainian literature by different authors who wrote about the horrors of war as well as the life of our people in the camps during the war in Western Europe, especially in Germany. I carefully read all of these memoirs; I carefully searched through them to find whether someone would say a good or bad word about Ukrainian Protestants, but unfortunately I was unable to find anything. The authors of all those memoirs were mainly Ukrainian Greek-Catholics, who in general, if they did not have something bad to say about us, they would not say anything good either. This has created the impression in many that we, Evangelical Christians, were not even there among the refugees. But this is not the case; we had formed a very large group, which was very lively and energetic. The members of our Evangelical Baptist family were scattered among all the camps of Western Germany, we had our printed publications, we had our Ukrainian Missionary Choir which travelled all over Western Germany, and many of our preachers were able to break through into every refugee camp with the message of the gospel. And all this great work would not have gone unnoticed within the refugee community.

I was an active participant in all this work to some extent, or I was able to observe it with my own eyes or experience it in my heart. So as not to forget all that had happened I have long desired to write it down on paper, because that which has been recorded in a book will never be lost. In my memoirs I am writing only those things, which I have experienced, endured and saw; therefore, my recollections are not based on any kind of historical research, but are completely subjective.

Our life and ministry in Germany was interesting and commendable and it should all be recorded for posterity, because that kind of time period happens once in a century. If we could have written everything about each refugee camp, about each of our congregations or groups, each of our postwar conferences and various celebrations, then this would have been an interesting historical book; unfortunately, our believers dispersed throughout the world, became absorbed in material things and forgot about everything else.

By the will of God I travelled a long and difficult road, from my native land all the way to Germany. I endured and suffered a great deal on that road but I sincerely thank God for it. In the turbulence of the events of the war I learned to love the Lord more; many times I was convinced that without His will nothing ever happens in the life of a person. For that reason I am sharing my experiences with you, dear reader. If you have the patience and the desire, then come with me along that road. And when you come to the final page of this book, then you can make your comments.

During the several years that I was in Germany I wrote in my personal journal without the slightest idea that I would ever use it to write anything. There were still several entries remaining in it but the majority was lost along the long road. Furthermore, not everything remained in my memory and therefore I recorded in my memoirs only a portion of what I experienced, only that which was imprinted in my soul.

At this point I would like to sincerely thank all those friends who sent me photographs for my memoir from our life as refugees, thank you to those who reminded me about many things, and those who gave me their advice. I would especially like to thank my publisher, *Doroha Prawdy* for publishing these memoirs.

Winnipeg, January 1963

The Author

HALYCHYNA

At the end of March of 1944, I crossed the Halychyna border, which at that time belonged to the so-called General Governorate for the occupied Polish region. I spent that night at a farm in Volyn and in the morning my gracious host showed me around his farm and then pointing in the direction of Halychyna said:

"You can continue following those bushes and when you reach the first curve in the road, that will be the border. There is nothing to be afraid of because the Germans are no longer as vigilant in patrolling this border as before. It is no longer important to them."

I walked on. It was a spring day. I remember that larks were singing very loudly on that morning. The sun had just risen. Flocks of larks circled above the fields, then swooping down among the farm buildings, they rose again like a grey cloud above the tall-uncut grass. The larks were singing, the ravens were singing, all the fields were singing, but my soul was sad and crying. I walked alone, broken. I had left my native home and set out into a distant foreign land without anything except an old torn sheepskin coat, a pair of half-torn leather boots, without a single coin in my pocket or any documents. Yesterday I had escaped from the Germans with only my life and now I was walking. I didn't know where I was going or what I was hoping to find. The long and difficult road stretched out before me.

The road crossed a field, which was bordered by bushes glistening with dew in the morning sunshine. I started walking down the road when I saw in the distance a horse-drawn wagon approaching me. I knew that this could be a German border patrol, so I got off the road and went into the field where there were many piles of manure that had been exposed from beneath the melting snow. I began to walk among the piles, occasionally poking a pile with a pole, pretending that this was my field and I was the owner who merely came to investigate whether is was time to spread the manure in preparation for seeding.

The wagon came alongside the field and I could see that this certainly was a German patrol. Two soldiers in grey uniforms were sitting behind the driver; they were holding rifles and were having a lively conversation with each other about some topic and did not even glance in my direction.

The wagon disappeared over a small hill in the distance and I immediately began to run to get across the border. I crossed a valley; I passed a farmyard and came to a wide road, which went from Brody to Pidkamin. There was no sign of any traffic on the road and it was clear that nobody had passed here for several days. Beside the road, on a mound covered with dry grass, stood a stone cross. It was covered with moss under which there was some hardly recognizable Roman letters chiseled into the stone. I climbed up onto the mound and as I stood by the cross I looked back for the first time in the direction from which I had come. I saw the grey fog beyond which was my beloved Volyn. I could see the outlines of farms, villages, fields, hills and valleys and on the horizon I could see the golden domes of Pochayiv Lavra[2] glistening in the morning sun. Yesterday, I was still there in those beloved villages. I was in Pochayiv standing in the galleries of the cathedral and from there I could see the tops of the tress and the buildings of my village. I had conversed with a friendly elderly monk for the last time and then I fled through Lidykhiv and several other villages.

Deeply troubled and deep in thought, I sat down beneath the cross and put my head between my knees. Until this moment, my native land had never seemed so precious to me. I looked ahead, but my heart was splintering into tiny pieces. I remembered my youth, which I had spent in these villages, which I was now leaving; I remembered Pochayiv to which, as a child, I used to walk with my mother, taking small steps trying to keep up with her, as we walked to the cathedral. I remembered Staryi Tarazh, which was close to Pochayiv and where I was baptized for my faith. I remembered Roztoky, Komarivka, Kolosova, Ridkodub, Baranne, -- and the pain in my soul increased. It seemed that Volyn was reaching out her arms to me. She was calling out to me with a motherly voice to return to her, but a different,

---

2 Holy Dormiton Pochayiv Lavra, a monastery in Pochayiv, Ukraine

terrible reality, which was approaching Volyn and was also driving me away into a distant foreign world.

The story of my past childhood and all the unfulfilled dreams of my youth replayed itself before my eyes. How many times had I stood inside the Pochayiv Lavra, squinting with my childish eyes trying to make out the faces of the ancient icons and fervently praying that they would help me enter the monastery and become a monk. Not knowing how to pray with my own words, I repeated the Lord's Prayer countless times, "*Otche Nash, Bohorodytse Divo, Viruyu*"[3]. I was convinced that those icons, by themselves, would be able to sort out the prayers of a sincere child pleading before them. Eventually my desire was fulfilled and mother gave in to my begging and allowed me to enter the monastery.

One warm day my mother took me to the monastery, but she did not go alone. We were accompanied by my uncle, because he was a learned person and my mother told me that he would be able to talk much better than she could with the abbot. We stood in a long corridor, which had a musty odour and waited to be called into the abbot's cell. My heart was trembling from the excessive excitement and I was hoping that our waiting would go on all day because I was uncertain how I would stand before the abbot. What would I say to him?

The door suddenly opened and we were asked to come into the cell. Behind a small table, piled high with books, stood the abbot; a tall dark monk with a long beard and a friendly smiling face.

"Ask for a blessing," whispered my uncle into my ear, but, as I stood before the abbot, I did not know how to ask for a blessing. My good mother came to my aid. She led me to the table and said, "Kiss the father's hand."

I did what she said, and she herself was somewhat embarrassed by my lack of a proper upbringing. However, the abbot with his gentle smile, quickly understood this uncertainty and patted me on the head and asked:

"Can you read Slavonic?"

"I can, Father."

"Do you attend church?"

"I do," I replied, and uncle added: "He even began singing in the choir."

---

[3] "Our Father", "Hail Mary, Mother of God", "I Believe" (Confession of Faith)

The abbot called a second man into the room. He was a tall, thin man who was not dressed in monk's clothing, but wore regular civilian clothing. This man brought a violin with him. He played a few notes and instructed me to sing the notes he played. I tried to sing the notes but I began to cough and mixed up the notes. He played another very *high-high* tone and I felt that my voice would tear like a thread.

We were told to go out into the corridor and after a short time we were invited back. The kind abbot placed his hand on my head and said to my mother:

"We are accepting your son into the monastery. He is well suited to serve God. You may bring him at the next Feast of the Assumption of the Blessed Virgin Mary."

Following the Ikva River we returned home. The fields around us were in bloom, quails were singing. My soul was singing together with all of nature. My mother, however, was wiping her eyes so that I would not see her tears while holding me tightly by the hand because the path we were following came close to the riverbank. Later, when we sat down to have a midday meal, she gave me a small piece of black bread, some sour milk, and a pickle and said, "My child, you will not be with me any longer." She began to cry. She hugged me to her chest and I could feel her hot tears falling on my face.

Before Assumption Day, I attended the first evangelical service that was ever held in our village. There I found a new way of life, I found Christ as my personal Saviour and He made me a very blessed person. I spent my youthful days with Him and I am still walking with Him on this long, unknown road; therefore, there isn't anything for me to be worried about.

Several German airplanes appeared in the blue sky above me; they seemed to be flying towards Pochayiv. Above Radyvyliv I could hear the continuous, ominous sound of gunfire. I knew that the German front was located at the Ikva River and that my Volyn was now flowing with blood and suffering complete destruction. Some unknown force was tugging at me, calling me to return. In my heart I was anticipating a lengthy wandering in a foreign world, but my heart was telling me that even in one's own country it was easy to die.

I stood up, wiped my eyes and returned to a nearby village in Halychyna. I soon arrived at the village and going to the first house, which was surrounded by a wicker fence, I knocked at the door. There was only the homeowner inside the house. He was sitting beside a sewing table, which was covered with various old pieces of leather and was mending a pair of boots.

"*Slava Isusu Christu,*"[4] I greeted him

"*Naviki Slava,*"[5] the homeowner replied without even glancing towards the door.

I didn't know what to do next, but the man, after glancing in my direction and seeing a stranger, angrily asked, "What do you want?"

"I wanted to ask you if you would permit me to sit and rest awhile in your home and try to determine what would be the best way to cross over back to Volyn."

"It is now possible to cross wherever you want because the Germans are not guarding the border as they had before," he replied. "Where are you from?"

"I am from Volyn. This morning I crossed into Halychyna and now my village is on the other side of the front. I was thinking of going to Lviv and from there perhaps going even farther but now I have decided to return back home. Whatever happens will happen, but my own home is never an enemy. If you are able, could you direct me to the best road so that I would avoid falling into German hands."

"If you are from Volyn, then I would ask you to please leave my house because I do not want any trouble," said the visibly frightened homeowner, lowering his hand in which he was holding the thread for mending boots. "There is a German army in our village now who have given orders not to accept anyone from Volyn. You already know what is happening in Volyn ... I don't want any trouble. The Germans have said that they will shoot anyone found hiding someone from Volyn in their house. I would advise you not to continue into the village because if you do you will be immediately captured."

---

4   Glory to Jesus Christ
5   Forever glory

"*Vuyko*[6], Can you advise me what I should do? Please help me." I begged.

The homeowner thought for a moment and then got up from his table, took off his apron and said, "If you wish, you can go and stay in the stable and later I will come to you. If it should happen that the Germans come I will tell them that I never saw you before; that you crawled into the stables on your own."

He led me across the yard and let me into the stable. I crawled up onto a pile of straw and sat down. The sun was shining through the cracks in the wall but it was cold inside the stable and I could feel myself getting cold. I made an opening in the straw with my feet and crawled inside. Somewhere deep underneath the straw I could hear the squeaking of mice and in the rafters above sparrows were chirping. I felt myself getting warm inside the straw and soon fell asleep.

Suddenly I heard, as if in a dream, a voice calling to me, "Hey, where are you? Come down here."

I crawled out from under my covering and shook off the straw, which was sticking to my clothing. Inside the stable stood a young man.

"Do you want to go to Volyn?" he asked me.

"Yes, I would like that, but right now I don't know what to do," I replied, not knowing whom I was addressing and afraid of trusting every stranger. "Yesterday I escaped from the Germans to this place. I was thinking of going farther west but perhaps it would be better if I just returned home. Who knows? After all, where can one hide from their fate; from that which is bound to happen?"

"Why would you want to return to that hell? Do you know what is happening there? People are using every possible road to escape from there. Some are making it to Halychyna. It is more peaceful there. So if you want to come with me to my village, from there you can eventually get to Lviv, and once there it will be clear what you must do. Why are you going into that inferno? You only have to go outside the village and you will begin to see what is happening in Volyn. There are fires everywhere. The German front is located there and ahead of the front there have been new directives. There are rumours that the Bolsheviks are already in Krem'yanka."

---

6   Uncle

I could feel a heavy weight falling on my heart. My beloved Volyn was on fire.

We went out into the farmyard, closing the door behind us. We proceeded through a gate into the orchard and crawled over a low fence into a field, then followed a hedge growing at the edge of the field. I followed the unknown young man who was leading the way. Beyond the village the field began to descend downward and from the top I was able to look out and see my Volyn for the last time. It was smiling at me underneath a blue spring sky. I could feel its breath upon my face, smell the fragrance of the black soil and hear the humming of bees. The rooftops of the Pochayiv Cathedral still glistened in the sun, but after a short time it disappeared from view. There were signs of destruction on both sides of Pochayiv; black smoke was rising above the treetops and spreading out into the sky. I was thinking that similar destruction had also occurred in Komarivsti and Roztoky. There were so many good and close acquaintances living there, fellow believers. Where are they now? Were they able to escape in time?

With a weight as heavy as a boulder on my heart, with my head bowed low and many dark thoughts, I walked down the hill. Each step moved me farther and farther away from the land of my birth. Each step pierced my soul with a new wound, which in later days would continue to fester and refuse to heal.

At around two o'clock that afternoon we arrived at a large Galician town. Along the way I discovered from my new acquaintance that he had been staying at a relative's home, who, because he was afraid of the Germans, had sent me to the stable to keep me out of sight. I further discovered from him that everywhere in the villages of Halychyna there were many Germans, as well as various rebels. To continue travelling to Lviv through the small villages without any documents was risky. It was best to keep to the main road because there, if the Germans caught one, the worst that could happen was to be placed on some transport and taken to Germany to work. The truth was that I did not have a single document on me, not a single piece of paper except an old Polish *Dowod Osobisty*[7], which at that time did not have any significance. I carried nothing in my hands except a walking stick, which helped me across the frozen fields and meadows.

---

7   Personal Identification

We arrived at a village where we spent the night and the next day I ventured out alone on the long road to Lviv. My young acquaintance happily accompanied me as far as the edge of the village and there he showed me a path through a field which he said I could follow to get to the main road which led from Brody to Lviv. The weather outside was beautiful, truly a Galician spring in its fullness. Groups of white clouds were sailing against a blue sky among which squadrons of German airplanes were continuously flying to the west and then returning.

My acquaintance bid me farewell and returned to the village. I found myself all alone again with my troubled thoughts, sensing fear and uncertainty about my future. If only I had taken some kind of identification for myself, then my fears would not be so intense. But now, if the Germans were to capture me, they would consider me a spy, and if they discovered that I was from Volyn, that would be the end of me.

Not far from where I was standing was the main road going to Brody. There were German military vehicles travelling along this road, cars and motorcycles were speeding by in both directions. I realized that this was the way that I needed to go; I knew I had to surrender myself to a terrible fate.

I walked off the road and descended into a small gully and there beside a tree I fell on my knees. Although a bright sun was shining in the sky, larks were singing around me and new flowers were beginning to bloom, a dark and terrible night had enveloped my soul. After several moments, as I fervently prayed and asked God for help, I felt a faint glimmer of God's grace beginning to shine through into my dark night. I got up from my knees, straightened up and looked down the road through tearful eyes. The blue sky smiled at me and I could sense within my soul as if a tender and gentle voice was saying, "Do not be afraid, go!"

When I remembered all that I had to endure in Volyn and those frightful years of the war, and when I counted the number of times that God rescued me from death, I felt ashamed by my lack of faith. If God is truly with me, then why should I be afraid? If He helped me yesterday to survive a hail of bullets and escape from the hands of the Germans, then, today, why do I have so little faith that He will continue to help me in the days ahead?

I gained new strength and courage and without any hesitation stepped onto the road. A German soldier on a motorcycle sped by in front of me, but he did not even turn towards me. He was followed by a second and a third and from behind a small incline a large German tank emerged which likewise passed by me, hurrying on to Brody.

The trees growing along the road did not have any leaves yet; they stood there, sad and resigned, as if they too could sense their fate. Not far from the road, underneath some trees, there were patches of trampled, uncut grass. I recalled that in 1939, before the beginning of the war, I had travelled this same way and rested under the shadow of the widespread trees. I remember drinking some clean cold water there before hurrying to Radyvyliv to attend services as evening approached. Those times were completely different from today, a different world and a different road. Back then it was straight and smooth, while today the road was beat up by tanks and other heavy vehicles. But it was not only this road on which I travelled to Zolochiv that had been damaged but also all of Halychyna, and the whole world was deeply ruined and deeply scarred. It seemed that today there wasn't anybody anywhere with a smiling face, only German soldiers in terrifying green armoured-vehicles and heavy tanks.

Just before I reached Yasinov, I could see many tanks coming towards me. They were all muddy and made a loud noise as they came along the rutted road. In every tank I could see the fierce faces of soldiers, which were just as dark as the tanks and as rough as the land. I walked far away from the road and leaned on my stick. I didn't even dare look in the direction of the road in order not to draw attention to myself. Suddenly a tank stopped, a soldier's head appeared and I heard a voice.

"Hey friend, is the road this bad all the way to Brody?"

I was completely dumbfounded with awe. The German soldier was speaking in clear Ukrainian.

"It's the same, and in places it is even worse," I replied.

"Do you want to smoke?" he asked.

"No thank-you, I don't smoke," I answered.

The tank continued down the road.

I stood and followed it with my eyes and wondered who this young man was who had spoken to me in my language. It was only when I arrived in Zolochiv that I learned that this group was a Ukrainian Division named "Halychyna", which was headed to Brody,

Soon I arrived in Yasinov. On both sides of the long main street there were straw-thatched cottages. Surrounded by a fence, the cottages stretched out in a long line until they were just dark specks in the distance. I knew that in Yasinov there was a fine Baptist congregation, of which I knew several members, but was it worthwhile now to begin to search for them? The yards were filled with German war-wagons; horses were tied to the fences, eating hay. The street was filled with military vehicles. Soldiers were walking among them but I could no longer hear any Ukrainian voices. The road here was all broken up and groups of prisoners, men and women, were using shovels and wheelbarrows to spread fresh dirt and stones to fill the ruts. Above them a German military person dressed in a grey uniform was standing holding a large stick. He turned and shouted something in German and then grabbed a woman by the shoulder. He had some type of badge on his chest and a black swastika on his left sleeve, the sign of the German wartime authority.

Passing the group of workers I could hear a loud German voice and I turned around to look. One soldier had rushed at a villager and threatened to kick him with his foot, but the worker had jumped aside, his face pale and frightened. I hastened my pace; my only desire was to get out of Yasinov as quickly as possible. Without a single document in my possession it was dangerous to begin knocking on doors to try to find the other believers. It would be better to continue on my way and depend on the will of God. That is what I did. I walked outside the village and continued farther down the road.

Soon a horse-drawn wagon caught up to me in which there were two people. They were seated on bags of grain and it appeared that they were going to a flourmill. After walking for such a long time my legs were beginning to hurt and so I asked these strangers if they would give me a ride. They agreed and I jumped up onto the wagon and sat down at the very back, on a sack of grain. They never asked me where I was going and I did not ask them where they were going. I learned from them that every village along the road was full of German soldiers. Farther down, the villages were filled with Ukrainian resistance forces that came in a large unified force from Volyn.

Near the road grew a sparse forest of young trees, by the forest was a stream of water over which there was a wooden bridge. We could see from a distance that there was a German military policeman standing on the bridge. My heart began to beat with fear. The policeman raised his hand, motioned for us to stop, and approached the wagon. He pushed aside the bags of grain, looked underneath the wagon and then motioned with his hand to his pocket. The wagon driver brought out some type of document. The policemen looked at it and motioned with his head towards the next passenger. The next person sitting beside me also took out his identification. I dug deep into my pockets and began looking for my Polish *Dowoda Osobistego*. I am not sure how it would have resolved my situation if I were to present to the policeman my pre-war document which now had no significance. To my good fortune, at that moment a military vehicle came up behind us and the policeman waved us on so that we would not obstruct the road. I began to breathe more easily and once more I was convinced that God was with me on my journey.

The sun was already past noon. I was very tired and hungry after walking for nearly the whole day. Several times I tried stopping at a farm to ask for bread but I didn't have enough courage. Eventually I overcame my fears and walked onto a property near the road where a wealthy landowner lived. There was a young girl outside, busy doing something. Immediately I felt embarrassed and asked:

"How many kilometers is it still to Zolochiv?"

"Maybe eight or nine," she replied with a pleasant smile. I was certain that she had not figured out that I had come onto her property for the purpose of asking for bread.

"That is still a long way to walk," I said sadly and turned towards the gate.

She did not have the insight to bring me some bread, and I did not have the courage to ask; therefore, still hungry, I continued walking down the road. As I walked, the world appeared to have a yellowish tint before my eyes and I had a wilting, gnawing feeling beneath my heart.

Soon I came to another wealthy home beside the road. "What if I went in here and asked for bread?" I thought to myself. "If they give me some, that would be good, and if they do not give me any I will go farther. Nobody knows me here anyway."

There were only two young people in the house who appeared to be the owners. On a bench beside the wall were some glistening, freshly baked loaves of bread right out of the oven. The aroma of freshly baked bread filled the house and I have never experienced such a wonderful aroma in my entire life. Being hungry and tired, I had firmly resolved while I was still outside to enter and ask for bread. But now as I stood inside the house, my courage left me. I had never in my life asked for food before and now I did not know how to utter a single word. The owner saw my frustration and rescued me.

"Did you want anything?" he asked.

"I was going to ask for some water and to ask how far it is to Zolochiv", I replied.

The man walked into the kitchen and soon returned with some water.

"It is nine kilometers from here to Zolochiv," he said, watching me as I reluctantly drank the water. "You should be able to get there before it gets dark."

He also did not conclude to offer me even a small piece of bread and again I did not have the courage to ask.

Again the difficult road loomed before me and again I met large tanks going in both directions. Nine more difficult kilometers stretched out before me. As I walked the sun also moved. It travelled across the blue sky; I walked on Galician soil. Although we travelled for different reasons, our goal was the same ... to keep moving to the west.

Towards evening I could see the village of Zolochiv in the valley ahead. I did not know anyone there but I had heard that there were believers in Zolochiv, either Baptists or Pentecostals. There was only one problem remaining, how was I to find them?

I sat down on a dry knoll to rest for a while. Below me in a valley was a town, shrouded by an evening spring mist. Looking at this town, unconsciously I began thinking of those years when after we had become a Polish nation, there was no salt in our villages. In those days people had to go to Halychyna to acquire salt. Some went to Ternopyl and some went to Zolochiv. My dear mother also went. Perhaps, she had walked the same road that I was on; perhaps she even rested at the exact spot where I was resting now, hungry and tired. She would arrive at home with a bag of salt on her back. She would walk barefooted for tens of kilometers. When she would return home she could barely sit down on the old wooden bench and would weep from her weariness. We children would come to her and ask, "Do your feet hurt, mother? Is it far to Zolochiv? Is there much salt there?"

"It is far, my children, very far," mother said, wiping the tears from her eyes. "If it was not for you I would not go any longer. I must feed you." She would hug us, pressing us close to her, kissing us. She forgot about her tiredness. The next day people would come, bringing flour, grain, or some money to trade for salt. They would weigh it on a scale, which was suspended on a long rope attached to a beam in the house. My smaller brothers and I would observe all this carefully from the top of the stove. Our curious eyes watched as the balance swung back and forth.

This painful image of my childhood appeared clearly before my eyes. How long it has been since all this happened. Images of the hard, dusty stove, the blackened walls of our poor house, the sad face of my mother. It was almost as if I was seeing it all again and once more I could experience the pain. Above, in the heavy ceiling beams, there appeared some large letters and beside them were blackened crosses, which were burnt into the wood with a candle every Easter Friday. The number of burnt crosses represented the age of the house. There was an entire row of them extending to the corner where there hung a smoky bottle of holy water from Epiphany and a bundle of dry weeds which was hanging there since the Feast of the Transfiguration. The holy water was kept because it was needed to bless the house on Christmas Eve. Sometimes a member of the family became sick and the holy water was again necessary. The weeds from the Feast of Transfiguration were kept in the event that if somebody died, it was necessary to place the weeds beneath the head of the person in the coffin.

"Dear mother, where are you now?"

I got to my feet and leaned on my walking stick. My boots had become very heavy as if they were made of lead. My head was splitting from severe pain and heavy thoughts.

Near the town there were some children who were watching cows grazing in the pasture. I approached them.

"Boys, do you know where there are Baptists living in this town?" I asked. The young herders looked at each other and I could see that they did not understand what I said.

"These are the kind of people who do not go to church, who do not cross themselves with their hand," I said again.

"Oh, now I know", replied one of the boys. "There are some Adventists in that house over there which you can see by the creek. Can you see it? By the willows..."

I thanked the herders and went to a small, solitary house that was standing alone in the hay meadows close to the stream. I knew that in Halychyna believers were sometimes called Adventists, Lutherans, Calvinists, Bible Students or *Shtundists* and therefore I expected to find in this home exactly those whom I was looking for. I was not mistaken; this was the home of a Christian family. They were members of a moderate Pentecostal group; they knew many Pentecostals who ministered in Volyn. In a short time we became acquainted, but more important, we became acquainted as members of one family in Christ. This kind, Christian family welcomed me warmly and sincerely invited me to have a meal with them. I could not remember how long it had been since I had a meal which tasted as good as the one at that home. That evening I learned from this brother in Christ that everything was still peaceful in Halychyna. It was being reported that the German front was still far away, in the direction of Brody, but the German army was moving continuously day and night. What was most interesting to me was that trains were still running between Zolochiv and Lviv.

I was truly like a newspaper and a source of real information for this family. I was able to inform them where the front was actually located, as well as informing them of the horrors which were taking place in Volyn, and the conflict between the Polish and Ukrainians. They had heard about some of these matters but not to the extent that I now informed them. Halychyna was still living as it had always lived in the past; there was still a post office, trains were still running, and a Ukrainian newspaper was being published in Lviv. In Volyn, during this time and in the years 1942-1943, its former lifestyle had completely ceased and now there were numerous skirmishes between Ukrainian dissenters and the Germans, as well as mutual conflicts between the Polish and Ukrainians. By the end of 1943, there was not a single telegraph pole along all the roads in Volyn because the dissenters told the people to cut them down and dispose of them. There was not a single bridge anywhere. Small detachments of Germans were found in the larger towns but they were locked down in fortifications, afraid to go anywhere. Whenever they were forced to move from town to town, they assembled a whole caravan of vehicles, armed with machine guns, often led by several tanks. The post office did not operate during the entire, long German occupation. All the villages were in the hands of the Resistance while the towns were in the hands of the Germans. Entire villages were burned down, people had scattered into the forests, into hiding places…

My host, his wife and children listened to all that I was telling them and I could clearly see the fear visible on their faces. They had not yet experienced anything quite so terrible, but they were aware that all the horrors that Volyn was experiencing, were now coming in their direction. In various ways, even small ones, they were coming to quiet and peaceful Halychyna. No one could save them from that which was coming; there was no power that could slow down the terrible troubles.

We went to sleep late in the evening, but before that, we read the Word of God together and prayed. I could sense that I was among my own people. Up until now we had never met each other; we had never in our lives been acquainted. This was not important, the important thing was that we were children of God, bought with the same price, and now it felt as if we were one family. What a great miracle God performs! Perhaps I had never felt this so deeply as at that time because I had never had the need for someone else's good heart, brotherly comfort and love. It is wonderful when God sometimes sends us some type of suffering and sadness because this all serves to unite believers into one family and into an inseparable Christian fellowship.

Many years have passed since that time. I have even forgotten the names of that Christian family in Zolochiv, but I have never forgotten their goodness and the Christian fellowship that we enjoyed in their home, and the pleasant, restful time I had spent together with them.

The following day I went with the brother, in whose home I had spent the night, into town. Zolochiv was not as attractive as what I remembered it to be before the war; but in comparison, it was nicer than any given village or town in Volyn. The stores were all open and some supplies could be purchased in them. Unfortunately there was a great deal of garbage on the streets, which nobody would sweep up. The houses, where Jewish families once lived, were all closed. Padlocks were hanging on many doors and all the windows were boarded up. When I had travelled though Zolochiv I would sometimes pass a small wooden structure, which was still standing beside the road. I would lean my bicycle against this booth and drink the cold lemonade that was sold by a short, plump shopkeeper. Beside the booth, curly-haired Jewish children would play on the filthy cement sidewalk, speaking to each other in Ukrainian. Today the booth was empty. Glass from broken windowpanes and paper was scattered all around. The owner was no longer there; that short, caring shopkeeper. His small children were no longer playing on the sidewalk. Where were they? The question needs not even to be asked. They were taken by force into some horrible gas chambers or they were murdered and dumped somewhere in the ditches surrounding Zolochiv.

We went to visit another Christian family. It was apparent that this family was quite wealthy because they lived in a very nice home. We sat there for a long time talking about the past, as well as the future that was still hidden from us by the darkness of the events of the war. This family also accepted me in a gracious and Christian manner and would not allow me to return to the solitary house in the hay meadow. They informed me that I was going to spend the night with them and that I could stay there as long as I wished. I accepted their invitation because I could not see any reason to hurry anywhere.

That evening I went by myself into the town to look at the army that was slowly approaching Brody. Then I went to the train station to find out when there would be a train going to Lviv. A conductor told me that there was not a regular train to Lviv but he thought that it would come tomorrow evening. The conductor spoke to me in Polish and I was quite surprised to hear the Polish language. It reminded me of the times before the war began and it seemed that this was still the same Poland. I imagined that I would soon board the train and travel through green fields to my nearby Volyn. I *thought-thought,* but the rumbling of tanks, which were moving nearby, and the drone of airplanes in the sky cut short my pleasant daydreams.

I walked past some doors and noticed that it was a barbershop. I realized that it had been a long time since I had a haircut and put my hand into my pocket for my wallet. I counted the few German coins inside and realized that I did not have enough money for a haircut. I only had a few coins; this was all my wealth. I did not have enough for a haircut and I did not have any money with which to go to Lviv. I would have to walk.

I spent another night in Zolochiv and the next morning I began getting myself ready for the long trip. "Since I already got this far", I thought to myself, "it is better to go farther, all the way to Lviv. Once I get there, it will be more clear what I should do next".

"You don't have to go so early in the morning, because the train, I believe, doesn't leave until the evening," said the good brother.

"I want to walk," I replied.

"Why do want to go on foot? It is a very long way."

I had to answer honestly that I did not have any money. My kind host shook his head and in a unhappy tone replied,

"My dear brother, why didn't you say anything? Do you think that we do not have any money?"

"I was not bold enough to talk to you about that, because when will I be able to repay you," I tried to defend myself.

"If we are alive and meet somewhere then you can repay us. In the meantime if something happens to you or to me and you never repay, that's the way it will be. I don't care about the money. The world is coming apart. Thousands of people are dying, so how can we compare that to our miserable money?" replied the brother and went into an adjoining room.

In a few minutes he returned and handed me some money wrapped in paper. I did not count it but hid it away in my pocket and thanked him. He also gave me a letter and an address where I could go once I arrived in Lviv.

Towards evening I found myself at the empty small train station in Zolochiv. The conductor handed me my ticket and told me that the train was going to leave in two hours. I went inside the dirty waiting room and sat down in a corner on a wooden bench. With the exception of myself, there was nobody in the building. Finally I took out the money from my pocket. I counted it and was deeply moved and began to weep. I don't recall today exactly how much there was but it was more than enough, not only to get to Lviv, but also enough to continue to Warsaw and support myself for a while. I turned towards a window, wiped the tears from eyes and prayed.

"Lord," whispered my troubled soul. "How good you are to me! I am so fortunate that I have such a large family in this world, my dear brothers and sisters. Help me to never forget this in my life, help me Lord that my hand would always be ready to help someone who is need."

Many years have gone by since that moment, I have forgotten the names of the Christian brethren in Zolochiv but I will forever remember their love for me. I never had an opportunity to meet with any of them again. I never returned there on any trip back to my home and have never yet repaid my debt, but I would like from a sincere heart to someday repay them.

The sun had set a long time ago behind the distant forest and it began to get dark in the waiting room. There was no light anywhere and it seemed that not only was Zolochiv shrouded in darkness, but all of Halychyna. It was a deep and dark night. Not only was Halychyna covered with darkness, but all Europe and the whole world as well.

The conductor came up to me, carrying a small flashlight in his hand, and said, "Sir, you may board the train. We will be leaving in a few minutes."

I had to walk through many train cars to the very end and sat down on a bench in the corner. I don't know if there was anybody else in the car because it was dark and I did not see anybody. I was sitting on a hard seat; I could feel a cold wall behind my shoulder and was aware of the fact that I was on my way to Lviv. I was travelling as I never travelled before in my life. I didn't even have a change of underwear; I didn't have a single possession with me. I left everything behind in Zolochiv. I even left my walking stick, which I had brought with me all the way from Volyn. I didn't have anything with me except my old, short, sheepskin jacket that was now keeping my back warm and my old long boots, which had become even more faded along the road. The toes were curled upward because they had become wet. I was worried the most about them. What would I do if my boots became completely worn out? They were not too far from being just that.

The train was swaying and rocking, causing me to become drowsy, but I could not fall asleep. I began to think. My thoughts carried me back to Volyn. I was back in my own village, walking along all the different roads and pathways that I had ever travelled in my life. I had never before been in such a tight and oppressed state. I knew that back at home there was still my house, my family and my job, but what was awaiting me ahead? Where is this road, on which I am now traveling going to take me? I knew that along this road I would have needs and encounter humiliation, hunger, sorrow, and sadness. The one thing cheering me up was that I was a Christian, and in this world I have a large family of my Christian brothers and sisters, who would come to my rescue during any difficult or critical time. I became convinced of this in Zolochiv. The other thing that gave me courage was that I was not the only one who was fleeing, but there were thousands of us. Beginning at the Romanian border in the south and up to Lviv and Warsaw, they were using different routes to leave. Every road was filled with those escaping; some were riding in wagons, bicycles, or walking on foot. They were going with entire families, carrying small children on their shoulders, lugging with them their scanty household goods. All were moving slowly, a hungry and ragged mass of people moving to the west. I too was also included among those thousands of hungry masses. However, my situation was much better than the others because I was by myself and headed towards familiar territory in Lviv where there were a fair number of acquaintances. In my pocket I now had some money that was now legitimate currency throughout the General-Governorate[8]. Most important, I had with me a letter of recommendation from Zolochiv to Christians living in Lviv so that they would accept me as a brother in Christ.

In Zolochiv, I was told that Lviv was full of fugitives, and that there were many of my friends from Volyn, who had escaped before the front came into our area. My heart yearned to go there to meet some friends. It would be much easier to endure hardships realizing that I was not the only one forced to go through these challenges because my friends were facing the same challenges. It would be easier to endure as a group.

---

8   An administrative region of a country

I was getting sleepy so I leaned against the wall and tried to sleep. I had a feeling that my tired body was here, travelling on this train, but my heart and soul I had left at home in my native village. The farms and villages of Halychyna blinked by through the train window. The train was going quite slow but always going farther and farther away, always going closer to that unknown west, but farther away from my native land. I had never imagined when I left that this road would be so long and difficult. Later, I often regretted that I had boarded that train in Zolochiv because I did not have any destination. I left to wander but it was now too late and there was no place to which I could return.

We arrived in Lviv. The sun had not yet set and the city was covered with a dense March fog. I walked over to a half ruined train station and was horrified by the image that I saw before me. There, lying along the wall, on the cold ground floor, were large masses of people; dirty duffel bags were placed beneath their heads, little children were crying and complaining to their mothers that they were hungry and cold. They were all frightened fugitives. There were people from all the eastern oblasts of Ukraine, who until now had been travelling by wagon or walking. Now, in Lviv, they were all trying to board a train, waiting in long rows for their turn to leave. Among those in the large crowds there were many from Volyn, Polish people and dark-skinned people from the Caucasus region as well as other nationalities. Everyone in this racially diverse mob of people was being persecuted by the front and had only one goal ... the west. The fleeing people did not always believe that the west would bring them good fortune, but there were no other choices available as they were forced to go always farther and farther ahead. They believed that somewhere in the world there was still humanity and freedom.

There were endless lines of people standing before the ticket-windows, but the windows were all closed and tickets were not being sold at that time. The men would stand in the lines until their wives or an acquaintance replaced them. In this way the line never became shorter but, on the contrary, with every moment continued to grow longer as new fugitives pushed their way in.

I walked through the waiting room and asked the conductor what I would have to do to obtain a ticket to Warsaw. The conductor looked at me and replied in what seemed a joking manner:

"First of all you need strong nerves, courage, a pound of butter and money."

"No, no, don't joke," I said, "because right now I don't have any of those things."

The conductor told me that the most important thing was to have a document from the district government certifying that I was a true fugitive from the front lines. If you do not get this certification they will not sell you a ticket. From that same conductor I also learned that trains were no longer going to the east, but were still running to Stryi, Peremyshel, Krakow and Warsaw.

Burdened with my difficult thoughts I went out into the street. Lviv was still asleep. Occasionally a solitary person or a German military policeman walked slowly down the street. Lviv was far from what I had remembered from my previous visits. There were piles of garbage scattered in the streets and the windows of the buildings where Jews once lived were all boarded up. This was the same scene everywhere in Halychyna during this difficult time of war.

The streetcars were still running but were almost empty. I sat down in one and showed to the conductor the address that I had been given in Zolochiv. "It's behind St. George's Cathedral," he told me. There I had to get off and transfer to a different streetcar. I did as he told me and began looking for the desired street name. For a long time I walked past the still empty streets of Lviv and finally found the street that I was looking for. I found the proper house number on a large stone building. I climbed the stairs to the third floor and knocked on the door. I could not hear anyone moving behind the door so I knocked louder. Still there was only silence. I stood for a few minutes, waited and knocked again. I stood and listened. Behind the tightly closed door I could hear some kind of commotion, and then a low voice spoke:

"Who's there?"

"It's one of our own. Do not be afraid," I replied.

"Who are you?" repeated the voice behind the door.

"I have just arrived from Zolochiv and have a letter from the believers there which is addressed to you," I said coming closer to the door.

The door opened slightly and a woman's hand reached out from the room.

"Give me the letter, but you can wait outside awhile."

I stood beside a window in the corridor. The streets of the city were becoming alive as more pedestrians filled the streets. They were all hurrying someplace as is normal in a large city, but here I was standing and waiting outside a stranger's door. After a short time the door opened and an unknown older man stood in the entrance.

"Please come in," he said, wiping his forehead with his sleeve.

I entered the room and saw the man, as well as two women and two children standing in front of me with frightened, sleepy faces and disheveled hair. I felt as if somebody's hand was holding me back in the doorway. I was looking at them with the same frightened eyes, not knowing what had happened.

"Come in closer", the man said showing me to a chair. "Come in and forgive us that everything is scattered around."

I sat down on the chair and finally saw that the room was in chaos. Shirts, children's dresses and paper were scattered all over the floor. The women were standing with tears in their eyes.

"What happened here?" I asked in a voice that sounded as if we were acquaintances for a long time.

The man tried the door to make sure that it was properly locked and then sat down beside me on a second chair and began:

"You know, we all are so frightened and distressed. Yesterday in the evening, around eleven o'clock, somebody knocked at our door. He said that there were two of them; they were fugitives from Ternopyl. They told us that they were believers and begged us to let them into the room. I opened the door and they came in. Suddenly one of them pulled out a revolver and told all of us to lie down with our faces to the floor. We lay down and they proceeded to tie our hands behind our back. Then they turned over every cupboard and searched every corner. They took all our clothing, they took all the money which we had in the room; they took everything that they could carry and then went out into the street. Before we could make sense of what had just happened and wake the neighbours, there was no trace of them. We were left just as you see us now."

"But did you report this to the police?" I asked.

"That would not have helped any. The police are not interested. They are only interested in the traffic in the street and keeping watch during the evening so that there is no light visible from any window. The police have simply given everyone instructions not to let strangers into their house, and if you did, it's on your own head. We had allowed two strange young men in their twenties to enter our home. So forgive us if we made you stand for such a long time outside the door. And now, who are you and where are you are from?"

The man's story had a depressing effect on me. I tried to encourage them but I could not find the appropriate words to say. It seemed to me that I was an accomplice in their tragedy because it was strangers like me who claimed to be fugitives but whose intent was only to rob the family.

In the foggy morning, I read God's Word together with this Christian family. We prayed together, and then I related to them what was happening in Volyn; where entire villages had been set on fire, people were looking for hiding-places in the forests, in ditches or in primitive homemade bunkers, which were often mutually dug by several families. My host and Christian brother heaved a deep sigh, waved his hand and emphatically told those present in the room:

"'We still don't have it bad. They took all our rags, but let it be. Thank God that we were left alive. There is nothing to cry about. It could have been much worse. Stop that crying! The Lord has not abandoned us."

The crying stopped. All that could be heard were occasional sobs from the wife and their youngest daughter.

After resting for a short time at this good Christian home, I went by myself into the town. I passed some kind of park and came to a street called Львівськик Дітей[9], where the magazine Післанец Правди[10] was once being published. I found No. 26. There was a lock hanging on the door. I stood on the small steps for a few minutes and then headed in the direction of St. George's Cathedral. Myriads of frightening thoughts and memories

---

9   Children of Lviv
10 Messenger of Truth

filled me. For some reason I thought of brother Nikodim Lukianchuk, with whom we had walked beneath these linden and chestnut trees. I thought of our Evangelical poet from Volyn, Oleksa Kostiuk, with whom, we were together before the war, at this same spot, sitting on an old wooden bench, weaving our dreams and sharing our youthful plans, which never came to pass. "Where are they now, my friends and brothers?"

People were hurrying to St. George's Cathedral. Somewhere a bell was ringing, its sound spread out among the sunny linden trees. Near a large cross above the cathedral flocks of pigeons and magpies were circling. Glancing up at the sky it seemed to me that nothing had changed from what it used to be more than ten years ago. White spring clouds were floating above, it smelled like spring but this was not reality. These were difficult war times and behind every home and every building some type of danger was awaiting every person.

That evening I attended a service at the Ukrainian Baptist church. There were many people from Lviv whom I had known before the war. There were an even greater number of fugitives from all over Ukraine whom I had never met before. I sat down quietly beside the door, ashamed of my old sheepskin jacket. After a short time I was called to come to the front and was forced to say a few words. Today, I don't remember what I had said but I do remember that the large auditorium of the church was filled with people. Later many of them approached me and asked me if I was in need of anything. Although I didn't even have a change of underwear, and only my faded sheepskin jacket and an old pair of boots on my feet which were ready to fall apart, when I saw so many of my Christian brothers and sisters around me, it seemed to me that I was very rich and did not need anything. I felt like going to a solitary place somewhere and having a good cry from the deep emotions and blessings I was feeling because of the kindness and compassion which I felt coming from the hearts of these believers.

After the service I discovered that many of my acquaintances from Volyn had been here recently but had left Lviv last week to go to Peremyshl. The people advised me that if I also wanted to go any farther then I should obtain a pass from the city government, because without such a document I would not be able to purchase a train ticket. I would not be able to obtain a card to receive bread or apply to start a new life anywhere within the whole region of the General-Governorate.

The next day I decided to visit an Evangelical congregation which was located between Lviv and Stryi. I wanted to visit some Christian friends and to rest for a few days from my travels. Conditions were terrifying and uncertain in Lviv. The Germans were arresting people on the street and were loading them into freight cars and transporting them to work camps in their own country. I, who had just recently escaped from their grasp, did not wish to fall again into their iron hands. There was an expectation in Lviv of the possibility of an invasion by Bolshevik warplanes and therefore I longed to go to a small village where it was quiet and peaceful.

I went to the train station and purchased a ticket to go to Stryi without any difficulty because a pass was only required to go to Peremyshl. The passenger cars were full of people with their bundles and suitcases who were all going somewhere. Among them I was a stranger to everyone. I didn't have a single document in my possession, which was very risky during a time of war. I surrendered myself to the will of God. As I travelled across the evenly harrowed black fields of Halychyna, I marveled at the vast difference in lifestyles between Volyn and Halychyna. Here the trains travelled peacefully and life was just as peaceful as before the war while Volyn was a total wasteland. Rebels had blown up almost every bridge over the main rivers. They had cut down almost every telephone pole. They had burnt down the farmhouses and destroyed the railroad tracks. And the same destruction was now slowly moving into Halychyna.

The train passed the small, quiet station of Mikolaev. Suddenly I glimpsed the silvery, gloomy Dniester River. I would soon have to get off so I began to slowly make my way to the exit. The train stopped beside some trees and I would still have to walk several kilometers from here to the village. I knew the way because I had traveled here many times. The sun was already sinking below the horizon, infusing with its beams the evening mist above the Dniester. In the distance, the white tops of the Carpathian Mountains were becoming visible. They seemed to be calling me to them and stirring many memories in me. It was here that I used to travel with a group of evangelical youth. We sang our songs and rejoiced in the springtime of our youth and now I was returning to those same young people by myself, poor and forgotten. I was embarrassed to go into the village in my ragged jacket so I waited until it got darker. I walked past the school; I passed the cemetery and went straight into the yard of a well-known Christian brother. There was a light inside the house and I boldly knocked on the door. I went inside and stood inside the porch. The owner of the house dashed out and threw himself at me. He recognized me but could not believe his eyes that it was I. There were tears in the eyes of both of us. They had not heard anything about me since 1939 and suddenly I appeared in their home.

That same evening many fellow believers came by and we conversed until late into the night. We prayed together, read the Bible and sang, "*Za Dnyamy Lynut Dni*".[11] Together we sorrowed and together we rejoiced.

I spent an entire week in the village, completely unaware of what was happening anywhere else. Nobody here had a radio; no newspapers and no news from the troubled wartime world were reaching this place. Sometimes German warplanes would fly over the village and then they would fly back. People continued working as if there was no war happening in the world. They were beginning to cultivate and plant their gardens. There were Polish families in the village, but none of the hatred and envy that existed in Volyn and Kholmachyna[12] had arrived here yet. Ukrainians and Poles lived peacefully together. The differences between Volyn and Halychyna during this time were beyond comparison; the fate of the Volyn people was more tragic.

I returned to Lviv from the village, but this time I was traveling much richer. I had with me a small suitcase in which I had several shirts, which were given to me by some of the believers.

The situation in Lviv had become worse. There were countless fugitives roaming the street in large groups. They had come from the east, looking for food and a place to sleep, but also looking for ways to get further to the west. Everyone was walking about, depressed and worried, expecting the worst. They were always looking upwards, wondering if there were any airplanes coming and listening for the sound of alarm sirens.

---

11 *За Днями Линуть Дні*. Translated "Days Following Days"
12 Chelm

I decided to leave Lviv and since the road to return home was closed for now, I elected to go to Warsaw. I discovered that some of the believers in Lviv were working in the city government offices so I had requested them to get me a pass. I received the pass after several days and soon found myself in a long line outside the train station waiting to purchase a ticket. Lviv was in a state of evacuation so there were several acquaintances with me who were also travelling to Warsaw. We settled down into a cold train car with broken windows, but were grateful that we had at least this space. We left hundreds of people standing in line in the station yard who were unable to obtain a ticket because there were ins cars.

Towards evening our train departed. The weather outside was foggy and damp. A light rain was beginning to fall, but the good thing was that the train was moving. The clicking sound of the train wheels counted off the difficult kilometers. Our hearts were pounding because rumours had spread throughout the cars that the resistance had blown up a railroad embankment, which threatened our train's safety. Therefore we prayed silently in our hearts as we continued to move forward.

Suddenly the brakes screeched and the train began to slow down. We stuck our heads out the broken window and saw a small station where several people were standing in the shadows. "Rebels..." someone in the darkness shouted and confusion started breaking out throughout the cars. But we were mistaken because these were not rebels but rather German soldiers. They entered the passenger cars and forced the people to get off, throwing their luggage out the windows, as they angrily shouted:

"*Raus, Raus!*"[13]

From that day and for the rest of my life I would remember that German word *Raus*. It seems to me that whoever uses that word must be a very angry, unhappy and fearful individual.

A tall soldier rushed into our compartment and waving with his hand pointed us to the door. There was a woman from the group of believers who was travelling with us to Lviv with her three small children. She rushed at the soldier and through tears begged him not to force her away with her children. The children huddled close to their mother and cried loudly. The

---

13   Get out, Get out!

soldier softened, slammed the door shut and left. The tears of the children had rescued us.

Later we found out that these soldiers had been travelling in a large army truck that the Ukrainian resistance army had destroyed and that was why they were so angry now.

Our train arrived in Krakow, stopped for several hours at the station and then proceeded on its journey. We were now travelling through Polish territory where there was danger of ambush, not only from the Germans, but also from the Polish. There were many incidents where the Polish would kill Ukrainians on the trains and throw their dead bodies out of the windows. This was the time that the Polish and Ukrainians were mutually attacking each other, taking revenge on each other. In this manner the largest number of people were lost on both sides, innocent people, often the elderly and children.

It was nighttime. Our train was travelling slowly through a forest. There was no light anywhere in the cars and we all sat in the darkness with a heavy heart and troublesome thoughts. I went out into the corridor, stood beneath a window and looked out into the dark night. Two young men walked past me and I could hear them speaking in Polish:

"Kazik said that he heard Ukrainian being spoken in one of the cars. We need to check this out."

Seeing me they became silent. Then one of them came up to me and asked me in Polish:

"Are you going far, sir?"

"To Warsaw," I replied and could feel something like ants running down my back.

"How were things in Lviv? Are the Ukrainians murdering Polish people?"

"Right now everything is quiet, but it is not clear what will happen in the future."

They walked away down the dark corridor and I quickly went into our compartment and whispered to my fellow travelers from Lviv:

"Sit quietly," I said, "but if you must speak, speak only in Polish."

Distressed and with burdensome thoughts we continued on. If only God would send daylight soon, but it was still a long time before there would be light. Outside the window all we could see was the thick darkness, the same darkness that was on our train, the same darkness that filled our hearts. Not only did we not speak Ukrainian any more, we kept quiet altogether awaiting the morning.

Day finally came, casting much light and heat through the windows into our train cars. Truly, the sun was pleasing, kissing and caressing everyone without prejudice.

WARSAW

Our train began to slow down and edge its way between damaged buildings, overturned fences and neglected streets. This was Warsaw. Once it was a familiar place, a beautiful and happy place. The train slowly crept into the main station and came to a stop. A multitude of people spilled out from the cars; each one carrying large suitcases and dusty bundles; a continuous mass of people struggling to force their way to the exit. Beside the entrance, wearing a grey metal helmet stood a tall soldier inspecting the luggage. Already there were many baskets, suitcases and bundles scattered about him, which he confiscated from the people. Whenever he took someone's suitcase or basket, nobody dared to protest. They quietly surrendered their belongings and continued to the exit with empty hands. The soldier did not shout at anyone, he did not hit anyone, he simply looked at them. That chilling glare caused many people to immediately give up everything that they had just to be relieved that their encounter was over. It would be interesting to know how these mean, dark looks developed; faces that appeared to be made from bronze. Later I travelled everywhere in postwar Germany but did not see such frightening eyes again.

It was now my turn. I had only one small suitcase and in the other hand I had the pass that I received in Lviv. The soldier looked at the pass, waved his hand, and allowed me to pass and not get in the way of others. The same thing was repeated with each of my fellow travelers from Lviv.

We walked onto wide Jerusalem Avenue. It was a beautiful morning outside. There was much sunshine and many thoughts. Warsaw, the goal of our journey, welcomed us with sunshine. But now? Where to next? We had the address of a sister-believer, an old acquaintance who lived not very far from the train station on Jerusalem Avenue. We went there and for the first time we found a place of shelter and rest. That morning, I was especially fortunate to meet with many former friends, whom, until now, I did not know if they were even alive. We had not met or even corresponded since 1939, but now we were able to meet again and rejoice together.

The home of our friend, sister Marta Kowalchuk, had several large rooms, which were already filled with fellow believers, residents of Warsaw as well as fugitives. Here I found a temporary place to rest, a warm shelter and the kind hearts of the local Christians; many of whom I had known before the war and others whose acquaintance I was able to make for the first time.

On Thursday as we sat down together for tea, one brother turned to me and said:

"You probably don't know about the fate of Sahryn?"

"No I don't know. What happened?"

The brother related to me the horrific story that fell like a heavy stone upon my heart, of the tragedy that took place in Sahryn. It was a story of bloodshed, human hatred for one another, and unrestrained revenge and cruelty.

Sahryn was the name of a large, beautiful Ukrainian village in Hrubieszow County. After the First World War, when a great spiritual revival spread throughout Volyn and Halychyna, the Word of God also reached Hrubieszow and came to Sahryn. A large and active congregation of Evangelical Christians was formed there. The believers lived in wonderful unity and harmony with each other. They witnessed to others through their words and actions, and from Sahryn the message of the Gospel spread into other villages.

In 1937, while attending a conference of Evangelical Christians in Warsaw, I became acquainted with the pastor of this lively and active congregation, brother Ivan Hrytsai. Later I visited the congregation and enjoyed wonderful fellowship with the kind and hospitable local believers. Now I sat sorrowfully listening to the difficult narrative about this congregation of God's children.

At sunrise, in the spring of 1944, while it was still dark outside, about three thousand Polish insurgents attacked Sarhyn from every side.

The attackers were on horseback as well as on foot. All were heavily armed. They formed a tight circle around the town and began shooting incendiary ammunition into it from all sides. Most of the buildings in Sahryn were covered with straw. The weather had been very warm for several weeks prior to the attack and the straw upon the buildings was very dry. In a matter of minutes the entire village was engulfed in a sea of flames.

Brother Ivan Hrytsai, pastor of the congregation of Evangelical Christians in Sahryn. He perished together with the entire congregation

Loud voices, moaning and crying could be heard in the village. People rose up, as if waking up from sleep, frantically began running among the burning buildings looking for help. There was no help to be found. Those who tried to escape into the fields from the burning village were shot by attackers who surrounded the village and were watching so that no one was able to escape.

The Ukrainian police, who were stationed in the village, formed a defensive line and carrying automatic handguns, they marched outside the village. They were able to break through the enemy lines and only one policeman was lost. With the help of the police, several people were able to escape but the numbers were very few. Some found other ways to escape by running through ditches, taking advantage of the darkness because it was still dawn and the sun had not yet risen.

The few people who acted immediately, healthy, young people and people who did not have small children, found it easier to escape. Those who tried to save their possessions, livestock, or children were left behind in the village.

As the sun rose, the Polish invaders entered the burning village from every side. Then began the atrocious work of the devil...

The Polish began shooting at every person, throwing small children into burning buildings, stabbing them with bayonets or hacking them with their swords. They had no pity on anyone, not sparing a single human soul.

When the merciful sun finally set over the village of Sahryn, everything was very quiet. The desperate cries of mothers and children were no longer heard because nobody was left alive in the village. The corpses of the villagers lay outside in their yards, on the roadways, and in the orchards and gardens. There were especially many dead bodies in the fields outside the village. These were the bodies of those who attempted to save themselves by fleeing. Black smoke continued to arise above the village as cattle bellowed from inside smouldering buildings, and dogs howled. The Polish rebels, having completed their horrible deed, had left a long time ago. Sahryn continued to burn.

Ukrainian residents from the surrounding villages approached the devastated village with fear and caution. Among them were a fair number of those who had escaped during the attack and were now returning to find their homes destroyed by fire. They came because they had parents and family members who were living in Sahryn. Many believers also came to find out what had happened to their Christian brothers and sisters. New tragic scenes played out as sons and daughters recognized their murdered parents among the corpses; mothers found the burned bodies of their children. It was impossible to describe the horrific and tragic images before them. The human language does not have the words with which to recount the scene...

On that spring morning in 1944, a total of 763 corpses were found and buried in Sahryn. Many people disappeared without any trace. It is possible that the Polish had captured and taken them. Perhaps they continued to be tortured elsewhere and later killed because none ever returned home.

This is the type of harvest of death that human evil and envy can produce. These were deeds that were carried out, not by primitive people in far away Africa or India, but by people who loudly proclaimed their culture, boasted of their civilized lifestyle and upbringing and considered themselves to be the most fair nation within the Catholic world ... the Polish.

The brother who was relating this tragedy became quiet and the rest of us, who were listening, also became quiet. There was a feeling of dread and sadness in the room, which was now in semi-darkness. I remembered one Christmas that I had spent in Sahryn. There was a Christmas tree and during the service the children wonderfully recited various poems. There were many children and young people. Now they were all gone ... the innocent and the pure were lost.

"Were any of the believers rescued?" I asked after a time of silence.

"Only one brother from the entire large congregation was spared" came the heartbreaking reply. "This brother was captured by two Polish horsemen outside the village and was ordered to undress, remove his shoes and to start walking away from them. The man removed his jacket and boots and began to run away as fast as he could across the field over the ploughed furrows.

The insurgents began shooting at him, but God turned the bullets aside; they mounted their horses and began to chase after him. The horses were large and heavy and began to sink up to their knees in the soft thawed earth and were unable to run. By this time the brother had run a long distance. Turning around he saw that the Polish were falling behind and he began to run with even greater strength. In this way he escaped. Later he told us about the horrible tragedy of Sahryn."

The room became quiet again. The only sound was the ticking of the clock on the wall marking the late hour; its ticking was keeping time with the beating of our hearts. We prayed together that evening, remembering in our prayers all the poor and forgotten, and all the innocent sufferers during this wartime calamity. There were at least a million scattered across the various countries of Europe who were suffering; the majority of them were in our native land. Nobody had ever counted them all and nobody will ever adequately document this horrible tragedy.

A wedding in the Ev. Congregation in Sahryn in 1941. Two years later, all these believers were lost. Seated in the middle are brothers Ivan Barchuk and D. Bolsunowski.

The following day the sun was shining brightly above Warsaw. I went by myself to view the city. I had lived here almost five years before the war. I knew Warsaw as I knew my own village, but now I could no longer recognize it. There were still many people on the streets, as before the war, but now they appeared sad, almost indifferent and crushed. Their capital city was in distress, in a deep state of suffering from the German occupation. The streets were full of German military vehicles, garbage was scattered everywhere. There were many broken trees and demolished homes. Many multi-storied buildings, blackened by fire during the air raid in September of 1939, were now standing with boarded up windows. Several buildings had only one wall, which was now washed clean by rain and faded from the sun, standing and staring at the sky as a witness to the horrible events of bygone days. At almost every street corner there stood an angry-looking German soldier, vigilantly observing the pedestrian. He was guarding an occupied people whose freedom was taken away by the Germans. In his hands he was holding an automatic rifle and there were grenades strapped to his belt. Passersby avoided him as if he was some unclean spirit. He continuously crossed from one side of the sidewalk to the other, with angry eyes staring from beneath his grey helmet.

I walked the length of Jerusalem Avenue to *Nowy Swiat*[14] Street, turned left and walked as far as *Krakowskie Przedmiescie*[15]. By the Nicolas Copernicus Monument I watched as German soldiers stopped a fully filled bus, ordered everyone to get out, and then searched the men's pockets for concealed weapons. After finding nothing, they let everyone go. I thought to myself that it would have been much better for me to have stayed quietly in my room and not to venture out into the city. I walked down streets that had less activity and then returned to the home of sister Marta.

I went to a church service for the first time on Sunday. There I met many fugitives from Volyn, Polesia, Halychyna, Belarus, Greater Ukraine and the Caucasus. There were many familiar and unfamiliar faces. They had now been living in Warsaw for several weeks, looking for ways to escape farther to the west on their own, avoiding any vehicles which the Germans might be using to daily collect and transport people into forced labour camps inside Germany.

After some time, with the help of the Warsaw Christians, I registered as a fugitive with the city government and received a card with which I could obtain bread and margarine. As long as I was just a visitor, others cared for me, but now it became my responsibility to take care of myself. Living in Warsaw was truly proving difficult and without assistance a person could easily perish. Every week new refugees came into the city and it was becoming difficult to find a place where one could spend the night. Thanks to the Warsaw Christian brothers and sisters we, Christian fugitives, had

---

14   New World
15   Krakow Suburb Street. The road connects Zamkowy Place in Old Town to *Nowy Swiat*

a place to stay because almost every evangelical family in Warsaw opened their homes and hearts to us. There were several Evangelical-Baptist services in the city and after each service, the pastors would announce that new refugees had arrived who required a place to stay and were in need of material assistance.

This was a time of spiritual revival in the ministry of the churches in Warsaw. In addition to the regular members of the Evangelical-Baptist churches, many of our preachers also ended up in Warsaw. Some of the refugees could not speak or understand Polish and so they began their own service during which Russian was used to sing Christian songs and to preach the Word of God. Those who could not understand Polish went to the Russian service. A choir was organized. There were many young people in attendance and it appeared to us that there was no war anywhere and after living in Warsaw for a while we would simply go back to our homes. But these thoughts were only temporary because in reality it was very different. Frequent emergency sirens kept informing us that we were living on a dangerous volcano and at a moment's notice it might be necessary to leave because with each day there was increasing unrest in the city.

Before the war I had many acquaintances in Warsaw, some of whom were doing quite well materialistically. Each one of them gave me something that I needed and I now could somehow survive. I still have a journal from those years in which I kept a complete list of those kind believers and friends who provided practical help for me and I will always remember with deep gratitude how dear those names are to me. Using the card that I received from the city government I could buy enough bread for the week, as well as some *krupiv*[16], and two or three spoonfuls of horrible tasting marmalade.

Later on, one Christian brother gave me a job at his business. He manufactured ladies' summer sports shoes in his own home and he taught me how to hammer down the soles. That summer, I sat for long hours in a room pounding with a hammer and struggling with many thoughts. I looked out through the window at the nearby glistening Vistula River, feeling lonely and sad. What was my family doing at this moment at home?

---

16 singular "*krupa*". Hulled grain broken into fragments.

Did they know anything about me? After two weeks we ran out of materials to make more shoes so again I found myself unemployed.

The Germans initiated a major resettlement effort in Warsaw. The Polish people were transferred from the more affluent parts of the city to a poorer region and replaced with German occupants as well as families of mixed German-Polish marriages. There were a fair number of believers who lived in these more affluent areas in whose homes refugees from the east were also living. I lived for a time with brother Mankowsky whom I knew from before the war, and now we often walked together on the ruined streets of Warsaw.

One day we were returning from a church service. The trams were packed with people, especially the last cars. The first car was almost empty. On it there was a sign written in large letters: FOR GERMANS ONLY. We stood for a long time at the tram stop. When the tram arrived, there were people hanging onto the last car from every side while in the first car with the sign, FOR GERMANS ONLY, there was hardly anyone.

"Brother Mankowsky," I said, "you have the right to travel in the first car. Find yourself a seat there while I try to hang onto the back."

He looked at me and shook his head in protest.

"No brother. I have never travelled with them, not even once. Let them ride alone. I want to ride together with my people, clinging together, suffering, and enduring hardships and discomfort. And believing in a better future for them....", he added in conclusion.

I will never forget that sincere, patriotic stance of brother Mankowsky towards his Polish people. The Ukrainian nation and other nations can learn something from him ... remain with your own nation, not only in good times but also in times of trouble.

Many so-called Volksdeutschers also took the same position[17], but unfortunately among them were also those who waited impatiently for Hitler's victory, which promised them control over the world. Fortunately this never happened.

We waited a little longer for another tram to arrive and then brother Mankowsky and I began pushing our way to the door. The first car was empty but the Polish people never even glanced in that direction.

---

17 People who had a German origin , but were living outside of Germany

UNFORGETTABLE PLACES OF MY YOUTH

One fair morning I decided to venture out alone, to travel throughout Warsaw, to walk along the familiar streets and recall the past. That morning I felt especially gloomy, regretting my lost home, so I went into the city to try to dispel my anxious thoughts, to calm myself and to put aside my disquietude. I walked down the entire Nowy Sviat[18] and *Krakowskie Przedmiesche* and finally realized the large extent to which the city of Warsaw was destroyed. I came to *Korolewski Dvoretz*[19], near *Stare Miasto*[20], where, before the war, there always stood an honorary military guard at the gate. It was now blackened by fire, surrounded by barbed wire and filled with broken bricks. The doors and windows were boarded up and there was not a single whole pane of glass or frame in any of them. Above the ruins of *Stare Miasto* grey clouds of pigeons were flying, perching on the burnt walls and then breaking out and flying away above the Vistula. Poor Warsaw, how much you have suffered.

I remembered that I had stood here at *Plac Zamkowy*[21] once before in 1939. I had just finished reading "Taras Bulba" by Gogol and I thought that it was here that there was a monument by Zygmont of Taras Bulba as he stood watching the Polish torture his son, Ostap. Somewhere here the powerful voice of Taras spoke the words:

"I hear, my son. I hear."

I was moved by this realization as I walked slowly along the banks of the Vistula.

I crossed the Kierbedz Bridge into Praga and continued until I arrived at the Orthodox Cathedral of Saint Magdalene. I found nobody there except

---

18   New World Street
19   Royal Palace
20   Old Town
21   Castle Square

an elderly priest or monk in a long robe who was sweeping the steps. I could see several candles burning near the altar; perhaps the service was to begin soon.

Leaving the church I followed the wide, green Jagiellonska Street to the military barracks. I walked slowly, absorbed in weighty thoughts. I arrived at the low, blackened, wooden barracks. It was apparent that nobody was living in them because the gate was wired shut and the windows of the barracks were broken. I looked through the barbed wire into the building. I could see the corner where my bed once stood, which the corporal of our company would turn over countless times, telling me repeatedly to make my bed. That was so very long ago in 1931. Here in these barracks I completed my two-year military service and there in that corner I would get up during the night and kneel beside my bed and pray and cry as I remembered my distant Volyn. An on-duty watchman would quietly come up to me and tell me to go back to sleep. Truly that was so very long ago, but now as I once again stood at the same spot, living images of the past flashed before me as on a screen. There by the fence was a well with a rusty pump where we would wash ourselves with cold water, undressed from the waist up. Behind the middle window was our *svitlitsya*[22] where there were various magazines and newspapers. Now, even that window was broken, and I could not see into the *svitlitsya* because there was a large board sticking out of the window.

Passing the gate, I continued down the street in the direction of some leafy linden trees that stretched all the way to the Vistula. I continued walking without any definite need or purpose. I walked and tried to untangle my bundles of memories. It seemed that walking made me feel better and more calm.

The street turned to the left and came to a wide field, which was now over-grown with very thick grass. Occasionally we would come here for "instructions". The entire company would stretch out in long lines with several corporals and sergeants in front:

" *Xloptsi*[23], sing!" the sergeant would call out. "Front row begin!"

---

22   living room
23   Boys

The first rows would begin to sing and others joined in as the song struggled to break out from the soldiers' chests like a bird trying to free itself. It struggled, but with no success. In our battalion were many men from the voivodships[24] of Krakiw and Lodz. There were some from Pomorania, Gdansk, and Selesia, but the majority of the soldiers were from Volyn and Polesia who did not know a single Polish song. Therefore, when several Polish soldiers began to sing about a gypsy-fortune teller or Krakowians, the song would never finish because the sergeant would angrily run between the rows and loudly yell:

"Stop, stop! What kind of singing is this? You sound like a bunch of grandfathers from *Gora Kalwaria*.[25] Enough of that noise!"

After wiping his perspiring forehead with a handkerchief, he again loudly called out:

"And now every man from Eastern Kresov sing in your own language. Show those old men how Polish soldiers are supposed to sing."

In the front row, a tall youth from near Kostopil, who always cleared his throat first, boldly began to sing as if he truly was a professional singer on stage:

> "Oy, on the mountain the reapers reap,
> And on the bottom of the mountain, through the ravine-valley
> Cossacks march…
> He-ey through the valley he-ey
> Through the wide one Cossacks march"[26]

Apparently all the recruits from Volyn, Polesia and Halychyna knew this song because, like a storm, the song floated above Praga like a majestic military wave. People began looking out of their windows with pleasure and waving their hands at our battalion. The sergeant walked beside the troops, smiling with satisfaction, as if he was the reason for the good singing. He lifted his glistening boots high in the air and loudly called out:

---

24   administrative region
25   Possibly a reference to Calvary Mountain, a town near Warsaw which had a strong religious significance.
26   "Oy, On the Mountain" from lyricstranslate.com. (*Oy na hory*)

"That is how the first battalion of the administration is supposed to sing. Shame on you old men ... bellowing like bulls being butchered. What a pity that you are only wasting military bread-rations."

I felt pity for the young Polish men marching in groups of four with very sad expressions on their faces, thumping their boots against the road. It looked as if they had just lost a major competition.

The wide field, where these exercises were once held, was now neglected and overgrown with thick grass. There was no longer a Poland, there was no army, and there was no Warsaw. There was nothing left. Only I myself, of the hundreds from that battalion, was here on that familiar field, searching for some comfort, some heartfelt consolation, and some type of companionship. And if today, it should happen by some chance, that I would meet someone from my old army friends, I would weep with joy and hug that person. However, I was here all by myself. Actually I was not alone because nearby on a high branch some kind of grey bird was perched, swaying in the wind and pitifully singing mournfully to me.

Nearby there were some crude shafts, which were thought to be some kind of military fortifications from a long time ago. I went over there and sat down on the thick grass and then lay down with my face looking up at the bright sun as I continued to recall the things that once happened here. I was a young believer then, only four years after my baptism. I had grown up in a small village in Volyn, I had never been to any large city when suddenly I was called into the army and had to go all the way to Warsaw. The life of a recruit was difficult, but my faith and my sincere prayers to God helped me to endure everything. After our training ended, our battalion came to this field to make our oaths. Thousands of new recruits filled the field, standing in straight rows as if carved out of marble. Each company was separated from the others. Beside each company were its officers. On the field there were several military orchestras with shiny horns. The sun was very hot and burning. The sound of military marches could be heard as more and more formations came onto the field. A sea of armies and a second sea of curious onlookers, who did not have permission to go onto the field, stood behind the fence that surrounded the field. All of a sudden a voice loudly called out *bacznos*[27] as a group of distinguished high-

---

27   attention

ranking military personnel, colonels, and generals came onto the field. We could see them clearly even from a distance. The music continued to play without interruption as what seemed to be a chill spread over my body. I wondered what would happen next?

The oath taking began. First of all, the Roman Catholic soldiers stepped out from their places in the rows. A priest, with the rank of a major, began a short discourse. He told the soldiers that they should consider themselves to be fortunate people because they belonged to the most truthful faith in the world and they also lived in the Polish state.

After the Roman Catholics took the oath, an Orthodox priest, with the rank of captain, approached the rows and all the Ukrainian and Belarusian Orthodox candidates, which was the majority of the battalion, stepped forward. To my great amazement the priest-captain began his remarks using fine Ukrainian. He reminded the Orthodox soldiers that their holy obligation was to be obedient to their superiors, to be sincere patriots of Poland, to cherish their Orthodox church and to fight for her, and if necessary to be willing to give their life for her. "Our Orthodox church currently has many enemies, the greatest number of which --", the priest-captain continued in a raised voice," are the various sects, those cursed *Shtundists,* who came to our country from America and are using American dollars to tear down our church. They refuse to join the army, refuse to fight, and refuse to take oaths to be faithful to our state. By these means they wish to weaken our army so that the enemy would come and take away our freedom, to ruin our peaceful Ukrainian and Belarusian homes..."

I was standing in the front row and hot sweat was forming on my forehead. It seemed to me that somebody had told him about me. It seemed that all of this time he was looking in my direction and devouring me with his penetrating eyes.

After the Orthodox, the Jews, Lutherans and Greek Catholics took the oath. I stood, waiting and not going forward with any group. A difficult battle was waging in my soul. "What was I to do? Should I stand together with the Lutherans and Greek Catholics? Who will know? Here nobody was asking anything, not comparing anyone. All I had to do was to stand and listen to a speech and that would be the end. However, deep down in my heart a different voice was speaking, my Christian conscience was responding and telling me to stay in my place.

When all the different faiths took their oath, an officer came before our battalion and said loudly in Polish:

"Perhaps there are Evangelical Christians or Baptists here. Please come forward."

Nobody even moved. It became very, very quiet. I could hear my heart beating loudly and my forehead furrowed. This was a difficult moment of decision for me. Should I go forward or stand here unnoticed. The officer took several steps in a different direction and repeated the same commands.

"Is there anybody here who is an Evangelical Christian or a Baptist?"

Again there was deathly silence and again my youthful heart began to beat. "Lord help me", I said to myself and took three steps forward. I stood and looked to the right and to the left. Was anybody else coming forward? But the battalion stood unmoving in a straight green line. I realized that I was the only one...

Nearby stood the Orthodox priest-captain who said something to another officer. Then that officer came up to me:

"What faith are you?"

"Evangelical Christian," I replied.

"That means, a Baptist?"

"That is correct."

The officer took out a New Testament and read for me from the Gospel of Matthew 5:33-37. I listened, standing there at attention and then returned to my place among the other soldiers. I could feel sweet joy and satisfaction filling my heart. A heavy stone had been rolled away from me into obscurity and the sun began to shine into my soul with its bright rays. The other men looked at me as if they saw me for the first time and I could hear their whispering: "*Shtunda* .... He is a *Shtundist*." But I didn't care. I thanked God that He had given me the strength to not be ashamed of Him and about what I believed, and I was glad that now everyone knew about it.

That evening in the barracks a soldier came up to me from the neighbouring building and immediately began to speak:

"Are you – a brother?"

"Yes, a brother. And you also?" I asked.

"Yes I am also a brother," he answered somewhat uncertainly and quietly.

"But why did you not step forward during the oath-taking?"

"I don't know. Frankly, I didn't have the courage. Now I regret it. God was not ashamed of me, but I was ashamed of Him..."

Tears began to glisten in his eyes.

"With what group did you take your oath?" I asked again.

"With none of them. The Catholics came forward, and then the Orthodox and I remained in my place. Who was to know, which soldier came forward and who did not?"

The following day, as soon as breakfast was being served, the corporal on duty came up to me and ordered me to follow him to the main office of the battalion. Fear gripped me and my heart mistakenly felt that something was not good.

In the office I presented myself to an unfamiliar lieutenant.

"Are you an Evangelical?" he asked.

"Yes, that is true, lieutenant sir," I replied, standing at attention.

"Then come. Please come with me."

The two of us walked into the street and then took the tram that brought us to the Ministry of Military Affairs; I think it was on Novomeyskaya[28] Street. A guard let us in at the gate and a second guard let us into a long corridor. The lieutenant left me in a small waiting room, told me to take a seat and then he left. I waited, my thoughts endlessly troubling me. Why did they bring me to this place? All the way to the Ministry of Military Affairs!

After a moment the same lieutenant returned and led me to a large beautifully carpeted room. In the middle of the room stood a wide table and beside it was an elderly general. The lieutenant left me in the room and went away. The general rose to his feet and approached me:

"Are you afraid son?" he softly said.

"No, general, sir"

"Why are you so pale, then?"

"I don't know, general, sir. Perhaps, because I don't know why I was brought here."

"No, don't be afraid, young man ... Yesterday I was present at the celebration of your battalion. I saw you when you came forward. I saw that you

---

28 New Town

were not ashamed of your faith in front of all those divisions of soldiers. Now you will work for me. *Dobzhe*[29]?"

"*Dobhze*, general, sir".

That same day I went to live with the general at his home at 25 Deluge. I never returned to those black army barracks. I lived apart from rest of the group and only my uniform identified me as being with the army. The general, for whom I worked, was a Catholic, but it seemed to me that this was only for external appearances because he never went to church. On Sundays he often sat and read the large Bible, which his mother had left, for him. It appeared to be a Lutheran one. He was in charge of a company of quartermasters at the Ministry of Military Affairs and was a very good person. His name was Karl Masny. My entire military service consisted of doing quiet, peaceful work. I was placed in charge of his entire domestic household. I was in charge of all of his keys; I had his entire trust. I had a special pass to go for supper in the city as many times as I wished. Often when I would be returning late from a special young people's service at the church or Pulawska Street or from the market, military patrols would come running to me from across the street hoping that they would have the opportunity for one more military arrest at this late hour. However, when I showed them my pass, they said nothing and quickly went on their way.

One time I asked General Masny why he had picked me to work for him from the many thousands of soldiers. He told me that a long time, before the revolution, his father owned a large steam-operated mill in Ukraine in which the manager and all the workers were the so-called *Shtundists*. During that entire time, not even the smallest item had ever disappeared from the mill. In the village, in which almost half of the people were *Shtundists*, there was never any drunkenness, theft or fighting. "And when I saw you standing there in the field, I concluded that you also were one of those *Shtundists*," said the General.

*****

The sun had already risen high in the sky. I still lay facing up, re-thinking about my completed journeys. As I reminisced and remembered, I felt

---

29   Good

a new strength filling my heart. "Lord, You were with me at that time, You helped me. Help me now. I gave You my youth, therefore, do not forget me now in my loneliness," I prayed.

I got up and looked around to see if anyone was listening but there was nobody here. All the same I was deeply convinced that my good Lord had heard me. O how good it was to realize this. How good it is to be with Jesus.

I returned to the city by the same road. Beside Wilenski Palace a German soldier detained me. He searched through my pockets and found my New Testament and opened it to the first page.

"*Was ist das?*[30]" He asked, looking at me with angry eyes.

"A New Testament", I replied.

"Polish?"

"Ukrainian."

He returned the New Testament and I continued in the direction of the Vistula River on Szeroka Street. I arrived at No 26, the building in which our Bible School was located in 1938. The gate to the building was closed but I could see through the fence a mailbox beside the door, from which I had received my mail at one time. I touched the gate as if it were some type of relic. Again a flood of thoughts and memories of my youth swept over me. They enveloped my heart like hornets, stinging it painfully and sharply. There was the large and unbroken window behind which our lessons were presented. A little farther was another window, which was the auditorium for worship. When Saturday came, our studies would be over and we would wait with anticipation for the evening. We would have a literary youth service, which included a Bible drama, "David and Jonathan". Brother Mankowski played the role of David and I played Jonathan. Many young people came from Pulawska, many older girls from the orphanage in Konstantin, as well as a large number from the other Warsaw churches. Everyone was happy and blessed. Afterwards, we would accompany the young people as far as the bridge in the centre of the city before returning to the school. We all regretted that the young people had to leave so soon, yearning and waiting for the following Saturday. Those were *chudowy chasy*.[31]

---

30 What is this?
31 wonderful times

My memories were flowing like a thread from a large ball of yarn. How beautiful things were then, how happy it was. But all of that will never return, because people have only one life and are young only once. And if a person misses and wastes their youthful years, then the rest of their life will be wasted. On the other hand, when a person finds a purpose for their life during their youth, if they find Christ, then all their life until their death will be useful and blessed.

I came to my residence. I fell on my bed and closed my eyes with my hands. Through the open door our beloved sister Marta saw me.

"What happened to you?" she asked.

"Nothing. Everything is fine," I replied, without uncovering my eyes.

"Do you want something to eat?" Marta spoke again.

"No thank you, I am full. I ate a different type of bread today. I am filled with my thoughts and memories of my past years."

Sister Marta closed the door. I was alone in the room, but in my thoughts I was together with all my friends with whom I spent my youthful days here in Warsaw.

The next day the weather was again beautiful, perhaps even better than the previous day. Early in the morning I decided to travel more than ten kilometers outside Warsaw to Radosc. Who had not heard of that wonderful relaxing location? All the residents of Warsaw were familiar with its abundance of fresh air, sunshine and its many green pine trees whose fragrant resin could be detected from a long distance. Believers from all over Poland know about it because at one time there was a Bible School there, which was known throughout all of Poland. The eyes and hearts of young Christian men and women were turned in that direction, everyone considered themselves greatly fortunate to have attended there for one or two winters. The same blessing was also mine for having been there.

I set out very early in the morning and in a few hours I was in Radosc. I walked alone from the station, along the same sand-covered path on which I had walked before. I arrived at the forest of tall pine trees, which resembled a long wall. Among the trees, bathing in the sun's rays, were elegant-looking vacation homes of different sizes surrounded by lilacs, cherry trees and other small bushes. The war had not affected this area, with the exception of the German signs at the station. It was an absolutely quiet and blessed place here. Everything was the same as it had been before the war. Birds were hopping about in the bushes. White-breasted swallows were flying low to the ground as if above a peaceful lake, predicting rain. The sun was unmercifully hot.

I walked beneath the trees and from a distance I could see the familiar fence and two tall fir trees. Beyond the trees a reddish building was becoming visible. This was the mission building, Bethel, where our Bible School was once located. Before the war, missionary conferences were organized here by W. Fetler's missionary organization. Every bush was familiar to me. I know every path. Every tree and flower was welcoming me. As I walked, many of my brothers, my friends and former students of the Bible School were walking with me. None of them were here now, but I could see each one of them in my heart and feel them in my soul and total being. It seemed we were walking together.

I opened the old, weather-beaten gate and I could see that my hand was trembling. I went in. There was the bench on which I once sat and "processed"[32] my lessons. Farther on there was another bench; they were all covered with dust and some type of twigs. Now there was nobody to sit on these benches, no one to walk on these straight paths, which were all, over-grown with tall grass. I went farther and wondered if anyone will meet me here.

I entered the yard. There was a wheelbarrow standing with a rake lying beside it. I concluded that this must mean that there was someone living here. An unfamiliar woman came out of the kitchen and asked me what I wanted. When I told her that I came from Warsaw to look again at a place that was memorable to me, a place where I once studied, the lady smiled and invited me into the kitchen. She served tea and told me that she also was from Warsaw. She was a believer and together with several other families had been living here since the beginning of the war. She told me that I could stay as long as I wanted, to look at everything and remember. I went into what was for me a precious "museum".

---

32 lit. translation "forged"

Mission's Building "Bethel" in Radosc where the Bible School was held

First of all I went to the large dining room where there used to be long tables but now it was empty. Each one of us students had our own place at the table, where we ate breakfast, dinner and supper. Here was my spot. In front of me sat brother Boris Wolosevich who always had a friendly smile. At the end of the table was a chair for brother D. Sheydy who always led in prayer before the meal. Before praying he often would ask:

"What should we sing today, brothers?"

"I am Standing in the Jordan"[33], somebody called out, and brother Sheydy would begin the song. This was followed by a moment of silence and then prayer.

I walked about the large room silently singing to myself, "I am Standing in the Jordan"[34] and then went out onto the veranda which was enclosed by green hops. The veranda was now old and leaning, the timbers were

---

33   Стою у Иордана я
34   **Припев:**   **Chorus**
     Отдохнем мы, друзья, в краю родном.   Friends, we will rest in our native land
     (Близок час!)   (The time is near)
     В свете берега, где нет зимы   On that bright shore where winter is no more
     (нет зимы),   (No winter)
     Песню Моисея воспоем,   We will sing the song of Moses
     (Близок час!)   (The time is near)
     С Иисусом вечно будем мы.   With Jesus forever more.

(Russian words taken from:https://vifania.org.ua/SongOfRevival)

cracked from the sun. From here, the pathway to our former orchard was visible. Once it was much wider, swept and sprinkled with fine yellow sand, but now it seems to have narrowed, overgrown with grass and sunk into the ground. I walked past the office window of the director of the school, M. Gitlin, and continued walking around the building. Crossing the grounds I followed a narrow path to our fine, sheltered gazebo which stood on a small elevation and which resembled a large green top hat. It seemed that nobody had been here for a long time because there was not a single human footprint in the sand. The bench was covered with dust from the previous year and its paint had peeled off and lay scattered on the ground. The sun's warmth never reached this spot because the gazebo was overgrown with wild hops which had become entangled in the wooden poles and spread unrestrained across the wooden structure in a green braid. From the thick shade of the hops came the melody of a solitary bird. It seemed me that this was the only living thing still left which had a happy clear song. Besides the bird there was no one else. Former students had all moved away throughout the wide world, some were still living while others were lost during the war.

From the gazebo there was a path leading to a small pond where a single grey duck was always swimming. It gathered food from the banks and would pick up the pieces of bread that we would throw to it. Today, even the duck was gone. The pond was deserted and overgrown with large leaves.

I went into the orchard and noticed that the large barn was still standing where there once was a horse. Behind the barn there was a shed beside which a tied-up black dog always sat. The grounds-keeper was a fine German brother named Emil. He spoke good Polish and was learning Russian. I recall that one time he was going to Warsaw and wanted to tell our housekeeper, sister Marta Kowalchuk, to give the dog something to eat while he was gone. Brother Emil came into her kitchen, hoping to impress her with how well he was speaking Russian, and said in a loud voice:

"Sister Martena, if I am gone for a long time, please eat my dog."

I wonder where good brother Emil is now?

I walked and walked around the orchard. Everything that once was here was still standing as a living, unforgettable picture before my eyes. Everything was very dear, reminding me of the past. There on the large wall of a building, where we stored our belongings, a sign written in Polish was still visible: "*Bo coz pomoze czlowiekowi, choeby wszystek swiat pozyskal a szkodowalby na duszy swojej*[35]". The letters were already faded but it was still possible to read them. I stood beneath the wall and read and reread this precious message several times. There were three of us who had painted this sign: brother Boris Wolosevych, who was lost somewhere in Germany, brother Wolodimyr Morhun, from far-away Volkavysk,[36] who was also killed in the forests of Belarus by partisans, and me. I am aware of all this and my heart *hurts-hurts*. Again I reread the lettering and wiped my sweating brow.

Brother Moses Gitlin, Director of the Bible School in Radosc

---

35 For what does it profit a man to gain the whole world, and forfeit his soul. Mark 8:36
36 Town in Belarus

I walked past the pond, across the wide yard, past the gazebo and hastened into the forest, which had now spread out to the Bethel building. Now the rustling of the tall pines were calling me. Feeling some type of weariness and apprehension in my heart, I walked beneath the pines. They were standing forlornly and quietly rustling. The wind was playing in their branches and singing some kind of song. Yellow butterflies were flying, searching for flowers.

I sat beneath a tall pine and gave in to my thoughts. I was transported on the wings of a fast-flying bird along the road back to Volyn. In my mind I could see my family, my acquaintances and in my soul I could feel bitterness and pain. There was not a single familiar person anywhere near me, not a single friend. I was all alone, surrounded only by what was foreign and unknown.

Returning to the green gazebo, I knelt underneath the thick growth of hops and in my deep melancholy I prayed for a long time. After that I felt as if Someone had brought an unexplained and complete healing to my heart and I felt so good. Many times in the past God had listened to me in this place. He heard me again and I thanked Him sincerely from my heart.

Towards evening I returned to Warsaw. In the home of sister Marta, I found brother Bychkowski present, and sitting on a chair by the window was an unfamiliar man. Upon seeing me, the man became fidgety for some reason and began to button up his coat, getting ready to leave.

"Sit brother, sit," sister Marta said to him. "He is one of us." The man settled down.

I stood by the door not understanding anything of what was happening. Later sister Marta explained.

"That you might know," she said. "This is brother... (I have forgotten his name) from the Jewish nation. His whole family has been lost and he has escaped from the ghetto. He has Polish documents and is now hiding among us."

I approached the short, young Jewish brother and kissed him in the fine evangelical Polish tradition. It seemed to me that I was not only kissing this unfortunate persecuted Jewish-Christian, but through him, I was kissing his entire nation, which a cruel regime had sentenced to death.

Later I sat down beside him and he told me the horrific tragedy of his family. His eyes were filled with tears. I, in turn, told him about what had happened to the Jewish people in Volyn. There were several Jews who were hiding in our village who, as I later learned, were escorted during the night across the border to Halychyna where they were turned over to unknown believers who later handed them over into other safe hands.

The Jewish brother *listened–listened*, then he breathed heavily and said:

"We rejected Him, so He rejected us, but I believe that He will still have mercy on us. I just don't know how long I will live or if I will be able to stay in hiding."

The next day I went to the church service and there I met the Jewish brother again. He told me that he was not alone here but there were also other Jewish-Christians that the Warsaw Christians were hiding. This was an act that deserved much gratitude and honour because these individuals exposed their life to danger in order to rescue those who were sentenced to death. It was especially necessary to thank those Warsaw Christians who were in mixed marriages with Germans. Many of them were allowed by the military leadership to live in the finer parts of Warsaw. The majority of them did not share the heart of Hitler and were hiding Jewish believers among them. This was the greatest danger for them at that time.

During this time I was searching in Warsaw for Dr. Price, a teacher at our Bible school, but he was no longer there. He was Christian, born into a Jewish family, who was lost, together with his family, in the terrible Warsaw ghetto.

IN THE FOOTSTEPS OF GREAT DESTRUCTION

In spite of the fact that the front was not very far from Warsaw, the mail was still running in the General Governorate and it was still possible to receive mail from Germany as well from the General Governorate region. Eventually I was able to make contact by letter with other young Christian brothers who were studying at the Bible school in Wiedenest and working at various jobs. I was also able to make contact with other believers within the General Governorate, who invited me to come to them. However, the General Governorate was burning with the fires of genocide. The Polish were destroying Ukrainian villages on a large scale and it was dangerous to travel to these parts.

One time, brother Bychkowski and I received a letter from the Baptist youth group in Rokitno to attend a special youth celebration. We set out. The train was exceptionally packed with people because residents of Warsaw were travelling to the villages where they could purchase or trade various urban goods for food products, which they later would re-sell in Warsaw on the black market. However, we were able to push our way into the overloaded car and we were on our way. It was the month of June and outside it was sunny and pleasant. Our train travelled across fields covered with lush grain, raced through a thick pine forest, and then re-emerged again across flat fields.

In the afternoon we arrived at Biala Podlaska and exited the train. In the courtyard several German soldiers were standing and checking the carry-on luggage of the passengers. We were not carrying anything so they did not bother to ask us anything, but again I noticed here, as in Warsaw, frightful soldiers in grey uniforms watching with iron fists over their occupied territory.

There was no regular train from Biala Podlaska to Rokitno, but rather a narrow-gauge train for which one had to wait for several hours. So we waited. We sat down in the shade of some shaggy trees and later walked about the empty streets around the train station. Biala Podlaska was bathed by sunshine and the smell of roses that grow in long hedges by the beautiful building. Before the war, while traveling on my way to Warsaw, when the train would stop for a longer time at Biala Podlaska, I was able to get off the train and go into the station. I still remember those beautiful red roses. They were the same as before, fragrant and beautiful. The horrors of the war had not affected them. In general there was no trace of the war here. The roses were blooming, the trains were running and there was no damage in the town. If it were not for the green German helmets at the station, there would be no sign of any occupation.

Suddenly, from behind the bushes, silently and imperceptibly, a round black train engine emerged, dragging behind it several small train cars. The conductor looked out from the car and smiled, showing a row of white teeth and waved his hand. Together, with other people, we sat down in an empty and very old car. Whoever wanted could sit down on the dusty benches or stand on the steps. They could also climb onto the top of the car, lay face-up on the even boards or sit with their legs dangling over the edge and travel in this way. The train crawled slowly through the dense forest, black smoke billowing behind it. The conductor was leaning on his elbow and dreaming. Wild cherry branches scratched against the car walls and we tried catching them with our hands. There were many hazelnut trees here with many clusters of developing nuts on them. It was a wonderful trip, one that I had not been on for a long time. It seemed enchanted, almost a fantasy. The forest swung in a wide arc and beyond the curve a wide field was visible. There was clover planted here and at the borders of the field were yellow piles of sweet clover. I had a desire to go there, pick some of those flowers and embrace them to the point of becoming oblivious and unconscious. However our box-like cars were again diving into the thick forest and the clover fields were becoming hidden behind the bushes. The coo-coo sound of a cuckoo bird could be heard somewhere in the distance, the dark shadows of the trees filled our cars and darkened our faces. What beauty! What luxury and extraordinarily wonderful greenery!

There was nothing like it in Warsaw. There were only army trucks, green tanks, and angry soldiers' faces. Here it was a completely different world.

We were again traveling through the forest and Bychkowski said that our charming voyage would soon come to an end. He had been here many times but for me it was the first time. Therefore I was examining every bush and becoming familiar with everything. I wanted to remember every small detail.

The group of Evangelical youth in Rokitno.
Seated in the centre of the second row, from left to right:
M. Podworniak, S. Bychkowski and Yuvko.

We arrived at the village of Rokitno. There were straw-thatched houses on both sides of a wide street. Gardens and orchards were becoming green. Pots and pitchers for milk were turned upside down and drying on the fences. At the edge of the road there was a beautiful house of prayer. I don't know who first brought the Word of God to this village or in what year this happened, because, unfortunately, we don't have, and never had, a record of the history of the Evangelical-Baptist work. So it is not clear when the spiritual work began in each village. But now there was a fine congregation of believers in Rokitno, all of them fervent in their love for the Lord and His work. With great respect they recall the many brethren-preachers who had visited them in the pre-war years. They especially remember, with a deep warm love, brother L. Dziekuc-Malej[37] who, in the past, had ministered a large amount in the region. And now, as we walked down the wide street, approaching the house of prayer, I had a pleasant feeling knowing that I am walking the same road that great workers for God had walked in the past. It was here that there was a portion of our history and spiritual work. Unfortunately nobody, anywhere, has yet written that story.

In Rokitno we met brother P. Hordiev, who had come here several days before us. The church was filled with people with happy smiles on their faces. Every window was wide open through which evangelical singing was flowing. No occupying enemy's shackle could suppress this song, which like a fast-flying bird, circled over the village, which had been tidied up for the celebration. All the believers were singing, the choir was singing, and brother Bychkowski and I sang a duet. There are many spiritual recitations, anecdotes, and among all these … the preaching of God's Word. The services were conducted not according to an American style, but according to our own customs. Nobody was guided by the clock, but by the sun. The sun was still high in the sky, therefore, the service could continue as long as necessary. Again the choir sang, more recitations, solos, and duets. All of this was spiritual food, which only the children of God could understand.

Each item presented during the youth services was either in Ukrainian, Russian, or in Polish because there were various people present here. Something had to be presented for everyone in their own language. We felt that we were all one family who understood each other, and there was never even a hint of any misunderstanding. There was no elevation of any one language or any humiliation. It is also in order to mention that although the congregation in the village of Rokitno was primarily Ukrainian, there were also Polish people present. In general, in the village and even now, there were many Polish families. There had not been the same hurtful enmity between Polish and Ukrainians that was manifested in Volyn, in the General Governorate, in Chelm and other areas. People lived together in harmony, awaiting the end of the German occupation.

---

37 Belarusian Baptist clergyman, 1888-1955

After the service there was a communal meal for everyone, followed by a time of getting to know each other. There were many believers there whom I had met for the first time in my life. Immediately it felt that even though we were meeting for the first time and our lands were far from each other, we were close and related as in a large family. What a great miracle God had created.

We spent the entire week in Rokitno. It was announced on the following Sunday that there was going to be a baptism in a different village. We waited for Saturday and in the meantime we helped the local believers with various work. We even went into the forest looking for some types of berries. Rokitno was surrounded on all sides by a very dense and luxurious forest. There were potato fields extending all the way to the forest, and in the autumn the villagers had to guard these fields against wild pigs.

One day, as we were walking through the forest, we saw a beautiful cemetery, which was surrounded by a green fence. There were hundreds of graves with leaning crosses standing in rows. These were the graves of German soldiers from the First World War. Before the war, German parents used to come here. They would sit on the graves of their fallen sons, leave flowers and draw crosses. But now, since 1939, no one had come here. The crosses were leaning and the paths between the graves were overgrown with grass. But the beauty of nature and the silence of the forest were unchanged. There was no sound of banging or of anything moving. Only the wind was rustling through the branches of the sprawling trees, singing its sad song to the fallen. Every day, towards evening, the silence was broken by the jarring sound of the narrow-gauge train from Podlaska, and then there was uninterrupted silence and peace again. I walked among those lonely graves for a long time, reading the darkened inscriptions and later thinking that only in a place like this was brother V. Gutshe able to write his wonderful story, "The Other Christ", which at that time was published in the Christian periodical, *Druh*[38]. This was the finest place to write, to create and meditate. It seems that the silence of the forest, under these overgrown shrubs and sprawling hazelnut bushes, is a source of inspiration, revealing vivid life-like images of the true essence of humanity.

---

38 "*Druh*" means Friend. Vladimir Gutshe was editor of the publication during the 1930's.

The following Saturday we got up very early in the morning and set out to a village where there was to be a baptism service. We walked along roads that were unfamiliar to me and followed several paths that went across fields. There was a large number of us because almost the entire Rokitno youth group decided to go on this trip. We walked through several villages and farms. The front had not been in this area but in the villages we observed the ruins of Orthodox churches, which stood as witnesses of a pre-war Catholic action. Some of the churches had shattered windows and broken doors. Only stones, which were now overgrown with tall pigweed, were all that remained of other churches. As we walked the local believers related to me the painful history of this land. For the first time, I heard that I was walking in the steps of a great destruction that raged throughout this region with unchecked power.

Baptism near the village of Rokitno. In the centre, Brother P. Hordeiv

In the beginning of 1937, the regional authority of Poland, at the instigation of the Catholic clergy, began its offensive against the Orthodox Church. In every church, during the service, a Polish policeman would sit on a special chair and observe whether the priest preached his message in Polish. Once the service was coming to an end, people would exit from the church and in this way they released the priest from having to preach the sermon, because there was no one to preach to. The Orthodox population protested firmly against the Polonization of its church and then the Polish authorities would charge the leaders with repression. On any evening a village would be surrounded by police armed with machine guns, preventing anyone from leaving. Then a drunken army would drive into the village and attack the people. Anyone whom they encountered was beaten to the point of death; women and young people were not spared. After completing their assault on the people, the army would begin to destroy their possessions, not excluding any house. In the homes they would break the windows and window-frames, destroy all the dishes, clothing and linens in the house. Pillows and quilts were torn apart and feathers were scattered outside. They had with them barrels of naphtha, which they poured, over the food. They climbed up to the straw-covered roofs of the houses and proceeded to tear off bundles of straw before they broke through the roof with crowbars and pickaxes. They then headed for the church, from which they threw out the icons, the shroud, and even what was commonly called the holy gifts[39], and books. They destroyed everything and burned it before the eyes of the people. Amidst the wild laughter of the drunken soldiers and the weeping of the village people, the soldiers would attach hooks to the cupola and pull it down with ropes, over-turn the outhouses and proceed to ruin the entire church. In many of the villages through which we were now travelling, the ruins of churches could be seen. In the wide green spaces surrounding the cemeteries, people had erected crosses and when walking past the spot where their church had once stood, they crossed themselves and whispered prayers.

In one village, we stopped for a short time at the home of a kind brother and noticed that behind his orchard was a large pile of dirt, overgrown with pigweed and thistles. The owner of the home related to me the tragedy that their village had endured when a drunken army invaded them and destroyed the Orthodox church. Such terrible events happened here that it was difficult to believe that such a thing could happen in Poland in the year 1938. That year I had lived in Warsaw and did not know anything of the

---

39 Holy gifts is a reference to the Communion elements which had been blessed by the priest.

tragedy that was taking place within these villages. The newspapers were careful that nobody would find out about this lawlessness and therefore hid these actions from even their own people. Everything that Poland was doing to the Ukrainian Orthodox church, it would later reap in abundance. God is just in His judgment. However, the Polish administration was not solely responsible for all the evil and abuse that the Ukrainian people endured but, rather these were the dark acts of the Roman Catholic Church, inspired by the Vatican's most Holy Father in Rome. Ukrainian newspapers published in the General-Governorate, which were controlled by Greek-Catholic fanatics, wrote that in Rome, "there is a great loving heart which, day and night, is concerned about the fate of the Ukrainian nation." This was a form of derision referring to the collapsed Orthodox shrines, because it was evident to everyone that this terrible ruin, which I was now seeing with my own eyes, was indeed initiated by that "heart" in Rome. From earliest times this "loving heart" had a great appetite for Ukraine; striving to bring it into its servitude; but the opposition to this goal was Orthodoxy. For this reason, whenever this "heart" had the power, it took revenge against Orthodox Christians with the greatest cruelty. In the past the Ukrainians of Podlaise[40] had painfully suffered from these attacks.

Soon we arrived at our destination, a small village where there was also a Baptist congregation. The day was exceptionally warm and pleasant. We gathered by a narrow stream that was crystal clear like a tear. Around us fields of tall grain were ripening and beyond the creek, stretching all the way to the forest, were level hayfields. The grass had grown very tall and was interspersed with multicolored flowers that were swaying gently and breathing on us its fragrant mist. What beauty was here, what luxuriousness. Waves were moving through the grain. At home we used to say, "Peter is tending the sheep". The river was glistening. Above it, water butterflies were flying and crickets were chirping. It all seemed like a fairy tale. It seemed to me that this was not a river in faraway Podlaise, but rather, this was my river Horyn[41]. On our hayfields, the river was also narrow and it was possible to step over it in several places. It appeared to me that this

---

40 A region in Poland
41 The Horyn is a tributary of the Pripyat which flows through Ukraine and Belarus.

baptism was taking place in the Horyn and my dear villagers were standing along the shore.

Lively singing of the hymn "*Nedaleko Za Rikoyu*"[42] awakened me from my reminiscing and painful reflections on my past, and I opened my eyes. Brother P. Hordeiv slowly walked into the water, holding down the bottom of his robe. He was followed in a single file of those who, today, will have the most blessed day of their life. Those who were making a commitment before God to serve Him for the rest of their life. I felt moisture in my eyes and turned my eyes to the field. I remembered my own similar celebration on July 12, 1926. Many years had gone by but whenever I witness a baptism of faith, I am always moved as I remember that day. My own baptism took place in the village of Stary Tarazh near Pochayiv. Processions of people, who were traveling to Pochayiv for the Festival of Peter and Paul, slowed down to witness how *Shtundists* are baptized. As I came out of the water, an old woman came closer to me, crossed herself and loudly proclaimed:

"Truly the end of the world is coming. Such a small child, and already he has signed away his soul to the devil."

This is the road that I have been traveling since that day, but I have always been blessed with my Lord and only those who have experienced it could understand this joy.

The baptism concluded and all the believers were still standing on the shore for a short time with a gentle wind kissing us. Suddenly someone started singing another song, which I heard for the first time on that day and later I wrote it down in my notebook:

> Talkative stream will not tell
> Anyone of my holy mystery,
> Silently through forests and fields
> Runs this cold stream.
>
> Will not tell what the waves have heard
> The secret of my humble soul,
> When my body was immersed in baptism,
> In the silence of midnight,

---

42 Literally translated "Not far across the River". This hymn was frequently sung during a baptism service. Sung to the melody, "O, The Deep, Deep Love of Jesus"

I renounced this world,
A vow to God I made
I promised to live according to His Word,
In my soul I rejoiced in Christ.

In the midnight hour, beneath the radiant moon
This holy promise was made.
With blessings and holy hope
I heard an answer from God.

And heeding to the sacred prayer,
That rushed from the water into heaven
Filling my soul with peace,
God sent a blessing to my heart.

That stream was a silent witness
Of my great holy secret
When the pure, shining water
Passed over my head.

Do not forget me lonely stream
When I sit by your banks in the spring
On that beautiful green shore
Where God completed His covenant with me.[43]

This song had a very moving folk melody. I think that I was more eager to determine the history of the composition of the song, but I was unable to find very much about the origin of the song. The local believers only told me that the song had come to them several years ago from Russia.

The following Sunday we travelled further all the way to the Bug River where another baptism celebration was announced. There was an Evangelical-Baptist congregation there. We arrived in time on Sunday morning. Again we had to walk through villages which were unknown to me and again we saw the same scenes of destruction of Orthodox churches

---

43 Translation of "Не расскажет ручей говорливый" as printed in Russian by the author. Modified from a translation found in → http://teksti-pesenok.ru/40/MAVYCe/tekst-pesni-0408-Ne-rasskajet-ruchey-govorlivyy. See Appendix 1 for complete Russian text of song.

by the Polish. Everywhere there was evidence of the tyranny of Rome, "the most righteous" Catholic faith in the world. I could not help but remember a Catholic procession, which I saw in Warsaw in pre-war times. The entire city was decorated with national and Vatican flags, every street was swept clean, all the lights were lit up, and bells rang loudly from every church, the sound soaring above Warsaw together with flocks of frightened pigeons. The procession, with countless banners that fluttered in the wind like shiny wings, moved slowly along the wide Krakowskie Przedmiescie in the direction of Nowy Swiat. On the sidewalks, barricaded from the street by a wall of policemen, were thousands of people from the entire nation. I also stood among those crowds of onlookers. I stood directly in front of the A. Mickiewicz[44] Monument and, together with others, was waiting to see that which had stirred the entire Polish capital and brought it to its feet. There was a sea of flags, a sea of school children, a sea of soldiers of various formations, and orchestras. Crawling slowly in the middle of the street was a shiny carriage, which was decorated on all sides with extravagant wreaths and live flowers. High up on the carriage was a gold-gilded coffin containing relics of the Roman Catholic saint, *Ignatius* Bobola.[45] Masses of fanatical Polish people began falling down on the sidewalks, until their foreheads were touching the concrete while crossing themselves, and sorting through small rosary beads. The carriage continued to advance. It was moving so slowly that it appeared to be standing still. Fat cardinals, wearing red and black mantles, walked behind it, carrying long sticks[46] that were curled at the top. Crosses were visible on their shoulders, crosses on their chests and crosses on their sleeves. Beside me two young Polish intelligentsia were standing and I could hear one of them say to the other:

"Look, they have hung crosses everywhere, on their shoulders, on their bellies; only in their heart there is no cross."

---

44   Adam Mickiewicz, a Polish patriot and poet
45   Andrew Bobola is one of the patron saints of Poland. *"Ignatius"* might have been used in error. St. Andrew Bobola belonged to the Society of Jesus founded by St. Ignatius Loyola
46   Croziers

Behind the cardinals and bishops walked the representatives of the government: the generals, the Marshal of the Seym[47], and diplomats and ambassadors from other countries. Everywhere there were cylindrical top hats and long black robes that reached down to the ground. All that lordship, puffed up like blisters, walked behind the carriage; meanwhile, their eyes were piercing the people who were falling down on the sidewalks. As their eyes surveyed the people, in their hearts they were probably laughing at the elderly Polish women who were stretching out their work-worn hands towards the shiny coffin, they were laughing at the national darkness. And what was there to laugh about?

Later I remembered the words of the priest, Father Hryhoriy Shavelsky, the head chaplain of the entire Russian army and the naval fleet. He wrote that during the time of the First World War, when their main headquarters were located in Baranovichi, Russian armies on the northern front were suffering defeat by the Germans. Russia had neither weapons, food nor clothing. They telegraphed Czar Nikolai about their situation and in a short time "help" came. The king sent an icon of St. Mikolai. They carried the icon into the trenches; the soldiers listened to the divine worship, received communion and their soldiers' spirits were revived. It seemed that there could not have been a greater incentive because it is evident to everyone how this comedy with icons ended. This was the same result in Poland with its Bobolas and other "saints".

Walking through the Ukrainian villages, I witnessed over and over again with my own eyes and became convinced that for our nation, as well as for all nations in the entire world, the ungodly, who are decorated with crosses, are more dangerous and frightening than pagans without crosses. And now, as never before, the words of Polish poet J. Slowacki became alive to me: "Poland, your destruction is in Rome." Unfortunately the Polish never heeded the more insightful voices of its poets, but went according to its "Bobolas" to a national catastrophe and submissively following wherever the black hand of the Vatican led them.

Thanks to God that in spite of the Vatican terror that ruled Catholic Poland in the past, thousands of people, including Polish, Ukrainians and

---

47 Seym (Sejm in Polish) or Diet is the highest governing body of Poland, The Marshal presides over the Seym

other nations, came to know God's truth and lived according to the teaching of the Gospel. And I also was now one of those people. We stood, all together, in a large group on the winding banks of the Bug River singing "*Nedaleko Za Rikoyu*". A sermon and prayer followed the singing. Sturdy poplar trees grew along the shore and we could see green hay meadows on the opposite bank. This was the beginning of a new world. The Bug was, at that time, the boundary of the lands occupied by the German forces.

From the Bug River we returned to Warsaw. We encountered great unrest and overcrowding in the city, even greater than it was before. We got together in a small group and again considered going somewhere else, perhaps into the villages. However, the elder brothers advised us to remain in the city and to stay together as a group. Whatever would happen would happen to all.

Conditions were becoming terrible and severe in Warsaw. Death was not far from every person and could encounter them in their residence or meet them in the park. More German troops appeared on every street of the ruined city. Their surveillance and cruelty increased tenfold. Anywhere one had to cross a street, a grey helmet or the black barrel of an automatic revolver was waiting to meet them. Because the German army had become more numerous, terror within the population had also increased as well as the resistance by the residents of Warsaw. Although this resistance was not always evident to any large extent on the outside, everyone felt that it was there somewhere. That it was organizing and waiting for the appropriate time to erupt with an unbridled force. Everything, everywhere gurgled like water in a boiling pot. Green tanks crawled by like turtles. Anti-aircraft sirens wailed, as a large assortment of fugitives from Eastern regions shuffled along the sidewalks. They had arrived in Warsaw from every city to save themselves from the approaching front; but from here, there was no longer any place to escape. To many it appeared that this was the final place of escape and only death awaited them here. It was especially dangerous for Ukrainians to remain in Warsaw because the Polish-Ukrainian enmity had crossed from Volyn across the Bug, and flooded all of Chelm, the entire General Governorate and now it had arrived here. It was dangerous to speak Ukrainian on the streets. In general, it was dangerous for any young or healthy person to show themselves.

Anticipating some type of danger or perhaps they were aware of it, well-intentioned Warsaw believers would come to us and say:

"Brothers, perhaps something terrible will happen. It might be better for you if you left Warsaw."

We fugitives felt and saw this ourselves but we did not have anyplace to go. We came here and this was the end of our road. Let the will of God be done in everything. There was no place for us to go any farther. We would sit and wait for the unknown.

We soon learned that trains from Lviv were no longer arriving. German newspapers in Warsaw, which were being published in Polish, printed announcements from the front on the front pages in large letters. Everywhere it was evident that the German army was "systematically moving into new positions". People, who were reading between the lines, understood the real situation. Sabotages became the regular activity of the Polish underground, and increased German terror was the answer. Often during the day, there would be the bodies of Polish men hanging from telephone poles along the street and on the following day someone scattered live flowers on that spot as elderly *babusi*[48] knelt there and whispered prayers. Warsaw was becoming more and more German during the day, but during the night it belonged to Poland. The Polish underground was exceptionally well organized. They crawled out at night from their hiding places and spread out throughout Warsaw looking for places where they could attack their captor. And when morning came they again hid somewhere in the ruined buildings of their capital. They hid in sewer holes and waited for an opportunistic moment. Every morning, on the walls of the homes, on the bridges and on the fences, one could read threatening messages: "Death to Hitler and Stalin", "We will not give Poland to the East", "Let independent Poland live". The Germans erased these unwelcome messages and searched for the guilty parties. However, the "guilty" were somewhere deep underground and the occupiers often caught and punished anyone who happened to fall into their cruel hands. They punished in such a way as to frighten others but now they could no longer frighten anyone. The patience of the Warsaw citizens had come to an end and no further acts could change that.

---

48   grandmothers

FARTHER INTO A FOREIGN LAND

One day we learned that the Germans had issued a proclamation that all fugitives must depart from Warsaw. Our elder brothers assembled for a joint meeting and prayer regarding our future fate. The Warsaw believers joined us to try to resolve this tough situation. We consulted, talked, discussed and made plans, but at every step and with every new plan we encountered insurmountable obstacles. It seemed that the only option was to go to Germany into forced labour and accept the hungry fate of Eastern workers. None of us wanted this for ourselves. The idea of going to a distant foreign country did not appeal to anyone, but the situation was such that we had to leave. First of all because of the approaching front, and secondly, one could feel in the air some formidable storm approaching which could wipe us off from the face of the earth.

Our brothers went into town, talked to various authorities, questioned, searched and consulted with local German believers. They studied different routes for our common rescue out of Warsaw. Later they came and notified us with the following news: if we, believers, wished to stay together, then we could leave with our entire group. At the station we would be assigned several freight cars as well as a civilian guide who would be one of the German believers.

Just when we were racking our brains, thinking about our hopeless situation, a German brother came from Germany to Warsaw specifically to rescue our group. Gracious German Christians in Westphalia, as well our brothers, who at that time were already in Germany, were aware of our situation and desired to help.

A portion of the believers on the eve of departure from Warsaw

We began preparing for the journey. On Sunday there was still a large farewell service for us. There were many tears, many fervent prayers and kind words and best Christian wishes for us. The following day we assembled into a caravan and slowly made our way to the large freight station in Warsaw. We were a large group of believers, gathered from all regions of pre-war Poland. Among us were also believers from Greater Ukraine, Belarus and deep Russia. We had all found a shelter in Warsaw and now, as a combined group, we were leaving the city. We were taking all our possessions with us, whatever one had. Some were dragging behind them wooden wagons, loaded with bundles and dusty suitcases.

At the so-called "spare track"[49] stood several empty freight cars. A young conductor told us that these were our cars. Two of them were covered and the rest were open. We began loading our belongings and everyone began looking for their own space. Families with small children occupied the covered cars, and we, especially the single young men, settled into the open cars.

July 26th, 1944 was a very warm day. Not a single cloud was visible in the sky and the sun was burning unmercifully hot. Our people were arriving from every street of Warsaw. Mothers were carrying small children in their arms, loaded with wobbling pots, pails and suitcases. There

---
49   spur line

were many Warsaw Christians here as well. Some wanted to come with us, others only came to say farewell one more time. The majority of them were wavering, trying to decide whether to go or not. It would be a pity to leave their homes, their churches, and their city. Therefore, some of them hesitated and then returned back to their homes. We seated ourselves in the cars and waited for them to bump together and begin to move. Anxiety and a lack of peace gripped our hearts. This will be a long and unfamiliar journey. I especially felt a great heaviness and sadness upon my soul because a foreign country had absolutely no attraction for me. I was raised in my peaceful village in Volyn. I grew up beneath the warm skies of my homeland, under the care of a loving mother, and therefore my yearning was to return to those times, to go back home to Volyn. However since my circumstances at this moment were forcing me to wander, and since I was already here, returning to my homeland seemed impossible. A grey fog caused by the conflagration of the war obscured any possibility of returning. Right now, there was only one road – to the west. Since there was such a large number of us, and all of us were believers, somehow the idea of wandering was not terrifying. It will somehow all work out. If only the train would already leave...

The sun was setting. We were settled inside the cars, but the cars remained motionless on the spare track, they didn't even budge. There was another long train alongside us, a passenger train. It was headed to Czechoslovakia and inside it was carrying all the Orthodox clergy of Warsaw. The passenger train began to move, some people, who were unknown to us, were standing at the windows and waving to us with their hands.

The sun had already set. The evening was warm and clear. The moon rose *high-high* over Warsaw. None of the Warsaw believers were approaching us because at night it was not lawful to be out in the streets. The long train of freight cars remained standing as we sat and waited. Hour after hour passed. All of a sudden shrill alarm sirens sounded above the city. The sound of airplanes could be heard from somewhere high beneath the stars. Nearby, from the centre of the town, anti-aircraft guns replied, as long beams of searchlights cut through the sky. In the distance the sound of exploding bombs could be heard.

We got out of our cars and searched for a hiding place beneath some buildings. What would happen if the airplanes came here? We were standing at the station from which there were tracks leading to all destinations. We were in a spot, which one expected could be bombed first. Around us were some tall buildings, piles of coal and wood. Among all this were a large number of railway tracks on which countless train cars of various types were standing. They were all standing motionless as if waiting for something. Our freight cars were also standing there, as the long night continued endlessly.

Again the sound of sirens was cutting through the night air and awakening the citizens of Warsaw. Again the search lights, again the firing of anti-aircraft guns. The long beam of light caught in its beam an enemy aircraft high in the sky and followed it across the night sky. The airplane, like a pigeon, was attempting to escape, but the light continued to follow it. We could see it flying directly above us and then turn away towards a field. Families with small children were already huddled underneath the train cars, children were crying, mothers were praying...

In the darkness, several of the brothers walked between the cars to the conductor's shed.

"Send an engine, please, and get us out of this place. We have small children and women..."

They returned disheartened.

"Well, what?" we asked.

"We are not going ...we have to grease..."came the reply.

"How?"

"Simply this, one of the conductors did not say it outright, but we understood that if we want to leave it will be necessary to 'grease the wheels'. We have to give them something. Do you now understand? This is not only the case in Warsaw but it is an idea that the whole world stands on ...If you don't grease... you will not go."

We immediately collected among ourselves several hundred of the wartime currency of that time and took it to the dark building. In less than half an hour an engine appeared and bumped into our cars. We were all grateful and breathed easier. Sirens were howling above Warsaw, anti-aircraft guns were thundering, searchlights were erupting upward as our freight cars began slowly to move away from the station in the direction of the open field. Farewell poor and weary Warsaw! Will we ever return to you? Thank you for the shelter you provided for us poor fugitives!

I don't know about anyone else, but for me it was difficult at this moment to leave Warsaw because it was here that at one time I spent the finest years of my youth. There were so many experiences here, so much reflection, so many plans; but, from all this very little came to pass.

It was night. Stars were twinkling overhead, and the moon was soaring among them. We were travelling through some kind of forest. Everywhere it was silent and peaceful. The trees were all lined up like soldiers. The wheels were making clicking noises and inside the cars tired fugitives were drowsing. There were so many of them, over one hundred people. This was not simply a group but an entire congregation, a whole church of Christ who were without a place to settle or a proper organization and leadership. Before the war, members of this church belonged to various missions and various independent conference and associations. Within this group were Baptists, Evangelical Christians, and Free Brethren. Perhaps in the past, when the world was at peace, these groups were not as close. Perhaps some human principle or other divisive barrier stood as a hindrance to their brotherly fellowship; but now all this was in the past, vanished like a fog. Because of our shared experiences, the events of war and common misfortune, we were now joined into one inseparable family. We looked out for one another like a brother for a brother, or a sister for a sister. We were all now equal in our situation, all the same, all forced by fate into an unknown pathway. At that time we conversed with each other in different languages, each using the language in which they were most fluent. No single nation stood as an obstacle to another. All were truly "one in Christ."

I would like to specifically emphasize here that Christian unity was what my soul longed for. Also this group of believers, which left Warsaw on July 27, 1944, became the nucleus, which paved the way for the great and blessed spiritual ministry among all Slavic nations in Western Germany. But more about that later.

A warm morning welcomed us far away from Warsaw. We were now travelling through wonderful fields and pine forests. There was no sign of the war anywhere here. The ripe grain was bending low to the ground;

green spruce trees cast their fragrance and stretched their arms towards us. The sun had risen *high-high* in the sky and it was becoming very hot inside our open cars.

Suddenly a town becomes visible in the distance. Our train came to some widespread bushes and made a large curve around them as its metal wheels scraped and screeched against the rails and then came to a halt on a distant empty "spare track". We all climbed out onto the green grass. Behind the cars was a field with the first sheaves of grain haphazardly scattered in the high stubble. Past the field were more freight cars, and further still was a town. We are not allowed to go anywhere because we didn't know for how long we would be standing here. Some of the brothers made a fire beside the cars and began boiling coffee. Mothers began preparing food for their children.

I walked the length of the freight cars, went out to the field and picked up a sheaf of grain. An elderly brother approached me.

"What is the day today?" he asked.

"27th of July", I replied to him.

A tear fell on the old man's chin. He wiped it with his sleeve and sighed like a small child. Then he said:

"Harvest has also begun in my home. It's already two weeks after Peter and Paul[50]. But who is harvesting there?"

He walked back to his car with his head down. I also followed him with a heavy burden on my soul. I knew that there was no field as wonderful as mine; the beautiful, sunny homeland that I would not be able to see anywhere in a foreign land. I might see large cities, boundless oceans, but nowhere is there the kind of place like my own. There is only one Ukraine in the world.

Life was buzzing beside our train cars. Some were boiling coffee, some were washing themselves by the water tap, and others were sitting on the green grass reading some old newspapers. Single young men, who were travelling in the same open car, collected long pieces of lumber and loaded them into their car, tied them down with wire and then covered them with green branches to create a shade from the sun. Our conductor went

---

50 A feast day celebrating the martyrdom of St. Peter and St. Paul, which is observed on June 29.

someplace and did not return for a long time. We waited and feared that we might again have to "grease the wheels".

This was the town of Kutno where we stayed for almost a whole day. We later walked to the small town nearby, came back and all the time we waited to continue our journey. Travel during this time was not normal and nobody knew at what time a train left or arrived.

Finally several conductors arrived and told us to prepare to travel. The red sun was setting beyond the forest in the distance as we set out again on our journey. We were again travelling across flat, Polish grain fields and past spruce trees. Here Poland was not the same as it was in the east. Everywhere there was evidence of the handiwork of a good landowner in the past. The fields were wide and even, in the fields there were harvesters, mowers, and herds of cattle. The train was travelling slowly and we were able to observe and admire everything. The brothers began to sing a song. The melody burst out from beneath our green covered shelter and settled on the harvested fields. We could hear others singing in the their cars: *Strashno zhityeve chviluyetsya moreh.*[51] The train was moving quickly now, blowing its horn occasionally, spewing black clouds of smoke that dove into the field, like into the water. Swallows were flying above our heads, vaulting over the cars. And the song soared and soared:

> Help me reach the shore quickly,
> I cannot go any farther:
> Only in You can I find an eternal harbour,
> Lord, hear me, Holy Lord.[52]

---

51 Страшно життєве хвилюється море. (Terrible Waves in the Ocean of Life)
52 Stanza 4 of "Страшно життєве хвилюється море". Traditional melody. Music published in Ukrainian Evangelical Hymn Book (Євангельський Співаник Відродження), Chicago, 1954, No. 430 and 430a

GERMANY

The outlines of some buildings were gradually becoming visible ahead of us when one of the brothers loudly announced:

"I believe that is Germany!"

The brakes squealed as the train began to slow down. Tensely we looked ahead. We could see a desolate looking field that had not been seeded. A white wooden pole was standing; there was one, and then farther --- a second, a third. This was the former Polish-German border. In the past there would have been vigilant border guards on both sides of the border watching over their land; but now the border guards were gone. Everywhere, on the right and the left, stretched out only one "Greater Germany"[53], as the German newspapers printed.

Our train stopped beside some kind of building which was overgrown with thick hops. Through an open window we could see some people; these were German police. They came out of the building, went around the cars, as we sat quietly like birds trapped inside a cage. The police went to the locomotive engine, conversed about something with the conductor, as well as with the guide who was leading our group. He wrote something down and then went to a telephone booth where he talked to someone by phone. In a few minutes a military person came and again talked with the conductor, looking over some papers. He walked the length of the train and then stood on the platform and waved his hand. Our train again began to move past the buildings.

"This, brothers, is Germany", someone from our group said. "Now we shall see how she will welcome us".

---

53 The Greater Germanic Reich (*Grobgermanisches Reich*), was the official state name of the political entity that Nazi Germany tried to establish in Europe during World War II.

"She will welcome us with hunger and hard work, as she did to hundreds of thousands of our prisoners", replied another voice.

We continued on our way without speaking. Each of us was thinking his own thoughts, each one trying to determine what was awaiting them up ahead. Not far from the forest was a glistening lake on which there were white swans swimming and some fishing boats with white sails were also in the water. Near the shore of the lake, a thick, green ring of bulrushes was growing and we could almost hear their tender whispering. We heard and repeated with Falkivsky[54], "Bulrushes were for me a cradle; in the mud I was born and grew up". In spite of the beauty and fullness of the German lakes beside which we were travelling, they could not compare to the Polish lakes and reeds about which Dmytro Falkivsky, so movingly sang.

Alongside the lake stretched an asphalt road, which glistened like glass in the sun. The fields had already been mowed and were full of sheaves. Harvesters were already resting underneath some kind of shelter. Our train was moving very slowly, as if it had become tired and would come to a stop at any moment. There were sheaves lying on the right side of the railroad track and beside them some young girls were working. Seeing us, they ran up to train and waved.

"Where are you people from?" they called out, chasing after us.

"And where are you from?"

"We are from Ukraine."

"And we also are from Ukraine. Sincere greetings to you from our native country."

"Thank you, thank you. Have a blessed trip."

On the other side of the tracks there was another harvested field. Beside more sheaves, another group of girls were saying something and waving their hands at us. But we could not hear them because the train had sped up and was disappearing over a hill.

We crossed another wide, shiny road, crossed several bridges, and travelled past green orchards and meadows. On the trees we could see an abundance of apples and pears; sturdy willows and poplars leaned above clean, clear streams. Beautiful Germany! Here every small piece of land was being used for growing grain. We could see sheaves of grain scattered

---

54   Ukrainian poet, 1898-1934

all the way to the railroad, some were scraping against our cars. We come to a hill on which we could see some metal poles and wires. Attached to the poles were thick cables on which black trolleys, used for carrying coal, were moving in both directions across a deep ravine. In one direction they were travelling filled with coal and then returning empty, moving slowly along the same path. Everywhere there was evidence of economics, culture, technology and civilization. But all of this did not appeal to us, because we had seen with our own eyes a different "culture" in Warsaw, in Lviv and in all Ukraine, and everywhere throughout the entire east wherever soldiers from this country, through which we were currently travelling, had come. Nothing that we saw here appealed to us or brought us comfort. Sometimes the only thing that brought a spark of hope to our gloomy hearts was that there were so many of us, all believers. If it so happened that some calamity would happen to us, we would be there to help one another. And furthermore, we knew that in Germany there were many believers with whom we had corresponded before the war and, if necessary, they would come to help us if we were wronged in any way.

It was almost evening when we arrived in Berlin. Realizing the fact that I am here filled my heart with emotions. This was Berlin! This was that small patch of earth in Europe where, behind closed doors, plans were devised to invade Poland and then to conquer the world. Terrifying directives were sent out from this place for the enslavement of the world, and every freedom-loving person in Europe now pronounced the name of this city with fear and disgust. On the other hand there was much about this place that reminded us of something more pleasant and good. Before the war a Russian Christian magazine, *Evanhelskaya Vera*,[55] was published here. This was also the place where brother Ivan S. Prokhanov[56] lived and ministered and where he was buried. Somewhere in this city brother J. Shnaidruk was carrying on a Christian ministry; but he knew nothing about us. There was a large congregation of believers here, and if they knew that we were here, they certainly would make themselves known to us and would send us words of comfort and advice which we desperately needed at this time.

---

55 "Evangelical Faith", edited by I.S. Prokhanov
56 Ivan Stepanovitch Prokhanov (1869-1935), ministered primarily among Evangelical Christians in Russia.

But nobody from among the believers in Berlin was aware of our arrival and nobody came to meet us. Brother Z. Reczun-Panko went several times to a number of public buildings and to the railway station trying to make contact by telephone with the Berlin Christians but, because of the continuous American air-raids, all telephone contacts were cut off and he was unable to speak to anyone about us.

The train stopped beside a bridge. It was almost evening. Two young boys approached our cars. Sewn on the left sides of their shirts was a badge on which was written the letters "OST." We already knew that these boys were from either Ukraine or Russia, so we began a conversation with them. They told us that every night American and English airplanes flew over Berlin, and we were standing in a dangerous spot because not far from here was a water reservoir and on the other side of the railroad tracks was the train station. And truly, as we looked around, not far from us we could see the blackened walls of some buildings and the burnt trunks of trees sticking up.

"But if there is going to be a raid," the boy from Ukraine said as he concluded the conversation, "there is a tunnel ahead of you. It will be possible to take shelter there."

They continued walking among the cars like two ghosts; like someone who brings terrible news.

Some of our brothers went to the station and brought back two large pails of black German *ersatz*-coffee[57]. We shared the coffee among ourselves and drank it without any sugar and without the least appetite. Several brothers went again to talk to the conductors who were sitting in the engine. They asked if they could take the train outside the city, but the conductors were as helpless and frightened as we were. We went to search for shelter in the event that it would be necessary to flee. It was very quiet inside the cars; nobody even stirred. It seemed that everyone was fearful even to speak, waiting for something. But in the sky, the stars were twinkling and it seemed that they were guarding our safety. All this time many of the brothers and sisters were standing beside the cars, constantly

---

57 "Coffee" made of different organic material (often acorns) to replace real coffee which was not available.

looking upward and praying fervently and tearfully. Many years later we learned how God heard and answered those prayers.

Brother F. Lewchuk, in the magazine *Seiatel Istiny* [58] for Nov-Dec, 1961, reminded all those, who spent that frightful night standing in Berlin, how God was merciful to us during that time. Many years later, already in America, one former American pilot told the daughter of brother Lewchuk, about how they were bombing Berlin daily for a whole month. He told her that one night they flew from England and were above *La Manche*[59], when suddenly they received a radio message to return to their base. This pilot was never able to find out why they had to return. This was the only night when there was no raid on Berlin, and this was the exact night when we were standing there waiting and praying. What a frightening and memorable night!

This was not the only vivid time when we personally witnessed that God was watching over us, His children. Several days after our arrival in Germany we learned that God had delivered us out of Warsaw, like He delivered Lot from a burning Sodom and Gomorrah. We had left Warsaw on July 27th and on August 1st there erupted a general uprising of the Polish against the Germans. Warsaw became embroiled in fire and destruction, but we were already far to the west. God had miraculously led us along His way.

We spent that memorable night in Berlin. We knew that our fellow-believers were living somewhere in this large city, but we did not know their exact number or the extent of their ministry. We learned later that the work here was extensive and blessed by God. More will be mentioned about this later.

Sometime after midnight our train jerked suddenly and began to move slowly among the ruined buildings. Above Berlin, the night was silent. There was only darkness, which swept into our open cars from every corner and from every lane. We stood, with our heads poking out above the sides of our open cars, and looked out at the streets of the city. Not a single person could be seen, not even a flicker of light in any window.

---

58 "Sower of Truth", a monthly periodical published by the Russian-Ukrainian Evangelical Baptist Union in USA, Ashford, CT

59 English Channel

Everything was sleeping, everything appeared dead, motionless ... this large European capital now resembled a desolate cemetery. It seemed that all of the living had died or had hidden themselves in some deep underground hideout. Occasionally a policeman would walk by on the sidewalk and a weak light would momentarily flicker beneath his feet. The bright moonlight cast long shadows of trees that fell upon our heads for the entire length of the train. The wheels were clicking as we slowly made our way farther and farther out of the city. Wide fields became visible and farther there was a sparse young forest. We had crossed the threatening danger. Praise you, Lord!

Berlin was left far behind us, but only now did we realize that we had not escaped the danger. Everywhere we saw evidence of the American air raids. When our train stopped at a small station we were horrified at the images we saw there. A thick spruce forest, which came all the way to the station, was now burned to the ground. Twisted pieces of zinc metal sheets were scattered among the burnt trees. Several trees were lying uprooted from the heavy bombs. Everywhere there were deep blackened holes and the bitter odour of fire and devastation. It seemed that there was a terrible raid here recently because the destruction was still fresh. The Germans had already managed to repair the tracks and all the trains were running and stopping here. We now stood there and waited, looking at the results of the bombardment. Not a single building was left standing by the station. Everything was reduced to piles of crushed rocks and refuse, but on a smoke-stained wall there still hung a large sign with the name of the station. I got out and walked through the burnt forest and looked at the ruins and then returned to the car. I finally realized that it was no better here than in Warsaw or in Berlin. As we travelled further west we saw more and more terrible destruction at every location. We saw that we were going into a very dangerous place. We were going into industrial Westphalia, where it would be necessary to constantly expect heavy air raids. But just as it is impossible to turn back the flow of a river, it was also impossible to change our course or our fate. Everything was now being controlled by the circumstances of the war. We were not our own but belonged to those who at this moment exercised power over millions of subdued people. Wherever the train was taking us, that is where our eyes were focused and what our hearts were deliberating. One of the brothers offered this encouragement:

"Brothers, it is not necessary to lose heart and give up. First of all we must resolve to stay together and then nothing will be alarming. There are many fine German Christians living in Westphalia. Somewhere in Wiedenest there is a Bible School where many of our friends are currently attending. They are already familiar with the local believers, so if there is ever a need, they will stand up on our behalf and will help us. We are not youngsters anymore whom the Germans can simply seize somewhere on the street and throw us, one by one, into this cauldron for torture and mistreatment. I remember a long, long time ago; this was just after the First World War, that I was receiving a magazine from Dusseldorf, *Vestnyk Lyubovi I Istini*[60], which was being published by the so-called Free Brethren. These were fine Christian people, and we were going somewhere into that area. Therefore, it was not necessary to whine and moan ... it was necessary to have faith and only faith..."

In the evening we arrived at a town; I believe it was Magdeberg. The station was clean and there were many people there. There was no sign of bombardment here. Our train stopped in front of the main entrance to the station. We could see that people were walking on the platform on this summer evening and many of them had sewn on their shirts the letters "P" and "OST". We know that these were Polish and Ukrainian or Russian. They were paying no attention to their badges; as if this is the way it should be, in order to differentiate them from the Germans. They were walking past the station, happily talking amongst themselves and laughing. Seeing our train cars, they approached us, but we began to move and there was no opportunity for any conversation or introductions with our people. The badges "P" and "OST" made an unpleasant impression on us because at home we had seen the yellow patches on the shoulders and the chest, which identified a Jewish person. Here we saw that Polish, Ukrainians, Russians and other nations from the east were being singled out with badges.

We continued travelling for some time. I cannot remember for how long, but I do remember that our train stopped briefly in a wide, flat valley where there was a small town. There were many red buildings and many

---

60 Herald of Love and Truth

factory chimneys that were pointing upward above the town. It was almost evening and we were told that we were going to stay here all night and tomorrow we will continue further. We were not worried because we did not have anywhere to hurry to. We exited from the cars and looked around the area. Surrounding the town we could see wide fields, birds were singing. The scenery was wonderful. Later that evening, several young men wearing "OST" badges came to us. There were from the Kharkiv region and had already been working for two years in this town. They were gaunt and unhappy. They told us about the life of a worker, but especially for a worker identified with an "OST" sign, life was very hard. They had to work hard for long hours every day. Food was substandard and insufficient. But what gnawed at and consumed these workers the most was a longing for their homeland. We gave those boys some biscuits, which we were still carrying with us from Warsaw. They were very grateful, but at the same time warned us not to give away bread too freely because we were going into a desolate and hungry Germany.

Night was over and a new, sunny morning welcomed us in a foreign land. Our train was travelling through some beautiful landscapes of Westphalia. At times it passed through green valleys, ravines and crawled alongside trees of dense forests, made wide curves around rivers before coming out again on a straight track. The scenery here reminded us of our Carpathian Mountains because there were many spruce-covered hills. On the hillsides herds of sheep were grazing. A shepherd stood beside the herds with a horn slung over his shoulders and long pole in his hand. Beside him, keeping watch was also a dog. The streams were flowing clean and clear, and quite swift. Sometimes they were quite wide and then became narrow again. The roads were all paved with asphalt. Trees were planted on both sides of the road. Running alongside the railway tracks, the roads were sometimes hidden by bushes and then disappeared somewhere into a ravine. The villages were all neat. The roofs of the houses were mostly covered with a red roofing material. Everything looked bright and cheerful. Only the women were working in the fields, while their husbands and sons were fighting on all fronts for a "new Europe". Women were using cows to haul hay, to plough narrow strips of land, which were surrounded by bushes, and to haul sheaves, brushwood and other types of plants.

Stretching upward in every village were the pointed spires of churches. A very large rooster was visible at the very pinnacle. In general, most of the churches here were Lutheran and because of this, everywhere there was evidence of order, cleanliness, progress and a high German culture. This is what Westphalia was like, where we were going.

Later as we often travelled throughout Western Germany, we were convinced that where there was a Protestant population, there was more culture and civilization.

THE END OF OUR HOPE

One sunny morning we arrived at a small Westphalian train station. We could read the name of the town from the sign on the station – Soest. It was Sunday. Our train stopped beside a dense growth of trees and we were told to carry out all our belongings. After we piled our suitcases and bundles on the grass, we all assembled together on an empty platform. The sun had just risen. Its beams flooded the shiny drops of dew and bathed the environment with gold. It seemed that it had rained here yesterday because there were still puddles of water between the railroad ties. Morning birds were singing, butterflies were flying and we were standing in a large group on the platform like wayfarers and homeless foreigners. Our conductors went someplace and it seemed to us that we would be arbitrarily left here. A heaviness and deep sadness had fallen on my heart. But as we stood there, looking at each other, one brother came to the front of the group, opened a hymnbook and said in a quiet voice:

"Dear brothers and sisters! Praise the Lord that we have come even this far. We do not know what lies ahead but let us put our fate into God's hands. Today is Sunday and in the entire world, wherever God's children live, they gather on this day to worship the Lord. We too must pray together and sing a hymn together to thank God for the completed journey thus far…"

Someone in the crowd began to sing, "Не пройди Иисус меня Ты"[61], a second voice joined and soon everyone united in song. We stood on the wooden platform that was still wet from the morning dew and sang. It was an emotional and moving scene! There was a solitary brother from far away Caucasus, standing and leaning on a long cane. In his left hand he was holding a well-worn coat; these were all his possessions. He was

---

61 "Pass Me Not O Gentle Saviour". Literal translation from Russian ,"Jesus Do Not Pass Me By"

captured by the Germans and taken into forced labour, but while in Poland he escaped from the camp and later became attached to our group. A short distance from him two young girls from the Chelm region were standing and near them a mother with a small child in her arms. The song continued to ascend high above the trees and its echo reflected back into our hearts. "Боже, Боже! О услыш меня, слыша люд молбой обятый, не пройди меня".[62]

One brother from Warsaw came to the front of the group and read Psalm 23. We listened with the greatest attention with our heads bowed low, and then we prayed. Many brothers and sisters were praying sincerely with all their heart and with tears in their eyes. The sun continued to kiss our bowed heads. An elderly German walked past us, stopped on the road and reverently removed his cap. Apparently he was an older Christian, but probably had never before in his life seen such a worship service by a group of refugees. Perhaps the trees that were growing near the station were witnessing such a service for the first time in spite of how old they were. Therefore, they, together with us, listened to the singing, bowing their branches, which were wet from the dew, and praying with us. Around us everything was silent and peaceful. The only sound was the chirping of a bird in the thick branches of the linden trees and a sobbing mother with a small child in her arms.

During my lifetime I have attended various conferences, attended large services where there were many people. But never, in any place, had I ever experienced such an emotional and gripping moment as during that morning worship service at the station in Soest. Perhaps this was because I never needed God's help and protection as much as then. And because of that, The Lord was so near to my heart.

Several very large cargo trucks came and we loaded all our belongings on them and drove past the station in the direction of the town. We came to an empty building, carried all our belongings inside and waited for what would happen next. In front of us were some wooden barracks surrounded by barbed wire and at the gate stood an elderly German guard. Behind the

---

[62] The corresponding English words in the hymn are, "Saviour, Saviour, hear my humble cry. While on others Thou art calling, do not pass me by". The Russian can be literally translated:" God, O God, hear me; listen to your people, who are pleading for your embrace, do not pass me by…"

wire people were walking, all of them were wearing the "OST" badge. A little farther past our building there was a large apple tree growing. It was filled with apples that were not quite ripe yet. A girl, wearing an "OST" badge, who had been sweeping out the building, approached the apple tree, grabbed a branch and pulled it towards herself. Several apples fell to the ground. The girl grabbed the apples and began eat them hungrily and then fled into our building. The German, who was standing by the gate, saw the girl and began to chase after her, throwing a heavy dry branch at her. But the girl, in a flash jumped out the door and the German, swearing angrily, returned to his position near the gate. This picture remained a sad memory in my soul. How many apples did this girl leave behind in her home! Not sour ones as those found here on trees growing along a road, but true, soft and fragrant apples. Here, in this foreign land, she was giving away her best energies to an insatiable regime, hungry and without any rights, craving only a sour, unripened apple...

We learned that we had arrived at a transition barrack for Eastern workers. We were each given a piece of doughy, dark bread as well as a ladle full of black coffee without any sugar. In the afternoon a wide gate was opened for us and we were directed into the grounds of the camp. Who knows how many thousands of people from our nation had passed through this gate. Who knows how many tears have been shed inside these dark barracks standing in forlorn rows inside a barbed-wire fence! On the walls of all the barracks were various names, written in Polish, in Ukrainian, and in Russian. In a corner beside a window there was a poem, inscribed with an ordinary pencil, which our girls copied and later brought to me. On the wall of this temporary barrack, some unknown Ukrainian girl, with fine even handwriting, had left a piece of her heart, writing the following poem:

> My dear *Matusia*, you can see it is spring
> Strolling through your own flowers!
> In this foreign land, bring me flowers
> And awaken memories in my soul.
>
> I am thinking now of last spring—
> Of planting poplar trees with you;

May they grow and bring delight,
That is what you told me, *matusia*.

The chirping of birds and the festival of spring
I have also observed here in a foreign land.
The sun is smiling pleasantly from above.
And the flowers in the grass are turning blue.

I will pick fragile blue violets,
I will leave them behind in memory of spring,
This is how I will remember your grief
And the silence in my native house.

The violets will wilt and lose their blossoms;
I would like to keep them forever
So that in a better future, when the world will be changed,
I would remember again this spring.

My dear *matusia*, accept my greeting,
May it soar like a bird in the spring!
I long for a spring of abundant blossoms
To share again with you.

From a sincere heart I desire for you,
Now when everything is being resurrected,
May the warmth of spring cultivate in your heart
Hope for better things.[63]

    A name was written below the poem – L. Lazareva. We stood for a long time reading these words, which were so dear to us who were experiencing the same feelings that this unknown Ukrainian girl had experienced. There were thousands like her in this camp. From here they were assigned like slaves to different jobs. From this location, roads spread out in all directions throughout Westphalia and these roads were watered with tears and strewn with difficult sighs. Now it was our turn and after us others

---

63   See Appendix 2 for the original poem copied in Ukrainian

would follow. It would continue like this until this oppressive war and the evil deeds of the frightful Hitler regime came to an end.

A short time later we were all called to an office that was located in a small wooden barrack. Within a few minutes several passport photographs were made of each one of us. We then had to file past several tables where government officials were seated and tell them, through an interpreter, the date and place of our birth, sign our name several times, get finger-printed, and then at the last table receive our documents which would allow us to remain in Germany. After receiving our documents we saw that we would all be included in the group of Eastern workers, and from now on were obligated to wear the "OST" badge. Beside the photographs on the documents we could see our identification number from which we could at least approximate how many other detained individuals had preceded us. My serial number was 11579. It was stamped under the picture on the document. Close by the picture, written in large black letters, was written the following: "THIS PASS MUST ALWAYS BE CARRIED ON YOUR PERSON. ANYONE ENCOUNTERED WITHOUT A PASS WILL BE TAKEN TO THE POLICE AND ARRESTED"

Towards evening we were ordered to go into the camp washrooms and take a bath in lukewarm water, without any soap. After the washroom we were handed our belongings that had been disinfected. Everything was now wrinkled, damp and stank from some type of chemical, similar to carbolic acid. We got ourselves dressed in our disinfected clothing and no longer resembled ourselves. The sleeves of our jackets looked like an accordion, the collar was turned around, the lining was hanging out and for some reason was now longer than the jacket.

We were again led through a gate where more barracks were standing. This was where the workers lived who had gone through the washroom and the disinfection. From here, those who were needed would be taken to the station for further transport. They allowed us to enter these barracks. This meant we were now clean and worthy of living on German soil.

The guard, who was leading us, pointed to a barrack and we all began carrying our belongings into it. The barrack was large with a black wooden floor. The windows were dirty; perhaps they had never been washed. Beside the walls stood some high, three-tiered, wooden beds. On every bed there was a bare mattress stuffed with chopped-up straw. In the middle of the room there was a large table on which were some empty tin bowls in which we could bring coffee for ourselves from the kitchen.

We rushed to choose our bed for the night. Those who had something to cover the mattress with, covered it, and whoever did not have anything, placed his duffel bag or suitcase beneath his head. This now became his bed.

I found a bed by the window and climbed up into the third level. From here I could see the outside. Wiping the pane with my sleeve, I could see the setting sun in the distance. It was disappearing behind the green hills, bathing my dirty window with its golden light. There were a variety of people walking about in the yard, frowning, unhappy and angry at their fate. Here, there were dark-skinned people from the Caucasus region, Uzbeks, Polish, Ukrainians, Belarusians, and Russians. There were representatives from all the nations of the East who had been reached by the arm of the war and brought here.

Two beds below me was a Christian brother that I knew from Warsaw. We talked for a long time until the only light, a single, small electric bulb for the whole room, was extinguished. As soon as the light was turned off I felt something fall directly on my forehead as if a fly had flown in and alighted there. And then something fell on my cheeks, on my arm...

I sat up in the bed and began searching for what was annoying me and not giving me any peace. Again I felt something fall on my head and begin crawling over my hair.

Suddenly someone from the opposite side yelled loudly through the entire room:

"Hey, will somebody who is beside the door please turn the light on! There is something here.... something is falling from the ceiling."

"Yes, yes there is something. A light please! Something fell..." I could hear voices from all the beds.

The light glowed dimly. We all got out of bed and began searching on ourselves for what had fallen on us.

"Here!...Here!. I found two fleas!" a man's voice yelled

"I have some too! ... Fleas! Fleas!...Without any doubt, fleas as big as beetles," another voice said.

The fleas now had come out of their hiding places and were crawling on the floor, falling from the ceiling, crawling out of the wooden walls and attacking their new victims.

"Nothing will happen to you," said a Belarusian. "Just go to sleep and when they bite you, you won't feel it. Nobody in the world has ever died from this. Go to sleep and that is all!"

He wrapped himself in his sheet, pulled some kind of sack over his head and stretched himself out on his bed. But not everyone was able to do this. One elderly brother, from somewhere near Kovel, got out of bed, tied the ends of the sleeves of his shirt and his pant legs into knots and walked around the room in this way saying:

"Well, so much for disinfection. We bathed and cleaned ourselves! Back home we were poor, but we never had this much of this type of filth. So much for European culture; they hope to conquer Europe but cannot even conquer bedbugs..."

It was impossible to sleep. A whole day without rest and the various experiences and thoughts were driving sleep away. I saw some people taking their blankets and going outside. I did the same thing and went out into the wide courtyard; the night was moonlit and warm. Our believers were sitting and dozing on the stairs to our barrack, tucked inside blankets or coarse bed sheets. The fresh air, like a hand, swept all sleep away and took it somewhere else. We sat, conversing, counting the bright stars and our days. It was dark inside the barracks; it was dark in the kitchen. Only at the gate, the guard from time to time struck a match and coughed, letting us know that he was still there and guarding his captives. In the east the sky was turning red, sunrise was approaching. Just before dawn, sleep finally closed our eyes and the conversation stopped. Each one of us, for whom it was convenient, slumped down and slept. Some slept on the stairs, some slept on a pile of chopped wood; as long as it was not on the bare ground. Night fell over the barracks and guarded our peace.

Morning came, cloudy and gloomy. A light rain began to drizzle like through a sieve. We were all on our feet. Everyone took time to wash themselves, to pray, to read the Bible and to drink our black coffee. Now we were just waiting for what was to come next. We did not have long to wait. Two large wagons were brought near our barracks and we were told to load our belongings on them. We were going to the station. We carried out everything that we had, as well as what we had received in that terrible barrack—fleas. They had crawled into our backpacks, into our clothes and travelled with us all the way until the end of the war. The Americans finally exterminated them with a white powder in 1945.

We were ready to leave and standing in a long line beside our wagon, when a girl came out from the office and in broken Polish-Russian told us to listen to what she was going to read. We held our breath, as she unfolded a sheet of printed paper in front of her and read out several names from our group. Among the names I heard my name being called. Something sharp pierced me in the heart. The girl folded the paper and firmly said:

"Everyone whose name I read, take all your belongings because they are going to a different place."

"What? To another place?" Voices of disapproval could be heard throughout the crowd. "If we are not going all together, then we won't go anywhere at all from here... We will protest. During the entire trip we were told that we would all stay together, and now they want to divide us! No, this will not happen. We came here only because we were supposed to stay all together..."

Confusion spread among us, we began searching for something. We soon appointed from amongst ourselves several of the elder brothers who knew the German language, and sent them to the office so that they would seek our rights and our protection. Everyone's belongings remained on the wagons and nobody touched them. We were not going to separate and that's all. That will be our united decision.

The brothers went to the main office and we stood and waited impatiently, looking at the green door behind which our fate was being decided right now. Very long moments passed. As soon as the door of the green barrack opened we held our breath, but each time it was a different person who came out. Our brothers, for some reason, were absent for a long time. The bargaining for our souls and our brotherly fellowship was long and persistent. The green door opened and our representatives appeared: P. Gordiev, Z. Ryczun-Panko and others. They appeared dejected and worried. Coming down the stairs, they approached us and waved their hands despairingly.

"Well, how is it, brother?" Several voices called out immediately.

"Not good", came the terse reply. "Nothing will help, we will have to separate..."

"No, we are not going anywhere! We will not separate," said those who were selected to go to a different place.

"Brothers and sisters -- that will not help anything", said someone's strong and serious voice. We are in captivity, we are in a foreign country, we are not our own, therefore, let us not protest. There are thousands such as us and each one of them must do that what they are told."

"That is true, that is true," someone agreed. "If they only divide us into two groups, that would still be a great favour to us. They could separate us one by one so that individuals would be scattered all over Germany and we could do nothing about it."

"True! True!"

Brother P. Gordiev climbed onto a nearby wooden block. He was one of the brothers whom we had sent to the office. He surveyed each one of us with his eyes and wisely said:

"Brothers and sisters, there is nothing that we can do. They have decided and here, we are ... as nothing. We must not cry but rather we must trust and be obedient to God. Later, we can search for each other through letters, and perhaps it might be possible to come together again. We will write letters to the brothers in Wiedenest and through them we will be able to find one another. Who knows, perhaps God has purposely done this for our good. We will see later..."

"So who is going where?" came the question.

"The larger group is going to Schalksmuehle[64] and the smaller one to Rüdersdorf.[65]"

None of us knew where these places were, whether these were cities or villages. We only knew that they are somewhere in Westphalia, somewhere among these green hills.

Reluctantly, and with great sadness and sorrow, we began to collect our belongings. Those who were going to Schalksmuehle were piling their belongings on one wagon and those going to Rüdersdorf on the other.

---

64 A municipality in North-Rhine Westphalia, Germany
65 A municipality in Brandenburg, Germany near Berlin

Although we would still be travelling to the station together, we could sense that we were already separated and this experience was very painful. During the time that we were travelling together we got used to each other, we became friends. We sorrowed together, we sang together, we prayed together, and now we would be separated, going to various places unknown to us. Those among us who were single young men and women felt this parting most acutely.

Once again we were all together at the station in Soest. One final time we gathered together to sing, "*Встретимся ли ми с тобою*"[66]. Following the singing one of the brothers read a passage from the Bible, and spoke briefly. He reminded us that we were in God's hands and that we should not worry or be sad, but we must have faith, pray and wait.

The group that was going to Schalksmuehle entered the empty train cars. There are so *many-many* of them. Almost all of our senior brothers as well as the single young men and girls were among them. They carried all their belongings onboard and waved their hands to us, but we, through tears, could hardly see anything. Finally they were all in the train, they were looking out through open windows, and we just stood there … just stood … The train slowly began to move. Our final moments together, a final wave of the hand and the cars disappeared behind some bushes. They were gone...

The total of those who went to Schalksmuehle that day were 85 people. Of those, 64 were members of the congregation and the rest were children. There were 16 preachers among them. A ministry began there immediately and a large church was organized. 19 individuals went to Rüdersdorf. The total number of those who left Warsaw was 104 individuals.

Suddenly the sky brightened and a bright sun smiled down as a large freight car rolled up and stopped beside our belongings. This sun reminded us that God's grace is limitless in spite of our little faith. We would be convinced of this many times in the days ahead. Later on we saw that it was necessary that we should be separated because there were many people in the place to which we were sent to whom it was necessary to witness about God. This separation was for our personal good and for God's glory.

---

66 Melody of "Shall We Gather at the River". The Russian words are literally translated as "Shall we meet with you "

Unfortunately, this is not how we always feel in our life. We did not feel this at the train station in Soest. Sometimes God sends us some type of pain, some type of testing, and we are ready to complain and become sad, but later we become convinced that this was truly necessary for us.

Before long our car jerked forward and began rolling behind the green bushes. We were now also moving, and although there were much fewer of us, we had among us brothers Barchuk, Bychkowski, Hryn, Antonowich and others, so this road also was not fearful. Thanks to God that although we were few in number, but at least we were together.

We were seated in the wide doors with our legs dangling and reading. I never knew then that a time would come when I would have to write about these memories. But inside the book, which I was reading during this time, which I still have today, I had written with an ordinary pencil the following line:

"We were separated and left Soest, on the 1st of September, 1944."

That same day in Warsaw a resistance broke out, but we were already far away from the inferno. How good God had been to us.

Our train continued rolling on as in a fairytale: among green bushes, between high hills, crossing valleys and through tunnels. Our surroundings were filled with sunshine, fresh mountain air and the fragrance of flowers. The door of the car was wide open and the sun was casting its rays upon us, the flowers were breathing their aromas on us and the tall evergreens were waving their hands. What beauty everywhere! There was a desire to take flight as a bird without any care and to fly above those hills, go to those green tops, gaining energy and strength. Our train turned before a mountain and we could see a village in the valley below resembling a flat tabletop. There were white houses with red roofs. The roads were all paved with asphalt, glistening in the sun and then hiding beneath overgrown bushes. There were no signs of war visible anywhere, only peace, sunshine and beauty!

Towards evening we arrived at the town of Siegen. Our train was left standing on a spare track, waiting, because we still had to go farther today. The tracks surrounding us were filled with train cars. As we looked we could see someone who looked very familiar approaching us between the cars. We looked closer and saw that it was brother Wasyl Siery. He had been working in Siegen for a long time. He knew some good German Christians in this town and by some miracle he found out that we were supposed to be here. He came to our car and greeted us. We were greatly moved by the efforts of our brothers and sisters in Wiedenest, as well as the local Germans, who had heard about our transport, stayed in contact with each other and looked out for us. That meant that we were not alone, we were not left abandoned to our fate.

Not less than a half hour later, we began moving farther. Again our train was crawling among trees, but now in a completely different direction. We were travelling alongside a small river. We could see piles of burnt cinders and rusty metal everywhere; all around there were bigger and smaller factories. We would travel a short distance and there would be another factory... and near it there were black wooden barracks for workers like us. Some of the barracks were new. It was evident that they had been built recently since the flow of enslaved workers began from the East.

We finally arrived and stopped by a small station which had trees planted around it. Above the door a sign was hanging on which was written in black letters – Deuz. We carried out our belongings, because a large cargo truck was already standing there, waiting. The truck brought us near a forest, then turned into a field and continued on a dirt road, constantly creaking loudly. We looked at one another and kept quiet. Each one had only one question ... where are they taking us?

We came to a wide valley with a river flowing between green banks. Close to the riverbank stood a factory with a tall chimney. Beside the factory there was a building. We were told to get off the truck and go into this building. Black smoke was continually rising from the factory's chimney and we had a feeling that this smoke was settling down in our hearts and our souls. From the open doors of the factory came the sound of clanging of metal, the creaking of metal sheets and the bitter odour of gas.

Directly behind the factory there was a narrow road going up a hill and there beside the forest were some uneven clusters of old wooden barracks. A barbed wire fence, on which children's shirts, towels and socks were drying, surrounded them. The area outside the barracks was full of people. Work at the factory had finished for the day and it appeared that the people were now free. Seeing us they came running down the hill.

"Where did you come from?" they asked, forming a tight circle around us.

"From Warsaw," we answered.

"But personally, where are you from?"

"From different regions of Ukraine. Some are from Warsaw itself. And you?"

"I am from Poltava"

"I am from Vinnytsia"

"Is there anyone here from Volyn?"

"Why not? There is...", replied a man's voice as he came forward. "I am from Lutsk, and another person here is from the Vladimir Oblast. The rest are mainly from Greater Ukraine."

"And how is your work here?" we asked everyone in general.

"You came here, so you will see. We are not allowed to say anything."

We walked about, talking to the people and becoming acquainted. The sun was setting behind the hills.

A bell finished sounding in the barrack and our new acquaintances left us because it was suppertime. We were told to also go and take with us out some type of container for supper. We went. We received a piece of dark bread. On the bread was a small dab of margarine, and in a cup we received some black coffee and a small piece of sugar.

There was no more room in the barrack, so we were given a small room beside the kitchen, which was also close to the river. After supper we gathered in our room, sat down on the floor like wandering nomads in the desert, as brother Barchuk opened the New Testament.

"Well brothers and sisters, the Lord has helped us until now. Let us thank Him for His protection, for everything."

We all got down on our knees and prayed. Several young ladies from the other barracks watched us through the open door and windows and did not know what kind of people these were who read the Bible and prayed so openly in their room. Hesitantly they entered our room and stood beside the wall. When our communal prayer ended we talked with them and gave them some Christian literature, which we had brought with us from Warsaw.

Late that evening we lay down on the floor to sleep. This was the best sleep of the entire trip. We were content that regardless of what would happen in the future, for now our journey was ended. We had supper, we prayed together, we were able to witness to many girls from Ukraine about Christ, and now we could rest. Fresh, healthy mountain air was coming in through the windows. Somewhere in the hayfields frogs were croaking and crickets were humming incessantly.

Morning came, bright and warm. Right behind our barracks flowed a narrow, shallow stream. The water in it was as clear as a tear. On a regular day one could see every pebble, every root, and every fish leisurely playing in the water. We washed ourselves in the stream and sat down in a row along the bank. Brother S. Bychkowski had his guitar with him and brought it out. He sat at the edge of the riverbank and began to strum the strings. One of the brothers sighed deeply and loudly declared:

"By the rivers of Babylon, there we sat and wept when we remembered about Zion. There we hung our harps on poplar trees."

Although our situation was much better than that of the Israelites during the Babylonian captivity; nevertheless, these words were very relevant and dear to us. They reminded us of our own captivity. They spoke about the things that we also hung upon the spruces of Westphalia as we sat beside foreign streams: our heavy thoughts, our troubles and our trials. We remembered our own Zion-Ukraine and there we soared with our thoughts.

That same day they took us to a neighbouring village for work. We worked for the whole day in a wide village square where we were required to carry weeds and dry branches from one pile to another. In the evening we returned to our building beside the glistening water. We sang evangelical songs and talked with more new people. We spent the next three days in this manner; every evening we held evangelical services that included the singing of hymns and a sermon. New people always filled our room. The Word of God found good soil for itself during these services because later we met young ladies from that factory who were affected by the good news of the Gospel.

A man came from one of the other barracks and told us that we probably were not going to stay in this place but would have to travel farther because the barracks were over-crowded and there was not an empty corner anywhere. This is indeed what happened. Very shortly some large cargo trucks came and we were told to pile our belongings into it. To our great delight, brother S. Yankowski, our long-time acquaintance since pre-war times, came with the truck. He had already been in Germany for a long time. He and his family were working in Rüdersdorf, and now he had come to take us to the same factory where he was working.

We were on the road again. We crossed hills, forests, and villages, always going farther and farther. The asphalt road vanished behind us as a new one appeared before us. One of the brothers said in jest:

"It would be nice if they would drive and drive us like this and during that time the war ended. And then – immediately home."

Our truck went under a bridge and then immediately turned onto the property of a factory. This was Rüdersdorf, the final destination of our long journey. Around us there was various kinds of metals, cast iron, wood, but mostly we could see all our good and fine people. They were standing beside their barracks which extended all the way to the factory and asking us with downcast eyes:

"Why did you come here?"

The truck stopped, but we did not receive any instructions to get off because it was not clear if there was any space available for us in the barracks. During this time there were so many various forced workers in Germany that all the camps were filled to the last corner.

An overweight German, who was limping on his right leg, dashed around, looking into every barrack and getting angry. He came out, waved his hand to our driver and said in German:

"Drive on!"

The truck turned around in the yard and then went out the same way that it had come in. It came to the neighbouring village and stopped in front of the small village school. This was the village of Gernsdorf. This is where we would live, from here we would walk to work, from here we were later liberated from our captivity by the Americans. From here we became scattered throughout the wide and distant world.

GERNSDORF

The room, which we were given, was large and bright. There were bunk beds standing against the walls and we began to claim our spot. We carried our belongings inside and prepared for a long stay. Local Germans gathered outside, crowded around the stairs, and stared at us as if they were looking at something that they had never seen before. We could not sense any hatred from their eyes towards us, only heartfelt sympathy. They all knew that it had not been easy for us to leave our homes and our villages to come to this place. But these peaceful villagers were not responsible for this situation, even as we also were are not responsible. They saw the small children among us and presented bread and candy to them. Hearing about the arrival of a large group of believers an elderly German brother came from the nearby town of Siegen, sat down on a wooden stool, sadly shaking his head as he watched us bustling around the room. We were unable to converse with him because we did not understand the German language but we could understand his heart. He belonged to a group of Germans who did not believe in the Fuhrer, but were ashamed of their nation, which brought so much evil into the world.

We went to sleep late that evening and in the morning, as soon as the sun had risen above the hill, we were already up. I had a great desire to become familiar with the village and its surroundings so I got dressed and went out onto the road. There was a row of houses stretching out on both sides of the street. There were not many of them because just beyond a curve the hayfields began and the road turned to the right and continued up the hill. There was a small bridge across a stream. Past the bridge there was a Lutheran church with a tall steeple. Only my footsteps were visible on the dew-drenched road as I continued walking up the hill. There was a forest. The trees were old and sturdy but not very tall because the ground was rocky everywhere which kept the trees low to the ground. There were many shaggy and thick hazelnut bushes, which reached out over the road with their green branches on which clusters of new nuts were beginning to develop.

I stood on a small hill from which all of Gernsdorf was visible. Hills and spruces surrounded this small Westphalian village on all sides. A shiny asphalt road, with fruit trees planted on both sides, stretched out from the village. There were flocks of sheep feeding on the hillsides. From somewhere below the sound of a bell reached to this height. Gernsdorf was blanketed with a morning fog, resonating with the sound of crowing roosters. This was a quiet, attractive corner of Westphalia unrivalled in beauty. Gernsdorf was especially beautiful now. The sun had long since risen behind the high hills but its light was still not shining onto the village. The red roofs of the houses were still blanketed with fog, which was rolling down from the hills, falling on the road, and then disappearing into the yards to make room for the sun. Stones, which had been dug into the ground, were placed beside the road. They looked like planted mushrooms and every Saturday the German women would re-paint them white. This was the location of our refugee group, the location of our work and our unforeseen trials.

Part of our group in Gernsdorf
From left to right: M. Antonowich, S. Bychkowski, D. Hryn, I. Barchuk, A. Sus, M. Podworniak, W. Siery

I followed a narrow path to the forest. When the path ended I found myself in front of a wonderful German cemetery. There were hazelnut bushes and flowers planted around it and at that moment it was filled with the singing of birds which, it seemed, had flown here deliberately to sing together in this place. There were many green graves and many wreaths and flowers. In the centre of the cemetery there was a high wooden cross. I took off my jacket and entered through the gate into the cemetery with such trembling and reverence as if I was entering some great cathedral. What a deep silence and peace in this place! Drops of dew were still sparkling on the flowers. The birds were singing, the hazelnut bushes were singing and my heart and soul were singing. I approached the wooden cross, sat down on a bench, which was still wet from the morning dew, and then I got down on my knees and said my morning prayers. For some reason I could feel a calmness in my soul, it was so clear and so sweet. I could sense that my Lord was the same here as He was in my native home, and that He would never leave me in my loneliness and misfortune. I sat for a long time on the bench, listening to the singing of the birds, thinking and dreaming. After that wonderful sunny morning, the small cemetery in Gersndorf would become my place of rest and conversations with God. I would come here on joyful days and on sad days. Here I would pour out my heart before God. Here I would search for comfort, peace in my soul, reassurance and consolation.

On Sunday, August 6th, 1944, we were visited by brother W. Siery from Siegen and brother S. Yankowsky with his family from Rüdersdorf. We held our first worship service. We sang many songs and rejoiced in the fellowship with our own people. Following the service we all went into the forest where we conversed and listened to the reports of brothers Siery and Yankowsky. They had been working here for a long time and knew the various working conditions and therefore informed us about this.

The sound of a bell ringing could be heard in the village, calling people to the small Lutheran church beside the hill. Women dressed in long black skirts and white hoods on their heads were making their way to church. The appearance of the women was the same as one can see in drawings in books by Kristina Roy[67]. Limping and supported by a cane, elderly grandfathers were also going to church; but there was not a single young man among them because all of them had been taken to the army. Therefore, women went to church by themselves. They cut hay by themselves, chopped wood, plowed the fields with cows, and sowed the millet. They worked, they listened to the worship service, but inside they were cursing Hitler as they waited for their husbands and sons.

On Monday we went for our first day at work. It was necessary to go to Rüdersdorf that was about a kilometer and a half away. As soon as we appeared at the factory our people immediately surrounded us. The majority of them were young women and men from greater Ukraine but there were also a good number of French workers, Dutch, Belgians, Danes, Polish, Belarusians and Russians. They began to overwhelm us with questions about what was happening in Poland. Each one of them wanted to help us in some way, to be useful in some way. At first glance, it appeared that there was great solidarity and harmony among the workers.

An elderly German took charge of us and showed us our new work. The three of us, Bychkowski, Hryn and myself, were led to a different room and given large leather aprons and dark glasses. We were told that we were going to use an *"elektron"*[68] *to* weld small metal parts together. Each of us was given his own small table. On the table were welding rods, hammers, and pliers. For several hours the old German hovered around us showing us how to perform different tasks and then we were left to work on our own. We were welding together some types of small metal plates and stacking them on a pile. We never knew and were never told what it was and what it was used for. This is how our work began.

Only foreigners worked in the factory, although there were also several old and limping Germans working there, but they were usually our supervisors. German women also worked here, but they were most often in the

---

67 Kristina Royova, Slovak protestant writer, 1860-1936
68 Possibly a reference to arc-welding. A process where an electron beam was used to create an electrical arc which heated and melted the pieces of metal and fused them together.

offices and in the kitchen. During this time in Germany, everyone who was able to walk had to work because all the healthy ones were at the front.

We knew that the owner of the factory in Rüdersdorf was considered to be a Christian, and so we were waiting for him to come to us, greet us and give us some words of comfort and take an interest in his fellow-believers. Unfortunately this never happened. He was a short obese man, who always wore grey clothing. Several times he walked among us and we hoped that perhaps *this-this* time he would come up to us, but he passed us by and never said a word. Although he was a so-called Christian, it seemed that we, the workers from the east, were as nothing to him. We were just a regular work force, material with which he could do whatever he wanted. This truly astonished us because up to now we had gauged the German Christians with the same standard as all genuine Christians. Now for the first time we were becoming convinced that they were not at all like that.

Later we found out that the owner of the factor had recently been released from prison for some type of opposition to the German regime and therefore they had no pity for him. It was forbidden for Germans to have any close relations with *ostarbeiters*.[69]

For dinner we were given a piece of bread with some margarine thinly spread on it, a ladle-full of soup and several potatoes. We were shown to a small room in the attic where we were supposed to eat. The French, Dutch and the other workers from Western European countries had their own separate dining room, which served better food. Workers from Ukraine were included with the *ostarbeiters*, who ate their dinner from a different kitchen with much worse food. We were included with them but we were not taken to their dining room because there was no room there, so they gave us a small room in the attic. We were content with that arrangement because we were always able to pray together before eating our food, and after dinner we could talk about different matters. For a long time our food was quite adequate, but as autumn approached the food suddenly worsened and did not improve until the end of the of the war. Especially disgusting to us were the turnips, the

---

69 Eastern workers

purple cabbage as well as some type of *krupa*[70], similar to grains of rye divided in half. Everything was simply boiled in water, slightly salted but without any type of fat and without any taste. Countless times we sat hungry until dinnertime, and after dinner we were still not satisfied and could still eat who knows what.

On Saturday we returned as usual from work to our Gernsdorf and found a great surprise waiting for us: brothers L. Galustyan[71] and Ivan Uhryn had come to visit us. They brought us news and letters from our group, relating many happy reports about them. The entire group, from which we separated in Soest, was working in Schalksmuehle. They lived in barracks and were all alive and well. They had already made contact with the Bible School in Wiedenest, and now had also made contact with us, having sent these cherished messengers to us.

That evening we had a wonderful service in our building, which was attended by workers from Rüdersdorf. We sang many songs and listened to sermons from our dear guests.

Brothers L. Galustyan and Ivan Uhryn were our first guests in this foreign land and they made a very good beginning, because after their visit other brothers began visiting us. On the third Sunday, we again had visitors from Wiedenest: brothers O. Harbuziuk and A. Sus. We again had a wonderful service and later in the evening went to the forest. The unwritten beauty of nature was all around us in this place and this same beauty filled our hearts. After many turbulent years I was able again to meet my friends in a distant foreign land.

---

70 Grouts can be a variety of different hulled grains broken into fragments.
71 It is not clear why the author uses "L" as the initial for Galustyan. This is again repeated beneath the photograph on page 195 of the book. Galustyan (also goes by the name John Mark), was an active minister among Slavic churches in Europe, North and South Americas. He was known by the first name of John (Ioann). He has published an autobiography, "History of My Life" (in Russian} in 1989.

Baptism service in Berlin-Spandau, 1944. Standing in front, is brother J. Shnaidruk.

The following day, brothers Harbuziuk and Sus returned to Wiedenest and we went to work, anxiously waiting for Sunday and new guests. We were not mistaken; guests did come. I believe it was brothers W. Ostapchuk from Wiedenest and W. Siery from Siegen. And now almost every Sunday we had someone visiting us and we would have a wonderful service.

Through letters we were also able to make contact with brother J. Shnaidruk, who at that time lived in Berlin, where he led a large and blessed ministry. He and his wife also visited us one time. That was on a Sunday. We were not working so everyone went to the forest. In a small clearing, covered with green grass, we all sat down on the ground and there we sang, prayed, and listened to the Word of God that was proclaimed to us by brother J. Shnaidruk.

Since Yakiw Shnaidruk and his wife visited us in Rüdersdorf, it is in order to mention the great and blessed ministry, which he carried on in Berlin. Unfortunately I had not written down any information, but I am familiar with this ministry from second-hand reports from those who lived in Berlin at that time.

**39 candidates for baptism in Berlin-Spandau in 1944.
Standing at the left is brother J. Shnaidruk**

1944 saw the largest influx of workers to Berlin from the East, but especially from Ukraine. In the city itself, as well as in many surrounding communities, there were countless factories and various enterprises in which thousands of our poor people worked. They worked as slaves. They were always hungry and without any rights. In addition to all these adversities, their lives were also in danger daily, because during that year, there were the largest allied air raids upon Berlin.

To help these thousands of unfortunate people God sent several of our preachers, among whom J. Shnaidruk and L.Pidhoretsky were especially noteworthy. These brothers were not able to help their people with clothing or food although they were involved in providing this assistance through good German believers, but what they brought to the people was the Gospel message in their own language. They went throughout the camps preaching the Word of God, and the results of their work were extremely abundant. This became evident among us as well as in many of the other camps. There were many young women and men from Ukraine who, after hearing the message of the Gospel, received it into their hearts and turned to the Lord.

Those were threatening and difficult days and since Germany was losing on all fronts, it increased the brutality within its territories, especially against foreigners. It was possible to end up in a concentration camp for the smallest offence, but our brothers did not pay any attention to this. Placing their own life in danger they visited the camps where our people were found and searched for various means to reach such camps and there proclaim the Word of God.

For example, in a region around Berlin there was a large camp, which our people called *Jundferhaide*.[72] It was impossible to enter this camp. Behind this camp there were some type of bushes growing as well as small hills covered with tall dry grass. At an agreed upon time the believers from this camp would go out among these bushes. They sat on the grass and there they would hold evangelical services and listen to the preaching of God's Word. These services were not the same as services we are used to having inside a church building. They were very simple, without any church furnishings but how powerful they were, how very much alive! People prayed, repented of their sins, turned to God and became new persons.

At an agreed upon time, believers went out behind the *Jungferheide* camp where they held an evangelical worship service. Preaching is brother Blaschuk.

---

72 This is possibly a spelling error, since the author uses *Jungferhaide* for the same location. This is likely the same location as *Jungfernhaide* which is an area of heath-forest located in Berlin. The name comes from is a combination of *"jungfer"* which means a young woman and *"heide"* which means heath.

One night there was a massive allied air raid on Berlin. Over 450 of our people were lost in that single camp. *Vichnya Yim Pamyat.*[73]

Not only were services held in a field under the open sky, but there were also baptisms, attended by many people, which took place in various canals and lakes. The candidates were taken into a forest where their faith was examined. The Lord's Supper was served on a sheet or blanket, which was spread out on the grass. This was done with utmost simplicity but at the same time in the greatest sincerity. God abundantly, more than abundantly, blessed this work.

Baptism in Berlin by Spree Canal, 1944

During this time of endless air raids over Berlin, a large number of our people were lost but I have no knowledge if any of our fellow-believers were lost. I am aware of only one believer who was lost during military action, a young believer from Halychyna named Kashchiy. Many believers, who were not heard of during the war, were later found when the war ended. But of brother Kashchiy, who was gifted in reciting evangelical poetry, nothing was ever heard of him again.

As I previously mentioned, I have no information about the extensive spiritual ministry, which took place in Berlin, and I don't know if anyone besides J. Shnaidruk was involved in this work. I mention this only because

---

73 Eternal memory to them

of the joyful fellowship we enjoyed when brother Shnaidruk visited us in Gernsdorf.

*****

The French workers advised us that since we were citizens of Poland we were allowed to enter their kitchen. We tried but we were not allowed to enter. We were told that this had to be arranged in Siegen at the labour administration. We sent our certificates stating that we were not only citizens of Poland but also residents of the Polish capital, Warsaw. We waited for a long time. Our documents wandered somewhere throughout all of Germany and later returned to us with many different stamps. We were now added to the kitchen where the French, Dutch, Belgians and others were eating their meals. However, having received such great "rights" we felt that we were now separated from our people; as if there was a wall created between us. We especially felt this when we first went into a different dining room. Our people were standing by the factory watching us with very sad faces. I felt very sorry for them and this first dinner in the "privileged" dining room did not taste good to me at all. Later we saw that there really was not much difference in the food. We were hungry before, we were still hungry now.

Once we knew that this would be the place where we will be working, we decided to properly structure the organization of our group so that it would be like a church congregation. First of all, we decided to hold our regular worship service every Sunday, and on Wednesday evening there would be a prayer service. This was extremely important, not only for us, but also so that the gospel would be preached to many of the people who were working in Rüdersdorf and the neighbouring villages. We appointed brother Ivan Barchuk as the leader of our group and he held this position until we were transported out of Gernsdorf. During our time in Gernsdorf we held a service every Sunday. During that time the Word of God was preached by brother I. Barchuk, and others, especially by S. Yankowsky from Rüdersdorf and W. Siery from Siegen.

The Lord's Supper beneath the trees led by brother L. Pidhoretsky. Berlin, 1944

News about our services and our group spread throughout the entire region by word of mouth. Every Sunday we had new people at our services, especially young girls. I recall a certain Sunday when several new girls came, who were working with employers in the neighbouring village. All of them were from the Vilna region in Belarus. We had a Belarusian songbook and so we sang several songs for them in Belarusian. Upon hearing their own language in a foreign land they began to cry. The following Sunday they came again and brought with them other girls; thus every Sunday our room was filled with new listeners. I remember those services and even now my heart is stirred with a good feeling. These were simple services in an ordinary room. We sat on benches and on wooden stools; but in that simplicity we experienced the power of the Holy Spirit; we felt the presence of God.

Every evening when I came home from work, I would go into the forest. I entered the cemetery, sat on the bench under the cross and read books, wrote letters, grieved and dreamed. Then I would walk about in the forest, I would go into the farthest thicket, follow a narrow path up the hill, and from there I could see all of Rüdersdorf, and farther still I could be see the reddish hues of another town. The sky above Westphalia was very blue, the air was clear and one could see *far-far* away, especially during those times when the fog settled to the ground. The trees here were not very tall because the ground was rocky and trees were unable to develop. Hazelnuts were growing everywhere and were beginning to ripen and would soon produce mature nuts. Underneath the bushes there were long vines of blackberries growing and now there were many berries on them.

Nature was magnificent in this place but people who grew up on the plains were lonely here, especially the people of greater Ukraine who longed for their steppes. For example, one could never see the actual rising and setting of the sun, when the sky was blazing with different colours as the sun, wrapped in mist, set below the horizon. Here, the sun had long disappeared behind the mountains, even though it was still daylight outside for a long time.

The warm, sunny days passed; autumn was coming. Everyday we went to work, everyday we returned as a group to Gernsdorf. Everyday there was something new to experience, but one can never write about everything. Our life was sad, but on occasions it was happy and interesting. We lived as a joint family. We lived without any misunderstandings. Each one helped the other; each one served the other. Every evening an electric light flickered in our room until late. Brother I. Barchuk was reading some kind of book. S. Bychkowski was strumming something on his guitar, composing new melodies and his only wish was that no one would bother him. Our beds stood next to one another and sometimes we would argue over something long after midnight.

Through our brothers in Wiedenest and through direct letters, we were able to establish full contact with our group in Schalksmuehle. They were all living together, working in various factories. They were also holding services, which were attended by many. There were numerous factories near every village and town where our people worked; therefore, there were always new listeners at the services. There were conversions and celebrations of holy baptism by faith.

The congregation in Schalksmuehle had organized immediately with 64 members. Initially the spiritual work moved forward with such great success that they had baptism services every Sunday, until the work diminished. Unknown to the authorities, baptisms were held in a small creek, which flowed into a forest not far from the barracks. The baptisms were officiated by various preachers who were in the group. The best evidence regarding the success of the ministry of this congregation was the fact that when the war ended in 1945 the congregation numbered 250 members.

Besides the good news from Schalksmuehle, there were also some sad news. One young brother who travelled with us from Warsaw had died. I don't remember his surname, but he was from Chelm Land[74]. He was no more than seventeen years old, gentle and pleasant, the son of Christian parents. He became ill with tuberculosis and because of malnutrition he quickly declined. He was buried among the green spruces on Westphalian soil and our congregation became smaller by one member.

"They buried him among the green spruces..."

---

74 Chelm Land or Kholmschyna, a region of Eastern Poland.

Towards autumn the Westphalian sky became covered with grey clouds that produced a constant drizzle. It seemed that the hills had become smaller; they seemed to have come closer and were shaking hands with each other. The protruding spruces swayed their wet branches. The flocks of sheep came down from the hills and hid inside covered enclosures. Every living thing was searching for shelter, rest and peace. But this was not available to us. Everyday, while it was still dark outside, we had to get up, drink our black *ersatz*-coffee without sugar and trudged wearily off to work. Inside the factories there was constant pressure; the grinding of metal, the crashing of falling sheets of tin, and the hissing of thick clouds of steam.

My boots, about which I was worried that they would not tear while I was still in Zolocheva, finally gave up. At the factory I was given a pair of wooden shoes, the kind worn by Dutch women in the pictures. They were light but not very practical because the soles did not bend and in order to walk in them one had to know how to shuffle their feet. Mud always stuck to the bottom of this block of wood, which was hollowed out for the foot. Often, when we would go to Rüdersdorf, we had to stop several times to scrape off the mud.

As autumn approached our food greatly worsened and real hunger began to pursue us. In the morning we would drink black coffee without sugar. For dinner we would get a cupful of purple cabbage and two cold potatoes, and for supper – again, coffee. It seemed that after breakfast, after dinner, and after supper, we were even more hungry than before. My head was spinning, some type of invisible cobwebs seemed to be spreading over my eyes, and a persistent dullness continued to gnaw away near the heart. We received one loaf of bread, which had to last for several days. We would make marks on it, dividing the loaf in a manner so that we would eat only the portion designated for that day. We hid the remainder of the bread so that it would not be visible and would not tempt us and waited for tomorrow. But not all of us had such a strong willpower and would eat all the bread at one time, and later we would be hungry.

I especially remember one such day when, after receiving my three-day ration of bread, I ate it all at one time. The following day I was so hungry that I barely crawled to work. Towards evening I went into a hayfield outside the village and sat down beside a small narrow stream. Everything appeared yellow before my eyes and my head was ringing. From the bank I could see small fish darting about in the clear water and I had a great desire to catch one. But when I moved even slightly, the fish quickly moved into deeper water. When I became still again the fish returned, swimming near the riverbank, scales glistening as if playing with hungry me. I got up and set out for the village near the hill. An elderly German woman saw me through an open window and waved her hand at me.

"*Komm nach haus*"[75], she said.

I entered the house and stood inside the porch not knowing what it was that she wanted. The woman brought out from the kitchen two large slices of bread with margarine spread over it and a bowl of soup, placed it on the table and told me to eat. Just imagine *dear*[76] reader, two slices of bread and a bowl of soup! And not only that, but I even found a piece of meat in the soup. I ate all of this before the eyes of the good woman and, up till now, never in my life had any soup tasted so good to me. I could not find the words to communicate with that woman, but I understood that her two sons were somewhere at the front in Italy and she longed for them very much. I sincerely thanked this woman for such tasty food, but from that time, for some reason, I avoided that house so that she would not notice me and perhaps think that I kept loitering near her house because I wanted to eat again.

I also remember one Sunday when, because of me, not only I, but also our whole group went hungry for the whole day. Every Sunday we took turns going by bicycle to the factory in Rüdersdorf to bring back dinner from the kitchen for everybody. On that unforgettable Sunday I went, taking with me two long pails, one for soup and the other for potatoes. I received the dinner from the kitchen, hung the pails on the two handlebars and slowly proceeded down the hill. Suddenly the front wheel skidded because the road was wet after a rain. Losing my balance, I, together with the bicycle, tumbled onto the road. In spite of the fact that I crushed my leg when I fell, the more important thing was that both pails had fallen with

---

75 Come to the house
76 Added by translator. This is an expression that the author often used when speaking to others.

me. Truly a catastrophe! The soup, containing some kind of *krupa*, spread out on the road as the potatoes rolled into the ditch. I stopped and spread my arms helplessly. What was going to happen now? Should I return to the kitchen and ask for a second dinner? I could not do that because there every spoonful was accounted for and dinner had already been distributed to everyone. I was embarrassed to go and face my people without any dinner; how could I look into their eyes? They were hungry, waiting for dinner, looking out the window and wondering why I was gone so long.

I looked at the spilled soup, gathered the potatoes into the pail, and walked the bicycle back through the village. I was already afraid to sit on it because I did not want to fall a second time.

With a burning face I entered our room and one of our brothers immediately said:

"See! Something has certainly happened."

I sighed heavily and set the empty pail down on the floor. My hungry friends looked at me...

Although we were all without dinner that Sunday, this situation became an inspiration for brother Bychkowski to write a poem that he dedicated to this event.

However, Sister P. Barchuk saved us from hunger. Gathering some *krupa* and asking the Germans for a few potatoes, she made some soup. Although none of us were completely satiated, the soup at least chased away our hunger and we were somewhat strengthened.

It is also in order to mention that sister P. Barchuk was our permanent housekeeper and hostess. Whenever we brought dinner or supper from the factory she would take all of it and divide it among all of us so that that nobody would have more or less. She also looked after the cleanliness of our residence and always when we returned from work we would find our room clean, the floor washed, and the beds, especially for the single young men, were neatly made.

One fall day a large number of young Ukrainian girls from the trenches near Holland arrived at our factory. They were distributed among the barracks near the factory in Rüdersdorf and approximately twenty of them were brought to Gernsdorf. We re-arranged our wooden beds to make space for them. All of them were from greater Ukraine, mainly from Kiev.

They had been working in the trenches near Holland and now they were brought here. They were poorly dressed, pale and worried but beautiful as true flowers from Ukraine. We soon became acquainted and became as one family. We walked together in our wooden shoes to work and together we returned. They came to our worship services and joined us in singing spiritual songs. Several of them heard the gospel for the first time. Some said that in their villages there were people similar to us, called *Shtundists*, but they were no longer there because almost all of them had been sent to Siberia.

When the girls came to us, our congregation increased in number and we were finally convinced that the tears that were shed during the separation in Soest were in vain. God truly did a wonderful thing when He brought us to this place. Who would have witnessed to these young girls about Jesus? From whom would they hear the good news of the Gospel? They all had grown up and studied in atheistic schools. From an early age the idea that "there is no God" was pounded into their heads and now with this mindset they found themselves in a faraway foreign land. Here their atheism increased and was reinforced, because they reasoned that if there was a God, then why doesn't He come to their defense? Why are they, who are innocent, suffering so much? And then they met us, heard the message of the gospel and listened to a spiritual song for the first time. Initially they observed us from a distance and later they came closer and closer. Eventually, they sat down on the benches during our services. Then they began to sing. Still later they began to pray and many of them were sincerely converted to the Lord. Their long-term atheistic upbringing dissipated like a fog, it vanished like the dew in the sun. Truly, in the words of professor W. Marsinkowski, "the soul of person – a Christian, could find true peace only in Christ."

A group of Ukrainian Christian girls in Siegen

Not far from Rüdersdorf was the attractive and quiet town of Siegen. It was hidden among hills and was not visible from any location. It was necessary to travel an hour by train to get to Siegen. There were numerous factories in which many of our people were working. Brother W.Siery was leading a fine spiritual ministry there, conducting services in the camp as well as holding services in the outskirts of Siegen – in Weidenau. In one factory in Siegen there were many girls working who were from Greater Ukraine; the majority of whom were believers. Their employer also was a very fine Christian man who took care of them as if they were his own children. The girls from Weidenau frequently came to visit us and we would travel to them. When we would go there, the employer would lock the gate to the factory with a key and then stand guard somewhere so that no one would notice us. During that time we held our service in a large room in his factory. *Ostarbeiters*[77], to whom we also belonged, did not have permission to go to any German church or to hold their own services. Although we did not have permission to officially have our own services, unofficially we had them; this all depended on the local commander of the

---

77 Eastern workers

camp. Therefore, when we occasionally visited Weidenau, the good elderly German brother closed the gate and watched during the time that we had our service if perhaps there were Gestapo patrolling the street. Later, he would let us out back to the road, in small numbers through various entrances of the factory.

Christian girls, behind their barracks in Siegen. At the end is a German brother who was helping them in their spiritual ministry

The first ministry among the Ukrainian girls in Siegen was started by Tania (later she became the wife of brother W. Siery). She was the only believer among all the girls, but afterwards she met another girl from Vinnytsia, sister Yusia, and the two of them began to witness to their friends about Jesus, read the Bible to them, gathered together wherever they could and prayed. God greatly blessed the work of sisters Tania and Yusia and after a short time a large group of believers was formed consisting of young girls from Greater Ukraine. Later brother W. Siery was added to this work, and later still, we were also included in the ministry to some extent.

I will never forget one very unique baptism that we had in Weidenau. We were not allowed to perform baptisms in the river and no German church had permission to release their baptistery to us. Nevertheless, the new converts desired to make this covenant with the Lord. Then the aforementioned German brother in Weidenau, whose surname was *Sheyloke*[78], advised us to hold the baptism in a large tub in his home.

On the designated Sunday we all came to Weidenau. The employer, with great caution, led us onto the grounds of his factory. We entered his beautiful house through some side doors where a large tub had been prepared for us. A table was set up in a separate room on which there was a goblet of wine and the bread for the Lord's Supper. We quietly sang "O Happy Day" and brother Yankowski performed the baptism for several newly converted souls. A second song, "Lord, when to His Disciples "[79], was quietly sung as the goblet of wine was passed around the table at which we were seated. An awesome, unspeakable feeling filled all of us, new converts and those of us who were older Christians. Each of us could recall several such evangelical celebrations on the banks of our rivers in Volyn, in Halychyna, and in Belarus. There were so many deep and emotional memories! And Here? Here there are even more. We would listen, if possibly there was an alarm siren and we would have to run for our lives into a bomb shelter. We were always looking out the window into the street to see if anyone was spying on us. Outside we saw only the elderly German brother who was walking about and indicating with a slight motion of his head that nobody else was here. Oh what a celebration this was!

Later there was another baptism in a tub, performed by brother Ivan Barchuk, but I was not present at that time.

In Weidenau, and later in other places, we were convinced over and over how virtuous the German Christians were. In many instances they placed their own lives in great danger only to help in the misfortunes of their brothers and sisters from the East.

---

78   Цейлокс
79   Господь коли ученикам

ALARMS AND AIR RAIDS

Our factory in Rüdersdorf was very close to the main railroad line, which connected Hagen and Erfurt. Every day dozens of trains, carrying various war materials, travelled this way, so we expected that English and American air raids would occur here at any moment.

The first reconnaissance flight took place on one fair autumn day. We had just gathered for dinner when the piercing sound of the siren at the factory announced an air raid. We rushed from the factory and headed for the forest as four white "airplanes with two tails"[80] were already above us. They circled, descended above the forests and then showered the factory with a hail of bullets. By now there was nobody in the building and the bullets only broke the windows. After that raid, the alarms sounded, initially every week, later every day, and then almost every hour. Outside the days were bright but we were working very little. We spent the majority of those pleasant sunny days sitting in the woods or inside a bunker in a high embankment under the railroad tracks. Everyone knew very well that the Germans were losing on all fronts. But we had neither a radio nor newspaper to read because these arrived very late. We were able to learn the news from the French and Belgian workers who were able to receive news by some means. Therefore, we knew that Warsaw, Krakow and Lodz had fallen a long time ago, and in the West the allies had landed in Normandy, having chased the Germans out of Africa and were now advancing towards Paris. The following day someone wrote on the bathroom wall with a crayon: "Paris". We already knew the significance of this – Paris had fallen.

In our Gernsdorf, the residents began digging a bunker in the hill, so that there would be a place to hide from the expected further air raids. The

---

80   Possibly a reference to the Lockheed P-38 Lightening, a long-range American fighter-bomber plane with two stabilizers in the back. The Germans nicknamed it the "the fork-tailed devil"

Germans brought in various tools, pick-axes, hammers and pry-bars, and began to dig from both sides of the hill so that the tunnel would join somewhere underneath the hill. Only elderly men and women were involved in digging because there was not a single young man left in the village. When we returned from work, instead of resting, we also had to go the hill and dig the bunker. Not only were the pick-axes and prying bars heavy for us, but even the small shovel was heavy because we were hungry and physically drained. Our men shoveled together with the German women and our girls. We were doing this, not only for the villagers of Gernsdorf, but also for ourselves.

In other places, there were frequent incidents where our people were not allowed to share the hideouts with the Germans during the raids, but in our village this was not the case. The people of Gernsdorf treated us favourably and had sympathy for us, as to strangers and travelers.

The air raids were now happening everyday. Around ten o'clock in the morning the siren in the factory began blaring so we dropped our work and fled into the forest. High up in the blue sky, an entire cloud of airplanes came flying above our village. They were roaring so loudly because of the extremely large weight that they were carrying that the earth trembled. They were flying in dense groups like crows. Reconnaissance planes were weaving back and forth around them protecting them against any enemy. We lay in the forest, with our faces up, waiting until they flew over us. They continued to fly on for a very long time, sometimes for several hours. Bombs were never dropped on our location, but they continuously transported them to larger centres. They were flying to the southeast and later returning by the same route. Again we would be in the forest, counting these frightening iron birds.

I recall one such sunny autumn day when brother Barchuk and I were again lying in the forest. I was counting the airplanes flying overhead and Barchuk was recording the numbers, so that we would know how many had flown by. I counted one convoy, then a second, a third, a fourth... in the end when we added them together, it was over nine hundred. And these were only the airplanes that flew over Rüdersdorf, but they were flying over all the territories of Germany! Elderly German women were looking upward, sighing heavily, crying and praying, because they knew that all of these airplanes were headed to their towns. And wherever these airplanes arrived, there would be no escape for anyone.

One day brother and sister Yankowski were celebrating the birthday of one of their children and invited our children from Gernsdorf to their family celebration. When the air raid began, the children were playing barefoot. It became necessary to turn the lights off and in the darkness put shoes on the children and then rush to the basement under the kitchen floor. In the confusion, mothers exchanged their children's footwear. The basement was already full of frightened workers, the most noticeable among them was an elderly man from Russia, who kept running around and shouting:

"We are lost…Now, everything is all lost!"

Sister Barchuk was a brave woman and never became flabbergasted. She came up to the old one and attempted to calm him down:

"But how are we all lost when we are all here? God will get us through this trouble and everything will be fine. Why is it necessary to shout for no reason and frighten the children and others?" The old man calmed down.

It was now getting late into autumn. Westphalia's beautiful hills were dressed in yellow garments as they kissed the sun. I have yet to see anywhere such a beautiful autumn as in Westphalia. The streams among the hills became even clearer than before and now yellow leaves from the trees were floating on the water. The sun rose later from behind the hills, and the dew was profuse. It seemed as if someone had dumped pails of water here during the night. In the mornings there was already a small frost, but during the day it warmed up. It seemed that the sky had become higher above the hills and shone with a blueness, as if it had been painted with the brightest blue paint. We were slowly becoming accustomed to the menacing Allied airplanes, which continued to fly across the sky every day. Every Saturday, when we were not working, we would go into the hills to pick mushrooms or search for nuts. On Sundays we had our worship services, which were very often attended by many sisters from Siegen. Towards evening we accompanied them to the train station and then returned to our Gernsdorf, walking along narrow pathways through the picturesque hills. The trees had dropped their leaves to the ground, which now rustled like music beneath our feet.

After work, together with brothers S. Bychkowski and D. Hryn, we would go into the forest. We would sit beneath the thick bushes and conduct endless, sincere conversations. We shared with each other everything that weighed heavily upon our hearts. We recalled the past and anxiously awaited the unseen future. We brought books with us, we read, we breathed the fresh air as if we were somewhere on an isolated resort or at some uninhabited location. S. Bychkowski always had with him a pencil and some sheets of music paper and would write notes, creating new melodies and songs such as *Ne Znayou Ya Shcho Ty Meni Poshlesh*[81], *Vechir Vyshyvaye Ponad Morem T'my*[82] and *Na Sertsi Kamin*[83]. These, and other songs, later became a part of his songbook *Ridna Pisnya Na Chuzhyni*[84], which was born on the slopes of the beautiful hills of Westphalia in the fall of 1944. Brother Bychkowski carried with him a pencil not only when we went for our time of relaxation, but also when we were running into the forest during an alarm. I remember, as if it were yesterday, one incident when airplanes were flying over our region, bombs were exploding somewhere beyond the hills and sirens were howling. Bychkowski and I were sitting in the cemetery in Rüdersdorf, when Bychkowski looked up, wrote something for a long time and emotionally said:

"*Hodut, hodut*[85], almost on purpose. A new melody has just come to me, but they won't even let me to finish it. Later I will forget it." He wrote down some notes on the paper, making some type of notations, as the airplanes roared and somewhere, beyond the hill, the sound of machine gun fire continued until midnight; the chords of a frightful, wartime symphony of that time.

Those wonderful days of autumn came to an end and the real frosts came. Then the first snow fell. We continued to walk to work, bundled up in our old clothing. Several times we had to stop on the road to scrape the sticky snow out of our wooden shoes.

---

81 "Не знаю я що Ти мені пошлеш", *I Don't Know What You Will Send for Me*, published in "*Ridna Pisnya Ha Chuzhyni*", No. 91. Words by M. Podworniak.
82 "Вечір вишиває понад морем тьму", *The Evening Embroiders Darkness over the Sea*
83 "На серці камінь", *A Stone on the Heart*, published in "*Ridna Pisnya Ha Chuzhyni*", No.103. Words by M. Ichnyanski
84 "Рідна Пісня На Чужин", "*Songs of the Homeland in a Foreign Land*". Published May 7, 1948, Germany
85 They "rumble, rumble". A reference to the continuous noise of the airplanes.

Christmas came. I remembered my native country, my dear village, and my loving family. I had a desire to fly as a bird and see my house even from a distance. Was anyone still living in it? Will my family be celebrating this great holiday there this year?

Towards evening I went to the forest and chopped down a Christmas tree. We placed it in our room, decorated it with some coloured paper and it reminded us that today is the Birth of Christ[86]. In the evening we had a beautiful Christmas service. The children of sister Brychukow, as well as those of brother and sister Barchuk and one other family from Greater Ukraine, who lived with us, recited Christmas poems. We sang many carols, listened to a Christmas sermon and then had supper together. There was much Christian warmth, many memories and much sadness. Our first Christmas in a foreign land.

The local Germans brought us some bread, some type of *krupa* and some candy for the children. We received our regular supper from the kitchen, black coffee, a piece of bread and two potatoes for each person. As soon as we finished eating our supper we heard the sound of airplanes howling above Gernsdorf and everyone scattered in all directions to escape: some into the forest, some into the basement. Perhaps it is not good to write much about myself, but I must say that among those who were escaping, I was always the first. Perhaps my previous wartime experiences had shaken my nerves, but as soon as the first alarm siren sounded I was already running into the forest. I wanted to live, to wait until there was freedom, to return to my dear fatherland, to see what kind of world there will be after the war.

I remember during one service as we were kneeling for prayer, when suddenly – alarm. Airplanes were roaring and somewhere bombs were exploding. I quickly got off my knees and in a flash rushed towards the forest. I looked back... no one else was running behind me. I had already reached the hill when I turned back and returned to our room where my brothers and sisters were still kneeling and praying. With an embarrassed look on my face for my lack of faith, I again knelt beside them. "Lord forgive me" ... my lips and my heart whispered.

---

86   *Rizdvo Khrystove*

The next day was Christmas and we did not work. The supervisor at our factory in Rüdersdorf agreed that we could use the large dining room to hold a Christmas service for all the workers. For a whole day we rehearsed carols, and brother Barchuk prepared a sermon. In the evening our entire group went to Rüdersdorf. The large dining room was filled with people. Among those who came were many local German women and many workers: French, Belgian, Dutch, but the majority were workers from the east; young and old, those who believed in the birth of Christ and those who did not believe. Now they were all standing here, perhaps they were thinking of their families, as they waited to see what was going to happen. We had prepared a small Christmas program, we had rehearsed songs, some had prepared recitations. Because most of the workers from the East were true Russians who did not understand everything in Ukrainian, we decided that Barchuk would preach in Russian.

The large dining room became quiet and a sense of expectation filled the room. Brother S. Bychkowski gave a tone and the quiet was broken with a carol: *Nova Radist Stala*.[87] The Germans, French and other foreign workers were looking at us, as if we were artists. They didn't even budge. They were hearing this melody for the first time. I am certain that the walls of this dining hall and the hills of Westphalia were also hearing it for the first time, because who had ever sung this song here before? Then we prayed, we sang again, recited poems and at the conclusion brother Barchuk preached. His words were alive and moving. Many of our girls were standing and whispering to the foreign workers, translating the message that Barchuk was speaking. The older people were listening, sighing and wiping tears from damp eyes. And then everyone was thanking us and greeting us as if we had never met before. After that service we felt that each worker had more respect for us, especially among the Protestants.

After Christmas the days became longer and warmer in the sun and we hardly noticed when it was already March. Dirty streams of water began flowing down from the hills, and buds were forming on the willows growing beside the road. Sparrows were chirping loudly and the sky had become even more blue.

---

[87] "A New Joy has Come"

Every day thousands of airplanes flew over Rüdersdorf and every day they would return the same way. Our villages were never bombed and we thought that there were no strategic military points of interest here and therefore there was no purpose in bombing here. But we were mistaken.

One evening we were sitting peacefully in our room, each was doing his work. I remember that Bychkowski was strumming on his guitar, Barchuk was writing sermon outlines and the other brothers were doing something as well. Suddenly someone opened the door, looked outside and yelled at the top of his voice:

"Put out the light! We are sitting here, but outside a terrible judgment is taking place..."

We ran out of our school and saw that suspended above the town of Siegen were several red flares. It was quiet outside, only the sirens were howling. The hills were silent, the trees were not moving and the people and everything else were waiting for something to happen. The wind was carrying the red flares from Siegen and they were already close to our village. They were burning in the air like terrifying comets and the entire region was now visible like the palm of one's hand. I dashed out of the school and began running towards the hills where there was a partially excavated bunker. The sound of airplanes could be heard above Siegen. Apparently, the first bombs were dropped there because the ground in Gernsdorf was vibrating and shaking violently. Large columns of smoke rose up to the sky as the echoes of explosions rolled among the hills. From Siegen, it spread through the valley and was coming directly at us. It seemed that airplanes were already close to Gernsdorf. We could hear them circling above the clouds. Abruptly bombs and flaming phosphor began dropping. The sky was burning, the hayfields were burning, houses, forests and hills; everything was burning and collapsing.

Several of our brothers and all the girls headed for the basement beneath the school. The girls from Ukraine all believed that God was with the believers, so they literally hung onto their clothing and cried with fervent tears. Bombs continued to fall and the door of the basement flew open from the pressure of the air. The bravest among us proved to be brother M. Antonowich. As soon as the strong air pressure forced the door open, brother Antonowich pulled it towards himself and held it with all his strength as Barchuk comforted the crying girls...

I began running together with brother Hryn, but somewhere beneath the hill we became separated in the darkness. I continued to run farther. There appeared to be some kind of deep opening in the rocky hill. Somewhere close by, a bomb exploded. A terrifying light flashed and lit up the opening, which appeared like some type of hellish abyss. I lunged towards the rock and fell to the ground to escape that, which was now happening in Gernsdorf. And hell was happening in the village. Houses were already burning, cattle were bellowing with terrified voices, dogs were howling, women were shouting, small children ...The airplanes were now above the village, rumbling and roaring and it was impossible to distinguish whether it was bombs falling or if the hills were crumbling, or if it was thundering with one thousand thunderbolts...

I threw myself into the dark opening and pressed against the wet rock. Suddenly a bomb exploded a short distance away and fire and smoke enveloped the rock. With all my strength I pushed myself further into the opening when suddenly I felt something warm near my feet. I reached down with my hand --it was the head of a child. "*Muter, muter*"[88]...the child was crying and firmly gripping my hand. Apparently he had been running with his mother but in the darkness and panic he became lost and continued running by himself towards the hill. I embraced the child and fervently prayed that God would take those frightening bombs away from us. But the hills continued to shake, dirt was pouring on my head and the acrid smoke from the burning phosphorus was stinging my eyes.

I don't know how long the air raid lasted, but when I came out from inside the rock, leading the small boy by the hand, the airplanes were no longer there. The sound of explosions continued to be heard coming from the town of Siegen. Gernsdorf was filled with smoke from the burning which was happening outside the village and from the phosphorus that was still burning everywhere.

That night there were casualties in the village. I do not know how many lost their life in our Gernsdorf; I remember only one woman with children, she was the wife of a German officer. Previously she had lived in a larger

---

[88] Mother, mother

town, but when the air raids increased she came to peaceful Gernsdorf. That night she was killed, together with her children.

The fine town of Siegen, which up till now had not been touched by the war, was completely destroyed that frightful night. Several towns, which were located along the Siegen-Rüdersdorf road, were also wiped out from the face of the earth. This frightening wave of destruction reached the hayfields and touched our Gernsdorf with its wing, but here it stopped.

When I visited Siegen a week after the bombing it was impossible to recognize. The streets were cluttered with various goods; bridges had collapsed. What had the most depressing impression on me was an image of a cemetery, which recently appeared so beautiful. Its trees were uprooted, the bones of the deceased were scattered over the ground, and crosses and headstones were over-turned and broken. This was a war on both the living and the dead...

I remembered many Jewish cemeteries in Ukraine, which the Germans had destroyed. The graves were desecrated and headstones were taken to build roads and various buildings. How true is the Word of God, which says: "What a person sows, that he will also reap."

The American raids doubled in number, then, increased ten-fold. Almost daily there was no light at the factory, there was no electricity and all the machines were standing motionless. Most of the time we were all sitting in the forest or in bunkers built underneath an embankment of the railroad tracks. American "airplanes with two tails" continuously circled our entire area and seemed to be searching for something. They would descend above hills and as soon as they noticed something, they would fire at it with machine guns. The French workers told us that they were searching for the place from which "V1" rockets were being launched against England. And perhaps this was the case because every evening when we were returning from the factory to Gernsdorf, we saw above the hills in the distance a rocket, resembling a long burning broom, which was flying north. One would fly, and after a period of time a second, a third ... It was rumoured that what we saw every day with our own eyes, were indeed those ominous V1 rockets.

It was a cloudy day in the beginning of the month of March. Rain clouds hung low over the hills as if they wanted to cover them. We worked from early morning that day but in the afternoon the alarms began to sound and we scrambled to find shelter. Barchuk and Bychkowski set out for the bunker beneath the railroad track, but for some reason I ran up the hill into the forest. Airplanes were droning over the entire area, but they were hidden above the clouds and were not visible. Somewhere bombs were already bursting, the sound of machine gun fire could be heard, its grim echoes rolling through the valleys. The edge of the forest extended all the way to a field. I sat down beneath some bushes. There was nobody there beside me because everyone had scattered into ravines or under rocks. The airplanes continued to roar; the skies were vibrating from their continuous thunder. A terrible storm was approaching...

I sprang up from beneath the bushes and began running across the field down the hill to the bunker that was located in the embankment under the railroad track. I was *running-running*; I could hear that the airplane was *almost-almost* above me, its heavy motors were roaring above the clouds until the earth was swaying. I quickened my pace when all of a sudden I felt as somebody's hand grabbed me by the shoulder and held me in place. So clear and certain was the feeling that somebody was running with me and holding onto my shoulder, that I stopped in the middle of the field. I lifted up my eyes and I could see some type of black strips descending to the ground from the dark clouds. This was only for an instant and then everything around me began to sway, everything was shaking, it thundered, there was a flash of lightening. The pressure of the air threw me down. I tripped over a furrow in the ploughed field and rolled into a small ditch. I pressed closely to the cold ground. I did not remember anything, but I had the impression that around me something terrible was happening. I could feel that dirt was falling on my shoulder and irritating smoke was biting my eyes. I could not move, I could not see anything because around me it was night and hell ... Bombs were exploding incessantly, bright lights were flashing, as again and again more dirt continued to fall on me...

I don't know how long this scene lasted but when silence returned the airplanes were already circling around a different hill. I got up from my small ditch and set out for the tunnel. I was tripping over new craters, which had been created, by the exploded bombs. I fell, got up and ran again. Around me there truly was considerable destruction. There were uprooted trees and telephone wires lying on the ground and beside a destroyed house a white hen with a bloodied wing was struggling to get up. Bombs had dug up the ground, hole upon hole. I could see that if I had not been halted on the field, I would have come precisely to this spot where the greatest number of bombs had fallen. But God would not allow me to come here. I clearly sensed His holy hand had grasped me by the shoulder and held me back. I endured terrible moments in the ditch, but now I was running through the area where certain death had awaited me.

Near the tunnel, underneath the railroad embankment, the bombs had created some fresh holes. Several bombs were still smoking and spewing the foul odour of sulphur. On a path beside the tunnel, there were signs of blood and in the doorway a person was lying. I looked ... it was brother Ivan Barchuk. He was pale and his head was all bloodied. Two German ladies were kneeling beside him, trying to wrap his head with a bandage. They managed to get him to stand but he could barely stay on his feet. There was also a second injured person, it was one of the French workers whose head was bandaged and there was a large, red blotch of blood on his face.

Brother I. Barchuk was a courageous man; he had very strong nerves and almost never ran away from bombs. Airplanes would be flying overhead, machine guns would be firing continuously, but he would sit quietly and read a book or write sermon outlines. And today, while he was sitting beside the tunnel reading a book, the powerful force of the bombs, which fell near the embankment, had flung him onto the path, and the stones that were flying in all directions had wounded his head.

When the airplanes could no longer be heard, people began coming out from their shelters. Bychkowski and I took Barchuk under the arms and led him back to Gernsdorf. At the beginning he walked very slowly, but just before Gernsdorf his legs refused to walk and his head began to droop from one side to the other. Again we could hear the sound of the siren alarms. Behind the hill the sound of airplanes could be heard, bombs were dropping. We continued walking, moving one foot in front of the other, one step at a time, because we could not leave our wounded brother on the road.

As we led Barchuk along the railroad tracks, we walked past the spot where he had been lying. I looked and could see that deep in the earth there was a long metal fragment from a bomb with one end sticking out of the ground. It was lying exactly where Barchuk's head had been. I pulled the fragment out of the earth and showed it to Barchuk, because this would have brought certain death to him. He took that fragment of the bomb with him to Gernsdorf.

That same evening I went to my "cathedral in nature" at the Gernsdorf cemetery. In the forest the first spring birds were chirping. Standing in the corner of the cemetery, shrouded by an evening mist, was the large wooden cross. Beneath the cross was a lonely bench. I sat down upon the bench as tears welled up in my eyes. "Lord, how good you are to me"... my heart was praying. "How merciful You are. Today I would not have been alive; my young life would have been cut short in the middle. They would have buried me in this foreign land and I would never return again to my native land. Never! But I am still alive, still sitting at the cemetery, thinking, and praying. And, because of today's miracle, my faith has been strengthened. If it is your will Lord that I should live, then I will live." I was convinced of this many times before. But today I was convinced in an extraordinary way when clearly and consciously I was aware that Somebody had taken me by the shoulder and held me back in that field...

I stayed at my cemetery late into the night, thanking God for my preserved life and in my thoughts flying back over the past years. I remembered the terrible night of May 15 to 16, 1943. In those days I was working as an accountant in the cooperative of my own village. When work had ended, I went into a field outside the village and walked along a green path to a nearby farm. These were horrible and evil days in Volyn. Every night, villages were being set on fire by the Germans, the Polish, Soviet partisans or the Ukrainian resistance. The Polish, together with the Germans, attacked Ukrainian villages, setting them on fire and murdering the people. In order to get revenge, the Ukrainian resistance did the same thing to Polish villages and farms, while Soviet partisans went against Germans, Polish and Ukrainians. There was true hell in Volyn back in those days, which until now has not been, described anywhere.

On the evening of the May 15, 1943, I had gone to an isolated farm outside of our village. A good Christian family was living there and I would often go to their place whenever I had free time. I went there again.

Green fields surrounded the farm, the sun was setting, a nightingale was singing in the bushes. There was nothing in the natural world that could have predicted that after today that farm would no longer exist. That today, among those green trees, a *terrible-terrible* tragedy would take place.

The people from the farm were at home. We were sitting on the *prizba*[89] talking, drinking tea and listening to the humming of maybugs and the singing of a nightingale. The father had gone to town and had not returned yet. Only the mother, three grown up daughters and a fifteen-year-old son were at home.

Suddenly I felt a great disquiet in my spirit. I could not understand what this might mean but this unease continued to increase and fill my heart. It seemed that an invisible voice was whispering in my ear saying: "Go, Go!" I tried to suppress this voice; trying not to think that something was not right, but my anxiety continued to increase and I could not gain control over myself. Then I got up and said to everyone who were sitting on the *prizba*:

"I am very sorry, but for some reason, I must go home."

They tried to stop me, asking me to stay for a while yet, but some unknown inner voice kept speaking to my soul: "Go, Go!... Quickly go!"

I got up and said farewell to everybody. I did not know at that time that I was saying farewell to them for the final time; that I was saying goodbye forever.

Their oldest daughter got up also and said:

"I am also going to the village with you. Things are now happening everywhere and I am afraid to spend the night at home."

We walked past the farm and through a valley. It was late, around eleven o'clock. We came to a path through a field and continued walking side by side.

Suddenly behind us, we heard the loud sound of revolvers being fired, and then came a second volley, then a third. At the same time a fire began

---

89 *prizba* is a mound along the outer walls at the base of wooden houses. It served to protect the building from freezing in the winter.

to break out at the farm. The fire was casting clumps of burning straw into the trees; it was rising upward, extending its terrible arms to the sky.

The girl, who was walking with me, screamed and began to run back to the burning farm, but I firmly grabbed her by the hand and would not let her go. We began to run to my village.

We endured a terrible night in the village. Many people stood beside their houses and watched as the nearby farm burned. At first the fire burned fiercely with high flames, which became lower and lower and towards morning it had stopped burning. None of us had the courage to go there because we knew that the hand, which caused this fire, did not have any pity or mercy.

When daylight came everyone from the village went to the farm. The girl and I went with them. A terrible scene awaited us there. The barn, some sheds, and the house continued to smoulder, but where were the people with whom I had been yesterday evening? They were not anywhere. We began to search for them in the orchard, in the bushes. They were not anywhere. We began to lift burning rafters from the barn, poles, boards, and burning straw and finally we found them. We found their charred corpses on which there was burnt, black blood. It was not possible to identify the bodies because their hands had burned off and their heads, which were badly disfigured by the fire, had fallen off. The terrible bandits and murderers had shot them and then threw them into the fire...

I cannot paint the scene to which the oldest daughter returned in the morning when she came home and saw her murdered and burnt family, or the picture that the father saw when he returned from town that same day. There is not enough paint in the world to paint such a scene. These images haunted me all the way to Germany and many times I would see them in my dreams and would get up suddenly and try to escape. The scene was still especially clear and fresh before my eyes when, after the terrible air raids, I was sitting by myself in the cemetery in Gernsdorf. If, on that terrible night in 1943, I had stayed at the farm for another ten to twenty minutes, the bandits would have caught me there. And today, if I had not been held back on the field for two-three minutes, I would have run directly into a hail of bombs. What could I say to God during those moments in the cemetery? Nothing except to fall before Him on my knees and thank Him, thank Him for being so merciful to me.

Late in the evening I returned to our room from my "green cathedral in nature". Brother Barchuk was lying with his head bandaged; his wife and children were sitting beside him. Bychkowski was writing new songs and one of the brothers was banging with a hammer, repairing his boots. We were waiting for a new day with new unforeseen experiences.

The railroad tracks beside our factory were destroyed during the terrible air raid and the trains stopped running; but this did not last for long. Machinery and workers came from Siegen, bringing all the necessary equipment and supplies, and began to repair the tracks. There was one German engineer and workers who were all our people, mainly from Greater Ukraine. They came with shovels, pickaxes and prying bars, which they could barely hold in their hands. They were all ragged, strained, hungry and, in general, indifferent to their situation and to everything in the world. They would work for several hours and there would be another air raid, the alarm would sound again and we, together with the workers, would escape into the forest. Among them there was an elderly man from Poltava. He sat beneath a spruce tree, with his head bowed low. He looked worried as tears flowed down his face.

"Don't cry *dyadko*[90]," one of us said. "God will make it happen and it will be over. There will still be peace on earth. We will go home..."

He wiped his eyes with his sleeves and began to cry even harder, like a distraught child.

"There will be peace," he said. "But who will be here to see it. I do not want to die in a foreign land. I lived my entire life in our sunny Ukraine, I was never attracted to any foreign place, but they caught me and brought me here. In my heart it feels that it will not be possible for me to ever return home."

I don't know if he ever returned to his Poltava or not, because we never met him again.

Guests from Wiedenest no longer visited us because travel was very dangerous. The majority of the railroads were destroyed. Many stations as well as entire towns were also destroyed. Brother S. Yankowski and I decided to go to

---

90 uncle

Wiedenest to see how our brothers were doing there. We received a three-day leave from the factory and went. Several times during the trip we had to stop and hide in bomb shelters, but we arrived safely. We saw Wiedenest and many fellow-believers who were studying at the Bible School and working in various factories at the same time. These visits were especially dear to me, because many years prior, still before the war, I had dreamed about the Bible School in Wiedenest. I had heard much about this beautiful *Rhineland*[91] region and now I had an opportunity to see it with my own eyes.

The town of Wiedenest is located among magnificent spruce-covered hills. Here it was green everywhere, both in winter and in summer. Our train proceeded among the trees. Spruce boughs peeked through the windows of the train car and on a curve it was possible to grab them through the window. I met many brothers and students of the Bible School, but especially I was able to meet again with old friends from former years: brothers I. Tarasiuk, O. Harbuziuk, W. Ostapowich, I. Polischuk and others. They were working and studying at the Bible School and at the same time they were doing Christian ministry; visiting the surrounding camps, conducting evangelistic services, holding gospel concerts and preaching the gospel. There were thousands of our people everywhere in this area. All of them longed for spiritual bread and therefore gladly accepted the Word of God. Especially blessed were the evangelistic services in Kierspe where many young girls from Greater Ukraine were working. Many of them, after hearing the Word of God, turned their lives to the Lord. The owner of the factory was a good Christian man. When these girls were sent to work for him, he immediately tried to find ways to obtain better food and clothing for them. He did all this in such a manner so that the authorities would not know, because he easily could have ended up in a concentration camp for what he was doing. When the girls accepted him as their guardian and friend, he gave each one of them a New Testament. The believers from Wiedenest and Schalksmuehle would come and conduct evangelical services here and as a result, out of the sixty young girls who lived here; almost all of them had been converted to the Lord.

---

91 "рейляндську" (*Rheiland*) probably is a reference to Rhineland. Wiedenest is in the Rhineland region of Westphalia.

Ukrainian girls from Kierspe with their Christian leader

When the Americans arrived many dishonest factory owners-exploiters escaped into the hills to avoid revenge from their workers. But this factory owner remained in place. Recently arrived *ostarbeiters* maintained a guard near his factory and would not allow anyone to do him any harm. However, many dishonest factory owners paid with their life for the way that they abused their workers.

The brothers from Wiedenest were in constant contact with the larger group of believers from Schalksmuehle and helped each other in their spiritual ministry. The Word of God, which was sown, brought fruit and because of this there were frequent baptisms in the lakes of the Westphalian forest. The German authorities were not aware of this, but good Christian Germans knew and in love helped our believers in their spiritual work. The ministry in Schalksmuehle was especially successful.

Returning to Gernsdorf, I was spiritually encouraged after witnessing the great work and dedication of our brothers and sisters in Wiedenest. I was also encouraged when I saw how many sincere German Christians did not bow their hearts before Hitler. They did not believe in his false promises, did not even fear concentration camps. They did whatever they could to help our people, but especially assisting them in their spiritual work.

I would like to emphasize one more time that the majority of the German Christians were the so-called Free-Brothers, who were very numerous in Westphalia. The majority of them did not believe in the efforts of Hitler and did not follow his leadership.

FREEDOM

The spring of 1945 arrived. The birds began to sing and the hills of Westphalia began to hum. We were still going to work every day, but for almost the entire day we were sitting either in the forest or in the tunnel under the railroad embankment. American and British airplanes were now flying very close to the ground, strafing the hills and valleys continuously with rapid fire. There were no newspapers coming to our factory and our correspondence by letters with Wiedenest and Schalksmuehle had been cut off. We did not know what was happening anywhere in the world. We only know from the French and Belgians that the Allies had taken back all of France and had crossed the western border into Germany. Knowing this, all of our workers, no longer concerned themselves with hunger and hard work, but were walking with their heads lifted high and faces glowing. Our freedom was coming nearer! On the other hand, the Germans lowered their heads. They were worried and treated the *ostarbiters* better.

Anticipating the imminence of freedom, brothers S. Bychkowski, D. Hryn and I agreed that as soon as the Americans arrived, we would go at once to Wiedenest or Schalksmuehle. Because we knew that the trains would not begin running right away, we began in advance to build for ourselves a small wagon on which we would be able to place our belongings and venture out somewhere on foot when the time came for this. Whenever there was an alarm and the workers were running into the forest, we stayed behind in the factory and welded the wheels, riveted and fitted the frame together, and earnestly prepared for a future trip.

On Saturday March 17, the short boss of our factory, whose name was Scheitz, told us that the factory was ceasing its operation and all of us must return to our barracks and prepare to be evacuated.

We returned to our Gernsdorf and began preparing for a journey. We took whatever we had, tied it up into a bundle, piled it up beside the wall and then walked close to the forest. The day was bright and warm. Airplanes were flying above Siegan and dropping bombs. Bombs were also exploding around Gernsdorf, machine guns were firing, but in the village everything was quiet. German women and children, as well as our girls, gathered beside the partially completed bunker under the hill. We sat down on some dry leaves from last year; focusing our sight and straining our ears and could hear the *far-far* away sound of machine-gun fire. It was easy to distinguish the sound from a bomb and we were now convinced that soon we would be free. The only thing we did not know was what would happen after freedom came. Will we live to see that fortunate day when now everything around us was burning and collapsing?

Towards evening grey clouds covered the sky and a cold drizzle began to fall. With every moment it was getting darker and darker outside. We were standing inside our room and with every moment it was also becoming darker and darker within our souls. After several sleepless nights we were feeling tired and weak. We were also hungry and frightened. Our hope was that this waiting and tension would finally end because we did not have the strength to live or wait any longer.

That evening the boss of the factory came and told us that our girls must go at once to the factory because today all workers would be leaving Rüdersdorf. The moment, which we were expecting, had come. The day came when we must separate and perhaps never meet again.

Our girls were crying as they gathered up their bundles and said their farewells to us. We still did not have orders to leave so we stayed where we were. We accompanied the girls all the way to Rüdersdorf so that they would not have to walk by themselves. The cold drizzle continued and the wind was blowing straight into our faces. We walked underneath the trees, along the same road on which we walked to work everyday. We tried to cheer up our girls, telling them not to worry, because *soon-soon* the war will be over and then we will search for each other by mail. Just in case, we gave the girls our addresses to the Bible School in Wiedenest instead of Gernsdorf. It would always be possible to find us there after the war.

Group of believers in Gernsdorf

The girls from the other barracks had already assembled at the factory. They were arranged in rows of four as if they were in the military, and proceeded in a long column through the village. I stood beside a house in Rüdersdorf and watched them as they passed by for the final time: hungry, pale and sad. The majority of them was dressed in green jackets, wore wooden shoes and resembled inmates of a concentration camp. Each one carried in her hands all of her possessions in a small packet wrapped up in a kerchief. The wind was blowing into their faces, a light rain continued to fall on them, but they continued to walk on and on... There was an old, tall German in front, followed by many dozens of Ukrainian girls. The evacuation had begun. Seeing this scene for the first time in my life, I had never felt so sorry for those poor girls as I felt at that time. Each one of them had already travelled a difficult journey in her life. They had often told us about the terrible hunger that they had endured in Ukraine while living under a difficult state regime and working very hard in the *kolkhoz*[92], before they were transported into forced labor to Germany where their cup of

---
92   Collective farm

suffering was completed. Now they were walking into the unknown in a foreign land. I stood there and looked at this sad procession. There was Marusia, Katerina and Ksenia who had lived in our room. They always came to the worship services and were later converted to the Lord. They walked by but did not see me in the shadows as I followed them for a long time with my eyes. I ran across a yard and again stood underneath a tree to see them at least one more time. They were still walking, and I continued to follow them with sad eyes. How destitute they looked! Hungry, weary, defenseless and abandoned by everyone.

Our group was still staying but no one knew for how long. We did not go to work the following day, but we did not have any peace at home either because of the continuous air raids. We either sat inside the bunker or in the forest. Towards evening we received a notification that we had to leave Gernsdorf and go on our own on foot anywhere to the East. We gathered for a final farewell service during which time there was much sadness and crying. After the service we discussed plans where we should go and what we should do. The factory boss told us that he will return in the morning and his wish was that we would no longer be there. Gunfire could clearly be heard from the front, though Gernsdorf was to the east of the German army. Wagons went rattling by, tanks were roaring, a cargo truck was pulling another behind it. The soldiers were over-tired, silent and angry. Frowning, they walked beside their wagon with their heads lowered. I remembered when they marched into Poland in the year 1939 and into Ukraine in 1941. How their boots used to shine during those times and how smartly they marched onto our land. It seemed that there was no power on earth, which could break those columns with the swastikas on their flags and on their tanks. Now the situation was different. Far away across the ocean a new power had arisen which was victoriously moving from the west and bringing with it freedom. This power was crushing the German armies and cities and in the concentration camps hundreds of thousands of people, speaking various languages, were praying. Each one in their own way prayed that God would send this power to them as soon as possible.

Bychkowski, Hryn and I placed our small bundles on our shoulders and were the first to leave. Barchuk and Antonowich also left with us, but their goal was to stop in some village to get away from the eyes of the boss and then return through the forest to their own people.

Beyond the village we parted and went our different ways. Barchuk and Antonowich went to the right, to a neighbouring village, looking for some type of shelter and refuge, and the three of us went directly into the forest. We climbed up the hill, found a dense clump of trees and decided not to go anywhere but to wait here until the end of the war. We knew that the front might be passing by here, that artillery fire might be flying through here. We might be in the path of cannon fire, but what will be will be. We were not going anywhere from this place. We piled our bundles underneath a tree. Finding an old stump whose thick roots had sunk deeply into the ground, we began to dig a hole underneath it with our hands and some branches. In the event of danger we would be able to at least hide our heads inside there. We dug for a long time but accomplished nothing because the ground was very hard and rocky and we became very tired.

A dark spring night found us in the forest. We had with us some bread and two or three potatoes apiece. We ate everything and waited for what would happen next. We sat there in the darkness among the dense trees listening to every rustle that came to us. In the distance we could hear the sound of droning airplanes and machine-gun fire, but the night was so dark that we could not see one step in front of us. The sky became covered with thick clouds and it seemed that it had fallen on the hills and valleys, covering them with darkness, and daylight would never come again. From Gernsdorf, which was down in the valley, we could hear voices and various sounds then the thump of wheels and the muffled sound of cars. Suddenly we heard someone crying loudly, someone called out, and again we could hear the sound of car engines and the thump of wheels. We were sitting and holding our breath. Various thoughts were going through our heads. We knew that the retreating German army would be passing through the village. When we heard the shouting we thought that perhaps they were evacuating or perhaps beating up the *ostarbiters* who were left behind in the village. We had heard various rumours that when the last of the German front lines retreated, they would murder all foreigners. And now, hearing the shouting and crying, we thought that, without any doubt, that moment had arrived. We sat there silently, listening to everything that was happening around us during that night and counting the long hours of our waiting.

Later that evening it became silent in the village. All was quiet on the road and in the dark forest. We ventured out onto a path in the forest and decided to send one of us back to Gernsdorf to investigate. I volunteered to go. Breaking off a tree branch, I began to walk to the village, waving the branch in front of me so that I would not bump into a tree. Bychkowski and Hryn stayed back and waited for me in the forest. The path went to the bottom of the hill and then turned to the right, but I could not see it and only sensed it with my feet. The darkness was so deep that I could see absolutely nothing in front of me. Knowing the direction of the path on which I had walked many times before, I walked slowly ahead, continuously waving the stick in front of me.

I came to the first house. I continued to walk into the village and it seemed that some type of danger was lurking behind every building. It appeared to me that none of our people were left in the village; the retreating Germans had taken everyone and at any moment would also capture me. Everything was silent and dark. Approaching the building in which we were living, I stopped at the steps and placed my ear against the door. I could hear noises inside and familiar voices. Not hesitating for a moment I opened the door. In our room, sitting beside the lamps, were all of our believers: I. Barchuk, I. Antonowich and all of the girls who had recently left us. The girls had returned today because the retreating German army was everywhere on the roads and therefore the girls were left to their own fate and were told to go wherever they wished.

So our girls returned to us. Where were they to go? Everything was on fire, the whole world was burning; our Gernsdorf was still the place of the least danger.

Baptism near Wiedenest, performed by brother H. Boltniev

Quickly I returned to the forest and brought Bychkowski and Hryn back to Gernsdorf. We were all together again. All conversing together, but no one was going to sleep. We just sat and enjoyed our peace until morning.

Towards morning the retreating German army again began to pass through the village in muddy green tanks, cargo trucks, in wagons and on foot. The faces of the soldiers were unshaven, sleepy, worried, hopeless and indifferent. They were carrying their army duffel bags and their rifles with the barrels turned down, resembling very much the retreat of Napoleon's army from Moscow. We watched them through our window but were afraid to go outside. The German soldiers were very angry with all foreigners and it seemed to them that it was because of us that they were losing the war and retreating. At least that is what we thought.

Around twelve o'clock that day the first round of artillery gunfire erupted in Gernsdorf as cannon fire battered the road on which the German army had just passed. The day was very bright and warm. An American reconnaissance plane came from somewhere and made a circle around the village before climbing into the sky. At the same moment gunfire was unleashed upon the village. A shell hit a retreating German car on the road. The car caught on fire. Fire and smoke spread through the village as everyone began running to the tunnel beneath the hill. We also began running. High above the village the American airplane was circling again. I think that it saw people running to their hideouts because immediately long-range artillery projectiles were fired at the hill.

Sister Barchuk hastily picked up her small child from a wagon and left the wagon by the hill while she and the child ran inside the shelter. At that moment two German women ran out from the shelter with two small boys and a child in their arms. They could not remain inside the shelter because there was a lack of air inside and so they began running towards their own basements. They passed sister Barchuk but as they came to the empty wagon that she had left, a shell suddenly exploded in front of them killing everyone. Five corpses lay beside the shelter. Their salvation was very close, but...

At that time we almost lost brothers Barchuk and Antonowich because, while they were outside, a shell flew so close to them that it almost killed them. A second shell struck a rock right above their heads in front of the shelter and covered both of them with dirt and small stones. Antonowich ran to the basement while Barchuk hid with us in the bunker.

We sat in the hideout and listened as shells were bursting all around us. Airplanes were droning and machine guns were firing. The tunnel was dug deep inside the hill, but there had not been sufficient time to dig through to the other side; therefore, the tunnel did not have an exit or access to air. Many people, who had gathered inside, did not have any air to breathe with. It was impossible to open the door because shells were exploding incessantly right by the entrance.

A woman began to faint and was carried close to the door so that she would at least have some air to breathe. Somebody was yelling to get some water, small children were calling out for their mother and father ... the situation was becoming difficult and hopeless.

I was sitting in the very corner pressed against the cold wall. Sitting beside me was Hanya, a young girl from near Kiev. I could hear her crying and her whole body was shaking like a leaf in early fall. At every moment it was becoming more and more difficult to breathe. All the saliva had dried up in my mouth and I decided to somehow make my way to the entrance.

Somebody lit a match but, without any air, it went out immediately. Inside the tunnel it was dark and frightening.

I lay down on the ground and pressed my tongue against a wet rock, but this did not help anything. I began to push my way through the people, moving against the wall to the entrance. One brave German jumped outside, ran to the nearest house and brought back a pail of water. A cup was passed throughout the tunnel and everyone received a drop of the precious liquid. Someone also passed the cup to me and I took several drops of water into my mouth, but still there was no air to breathe with. People were literally suffocating, fainting and everyone was pressing to get to the door. Suddenly it became quiet outside. The airplanes had gone away and we opened the door. Oh how precious and priceless was that air which was blowing into our faces. It seemed that there was nothing better in the world than that healthy mountain air.

We sat near the shelter by the forest for almost that entire day, ready at any moment to throw ourselves into the deep opening among the rocks. This was the most frightening day of our entire stay in Gernsdorf, but it would also be the final day of our terror.

That evening the sky was bright and a round moon shone above Gernsdorf. Again we were sitting in the shelter beneath the hill because shells were still falling upon the village. All at once everything was quiet and still as if someone had cut short the gunfire with their hand. We could no longer hear any gunfire. We could not hear any airplanes. We could not even hear each other. Suddenly the sound of people's voices could be heard in the village. Somebody was loudly knocking on the door of the house near the road. Somewhere a window rattled and a voice yelled out in German:

"Polish, Ukrainians, you can come out now!"

One of our brothers said in a whisper:

"This is perhaps the end of the German front line and now it will be the end for everyone."

I do not know what happened beside the tunnel because in a flash I dashed up the hill and with all my strength headed into the forest. Dry leaves from last year, which had been burned from the falling artillery shells, were still smoking beneath my feet. Irritating smoke was biting my eyes but I did not pay any attention to anything. I just ran, ran... In the dark I became entangled in some kind of branch. I fell face down to the ground, and then I ran again. Farther and farther...

When I was already far into the forest I came to my senses. I stopped and listened. A rocket soared upward above Gernsdorf, lighting up the entire region, and then fell into the forest. In the distance the sound of airplanes could be heard. Guns were firing, rapid-fire shells were whistling, but here, beside me, everything was quiet. I noticed that at the beginning brother Bychkowski and one other brother were running after me but all of a sudden they had disappeared somewhere and I was running alone. I stood for a moment and then began to quietly call out to them but nobody was answering me. I thought that perhaps the Germans had captured them, and I alone, was left. What was I to do now? There were so many of us, we lived together, we worked and now I am all alone, like a branch broken off a tree.

I continued farther into the forest and finally came out onto a road that led to a neighbouring village. I stopped on the road and fervently prayed that God would show me what I must do next. At that moment, more than ever before, I remembered my whole journey thus far, the entirety of my difficult life and realized that now it was more difficult and strenuous than when it all began. Up till now, at least we were given something to eat at the factory, I had my wooden shoes, and I had friends, my brothers and sisters. I had a place to live and a place where I could sleep. But when morning comes, where will I go? Where will I find shelter and a refuge? I could spend the night in the forest, but will happen tomorrow?

I followed the road to a field, which led straight to the neighbouring village. I knew the house where a Ukrainian lady lived who attended our services. I came to the door of the house and quietly knocked on the window. Marusia stuck out her head and recognized me.

"What happened?" She asked, frightened.

"I am running away from the Germans," I replied. "The final line of the retreating German front has come to Gernsdorf. I don't know what happened with our people there, because I ran away into the forest."

"But that cannot be," Maria said again. "The Americans have already come to our village. Come, let us go to the road."

We came to a large village square. There certainly were many American military vehicles and several tanks standing there. Soldiers with machine guns were walking about, talking among themselves and laughing happily.

"Marusia, are you sure that these are Americans?" I asked, not believing my own eyes.

"I am sure that these are Americans. Who else could it be?" answered the bewildered Marusia.

"What if these are Germans, dressed up as Americans to deceive the foreigners and then capture them? What will happen then?"

"No, these are truly Americans. Look, the Germans have hung up white flags everywhere," Marusia said again.

I ran headlong back to Gernsdorf. I could feel wings growing on me; I was not running but flying, conscious of the fact that I was free.

Everyone had gathered in our room and were waiting for me. We were all together once more, we were all alive, and we were all well.

That night none of us could sleep because how can one sleep when we had seen the Americans with our own eyes! They had given candy to our children and we all received some type of biscuits and several cans of food. We no longer had to go to work. There would be no more running for the shelters. Freedom had come. O God, we are free and alive! The emotions that we felt at that time cannot be expressed with words.

All of next day we watched the American army as it passed through Gernsdorf. They were all riding in small army jeeps with their legs dangling over the side as if this was some kind of sports team and not an army. They were all chewing gum and smoking shiny white cigarettes, which after smoking only half of the cigarette, they would throw the rest onto the road. Elderly Germans later gathered these and smoked them entirely.

Although the Americans were already in the village, heavy machine gun fire did not cease in the hills surrounding Gernsdorf; therefore it was dangerous to go by the road into the hills. However, our brave brothers went to see what was happening there and returned with much treasure. On the road in the forest there were destroyed German army vehicles. Beside them were scattered cans of meat, bread and sugar; this was not an insignificant matter to us hungry people. The brothers shared with those who did not go into the forest. For me it seemed that there were not any better cans of meat in the whole world than those that we ate at that time.

Gathering courage I also went down the road to the forest. In a small clearing I could see many broken trees and several green German vehicles. On the ground there was a large amount of scattered paper and some type of empty sacks. I stepped behind one vehicle and there, lying on the ground, was a dead German soldier. His face was all distorted, splattered with blood and his hands were crossed over and resting on the grass. I began to run back to Gernsdorf at a breakneck speed. Along the way I met some Germans from the village who were going into the clearing with shovels ... Therefore, whatever I had when I went into the forest, I came back with the same thing. This was the only time that I saw such a scene, which was repeated frequently in Germany during that time.

In the morning we went to see what was happening in Rüdersdorf. The scene there looked as if a hurricane had passed through. The wire fence around the barracks was knocked down, the gate was broken, the shed in which the guard had once stood, was upended. The French, Belgians and Dutch were preparing to go home and large American cargo trucks were already waiting. In the barracks there was singing, shouting and much noise, which made the ears ring. Ukrainian and Polish books were scattered on the grass beside the kitchen where the library for western workers was located. Many books were torn but the majority was whole. Nobody needed them any longer. They were scattered around and the wind was turning their pages. The factory was closed, the kitchen was closed and the Germans were all in hiding, fearing revenge for mistreating their workers.

We returned to Gernsdorf. Coming to meet us was a group of boys, recent *ostarbiters*. They were carrying bread, milk, meat, boots, and various types of clothing. Approaching us, they showed us all their goods and called out:

"Go to that house over there and take whatever you want. We have been carrying stuff since early morning. They had sucked enough of our blood and now it is our turn. We will show those '*nimaki*'[93]."

Unfortunately, many of the recent *ostarbiters* did take harsh revenge against the Germans; but it was mainly against the innocent ones. They

---

93   Derogatory term for Germans

roamed through the villages, breaking down doors, breaking windows and looting everything. This did not last for very long because the American military authority quickly brought this to an end. Thank God for our believers that none of them went down that road.

The next day several of us walked outside the village, following the route, which the American army had just travelled. There were still several cars on the road that were filled with German prisoners. German women were watching them through the windows and crying. For some reason we had no sympathy for those tears. The Americans will not mistreat any of those prisoners. They will transport them in this manner and later set them free to go home. Did these women know what the Germans did to Polish or Russian prisoners? No, they probably were not aware of the terrible incidents, which happened in our lands.

Retuning to our village we saw a beautiful house beside the road. It was reported that a German sympathizer had lived there but now he had escaped. The house was standing with the doors and windows wide open. We went inside and heard rustling coming from the basement. We went down the stairs and saw a German soldier sitting on the floor in the corner. He was in his military uniform with a swastika on the left sleeve, but he did not have a gun. We became frightened and began to turn back but he got up and with his whole body trembling asked:

"*Sprechen zi Deutsch?*"

"*Nicht,*" we replied.

"*Polnische?*"

"*Jawohl*"[94]

"I speak some Polish", replied the soldier. He began to cry and begged that we would not beat him but would help him get to the village.

We helped him out of the basement, walked with him through the forest, and then quickly led him from the forest to our room, making sure that that nobody in the village saw us. We gave him some breakfast; he shaved. We collected whatever anyone had and dressed him in civilian

---

94   "Do you speak German?"
"Nothing," we replied
"Polish?"
"Yes sir"

clothing. He spoke Polish because he had come from near Danzig. After resting for a while he sadly said:

"It is still not evident if we lost the war. Germany is a large country and our glorious army is still fighting on many fronts."

One of us interrupted him and said:

"Look man, do you still want your regime to win the war? Can you not see how much harm you have already done in the whole world? How dare you say that? You are fortunate that you happened to come among people who do not seek anybody's blood, but do not forget that your government has done a great wrong to us. We will not take our revenge on you, because we are Christians. So go with God and don't tell this to anyone…"

He apologized, thanked us and went into the village.

Two or three days later a German, accompanied by an American soldier, came to Gernsdorf. He said that all of our girls must come to the factory. From there, together with all the Eastern workers, they would be taken to collection points to be transported back home. Our girls became worried and lowered their heads.

"What are we to do?" we asked the American and the German.

"You are Polish citizens. We still do not have any orders regarding you," they replied. "Stay where you are, but the girls must go. Those are military orders."

That day we had a farewell service and then accompanied our girls far past the village. They walked in single file, carrying in their hands small bundles containing all of their belongings. Several of them were crying. They had suffered once at home, they had suffered enough during their in forced labor in Germany, and now they were going to new suffering. Although at times they had longed for their home when in the evenings they would cry for their parents, but now their homeland did not appeal to them. They knew that another guardian would now be observing them from which there was no way out. There was nothing we could do to help them because it was not yet clear what our fate was going to be.

Outside the village we said our farewells to our girls. We shared their grief and cried with them. We stood for a long time waving our hands at each other and then we returned to Gernsdorf. A terrible weight and sadness lay on our hearts. Our room had become empty. Long rows of empty, unmade beds stood against the wall. The poor Ukrainian girls were no longer there beside the beds; they had gone into the unknown and disappeared like a rock into water. The only thing that was left for us were memories and good impressions of when we worked together and the evangelistic services when we worshipped together.

The girls were gathered into large camps where true hell reigned. Soldiers with guns and hearts of stone stood at the gate and guarded them as if they were criminals. This was the beginning of new suffering for them, new troubles and more abuse.

Spring came very early to Westphalia. The days were now very warm; the grass was becoming green on the slopes. The first leaves were beginning to form on the trees along the road. This spring brought us freedom and will never be forgotten. Our nerves gradually became more relaxed, but still whenever airplanes would fly overhead, heading somewhere towards the east, a chill and fear would run through our whole body and we had an instinctive desire to run to a shelter.

JESUS, TAKE MY HAND

After a short time, no longer than five or six days, the Germans took down the white flags, which they had hung up when the Americans arrived. In the hills surrounding Gernsdorf machine guns continued to fire and heavy artillery resounded near Siegen. Rumours had spread that in the hills the German were reorganizing their retreating army and presenting a stubborn resistance. This appeared to be true because the Americans seemed upset as they drove their jeeps faster and were now driving in different directions through the village. It seemed to us that we were living on some kind of wild island that was threatened with danger at any moment. Although we did not cause any kind of wrong to the Germans in Gernsdorf, or they to us, we feared that when they saw our joy with the arrival of the Americans, we might lose our lives for this joy if the German army ever returned here.

Some of the brothers had families and could not venture out on the road, but we were single and not tied down by anything. In the morning the three of us, Bychkowski, Hryn and I, piled our packages onto our completed wagon and set out, heading somewhere to the west. It was difficult for us to part with our group, but the shooting in the hills and the various rumours were not giving us any peace. We had previously decided, a long time ago, that as soon as the Americans came, we would immediately go on foot to our own people in Wiedenest or Schalksmuehle. The Americans had already been here for a long time and there was no reason for us to continue to wait here; perhaps the Germans might return.

We went outside the village, pulling our wagon. I turned around and could see in the distance the cemetery in the forest. I felt an ache and a yearning in my heart. This had been my cathedral, a place where I came almost every day to read books, write poetry, think, dream and pray. Now

I was leaving this quiet corner of God's creation and going again into the unknown. Where? We truly had no idea where we were going but continued to travel in the direction of the setting sun. That was where the Americans were, who brought freedom for all those like us.

Past Rüdersdorf we came out onto the main paved road. When we saw American cars and tanks coming towards us and we would pull our wagon over to the side to make way for them. By the road and scattered in the ditches there were broken German military vehicles and tanks. There were dead cattle in the fields and everywhere there were large craters from the bombs. There were many fresh graves beside the road; most of them had a German military helmet placed upon it. Walking past those graves I recalled the year 1941 when the Germans forced a group of hungry Red Army prisoners down our Ukrainian roads. The German soldiers shot those who could no longer walk. There were also graves along the road. After several years, retribution had come here in Westphalia.

As we were walking we saw an American military vehicle approaching and pulling behind it was a shiny German limousine. They brought it to a deep ravine, unhooked it and with all their force pushed it over the edge. The car creaked and turned over several times before it hit the bottom with a thud. Its sound echoed throughout the valley. The Americans laughed, photographed the falling vehicle and continued on their way. From a nearby house we saw as a German women, with two teenage boys, ran out and fell upon the broken car. They pulled out some leather suitcases and other valuables. I believe they were delighted that riches had come rolling right past their house.

That evening we came to a village, which had a wide street going through it and a tall Lutheran church. It was necessary to find a place to sleep for the night but we did not have the boldness or courage to go into any of the German places. We approached an American soldier and using words, head and hand gestures we tried to tell him in every way possible that we were hungry and did have a place to sleep. I don't know if he understood us or not but he shrugged his shoulders, pointed at something in his tent and we went further. Past the church, by the forest there was an empty shed with a wooden floor and we went to it. We spread some dry grass beside the wall and lay down to rest. It felt as if we were inside a sack with all the noise around us. The hills were shaking and shells were exploding. Bullets and artillery shells were whistling above our shed.

Later, several Latvians, who were also travelers like us joined us and it seemed to be less frightening.

When it became dark, the same American soldier came to the shed and brought us a large loaf of white army bread. How good it tasted! I had never seen or eaten bread like that before.

The guns did not allow us to sleep for the entire night. Our shed was shaking and it seemed that it would disintegrate into small pieces at any moment. We would drowse off, then awaken and go outside, keeping guard so that nobody would come in and strangle us here.

Teachers and students at the Bible School in Weidenest

In the morning as soon as the sun rose, we were already on our feet and began to pull our small wagon farther. It was a beautiful morning. The sky was a bright blue, but the ground was black and frightening, completely carpeted with deep holes and horrific ruins. We witnessed the same scene wherever we went: destroyed villages, towns, factories, bridges, roads and residential houses. Nobody was attempting to repair those ruins, nobody was even paying any attention to them, because the people had become used to them. Underneath a green shelter in a deep ravine beside the road there were American artillery guns, which were continuously firing into the air. There were several destroyed German vehicles along the road as well as several fresh graves ... the war was here yesterday. It was still here because the enemy had hidden it in the hills and American airplanes were diligently searching for them. The three of us were travelling through all this destruction and seeking some type of hiding place and some peace. My mind was continually on Wiedenest, but we did not have a map and we did not know where it was. We only knew that it was in the west from us and therefore, that was where we were going.

In the afternoon we came to a beautiful river. We sat on the riverbank, prayed and ate our last can of fish, which we had received from the Americans. Close by stood the village school. Its windows were all broken and there were many holes in the walls. We went to it. The large rooms were demolished; portraits were destroyed. There was ink spilled on the walls and the floor. In one corner stood a piano. It seemed that it was left there on purpose for us. It was covered with a thick layer of dust but otherwise it was completely whole. Bychkowski sat down at the piano. He thought for a moment and then began to play. Hryn and I stood beside him and began to sing softly a song that we needed the most at that moment. Our wondrous song spread throughout the empty rooms of the large German school:

> Take me Jesus, in Your hand!
> And lead in holy pathways to Your eternal throne.
> For I cannot take a single step without You,
> Along the road my Jesus, hold my hand.[95]

We sang sincerely, prayerfully and with many emotions because this song was exactly what we needed at the moment -- that the Lord would lead us. I will never forget that demolished school beside the clear river and our song. It inspired us for our long journey and gave us spiritual strength and hope. Truly what can be better for a Christian? Nothing! It is

---

95 Візьми мене, мій Христе, за руки Сам!
Й веди Ти шляхом чистим в Твій вічний храм!
Бо кроку я не можу без Тебе йти, -
Мене в дорозі, Боже, підтримуй Ти!

the best there is when the Lord leads a person with His hand. God can lead through fire and water, through destruction or a blazing inferno...

In the evening we came to another village. There were Americans stationed there and again we asked them for bread. That night we slept in a shed out in a field and the next day we went farther. We crossed fields, villages and farms. Especially memorable for me was a circular clump of young oak trees which were growing in a large field. Evidently the allies overwhelmed a German military group several days ago in that forest. All the trees in the forest were severely burnt, some were completely uprooted, and others were lying on the ground broken in two as if a fierce storm or the most powerful tornado had passed this way. Not only the trees, but also the grass in the forest was also incinerated by phosphor. The earth was gouged so severely by bombs and exploding shells that it was impossible to find a spot to place one's foot. Scattered everywhere were burned-out vehicles, wagons and horse harnesses, empty bullet cartridges, helmets, and metal twisted by fire. In the field, close to the forest, there were many black mounds of new, freshly filled graves. I believed that soldiers as well as their horses were buried here. How frightful war is! All of Germany, through which we were now travelling, resembled that destroyed and burned forest. It was like one enormous grave.

It was already in the afternoon of the following day and we had not eaten anything yet. We could hardly move our feet and still we had to pull a wagon loaded with various pieces of clothing and books. We had already thrown away much stuff along the way, but we were still carrying things, which we thought were essential for us. Bychkowski insisted in protecting the new songs, which he had composed in Gernsdorf while surrounded by the noise of airplanes. I was carrying several books, as well as my notebooks containing the poems and stories that I had written. Hryn also had some medical books with him and some old evangelical songbooks with notes. We were beginning to feel that we no longer had the strength to drag all these possessions and so wearily we sat down beside the road and waited for help. We got up and continued for a distance but always moving slower and slower, going step by step because we were very hungry and no longer had any strength.

We came to a curve in the road when an American soldier held up his hand, motioning for us to stop. He approached us and took all our packages, piled them up on the grass, and then picked up our wagon and with all his strength threw it into a deep ravine. We could hear it as it fell, striking rocks and then softly hit the bottom. I looked down into the ravine and saw that there were many wagons similar to ours; there were also bicycles and motorcycles. People, like us, were sitting on the grass waiting for something.

Two young boys approached on bicycles with bundles tied to the back of them. The American soldier again held up his hand, signaling to them to stop. Then he took their bicycles and pushed them also into the ravine. The boys were quiet because first of all, they are unable to speak to him and secondly, they did not understand what all of this meant. They also sat down beside us.

Soon a military vehicle arrived and we were told to climb aboard. We sat on our belongings as we travelled through forests, hills, valleys and villages and then finally we came to a small town and stopped in front of two gates. An American soldier approached the truck and said in Polish:

"Those who are from Russia will go to that gate, and those from Poland will go to the other gate."

We immediately assessed the significance of this choice and said that we were from Poland. Our documents said that we were *ostarbiters* but we had already either thrown them out or they were hidden somewhere down deep among our belongings. We had nothing to prove that we were from Poland but what saved us was our knowledge of the Polish language. A man at the gate sized us up with his eyes and then asked in excellent Polish:

"If you say that you are from Warsaw, then where in Warsaw is the street Nowy Swiat?"

One of us came forward and answered in equally excellent Polish:

"Nowy Swiat goes from *Plac Trzech Krzyzy*[96] all the way to the Nicholas Copernicus monument. And there begins *Krakowskie Przedmiesche*[97] which goes all the way to Plac Zamkowy[98]. On the right will be the

---

96   Three Crosses Square
97   Krakow suberb
98   Castle Square

Kierbedz Bridge over the Vistula River, then there is Praga, Wilensky Palace, *Ulica Sklepowa*[99]."

The man smiled and did not allow us to speak any more and shook everyone's hand.

"Please, please enter, countrymen!"

He closed the gate behind us and we found ourselves in a large Polish camp. First of all, they poured some kind of white powder into our sleeves and behind the collar then gave us tickets with which we could go to the kitchen where we were given a very good dinner. We were told to find a spot in the camp and so we went looking throughout the barracks. There were countless people here, mainly young men and women, and the only language everywhere was Polish.

We found a small room for ourselves with three mattresses on the floor. We piled our belongings on the mattresses and lay down to rest, closing the door behind us. Amongst ourselves we talked strictly in Polish and very loudly so that everyone would hear, but deep down in our souls there smouldered uncertainty and fear. What would happen if they came to inspect our belongings, which were full of Ukrainian handwriting, notes, books, and filled notebooks?

For a long time during the evening, the sound of Polish songs and voices hummed throughout the camp like inside a large beehive, but the three of us lay silently on our mattresses and did not go anywhere. We locked our door and then quietly spoke in our own language. All our belongings were beneath our heads as each one of us guarded his own possessions. These were our only material assets and we would not want to lose any of them.

In front of our camp was what the Polish guard said was the "Russian" camp. An accordion continued to play in the camp until past midnight and the sounds coming from there caused us some concern. We could hear drunken shouting and coarse language. There was less light there and the barracks were darker than ours. It was surrounded by barbed wire and a guard in a long, grey, military coat stood at the gate. Above the gate a red flag waved like a pair of frightening wings. The barrack was directly in front of our window and we could hear as a young girl was talking to the guard:

---

99 Market Street

"Tovarish commander, tell this one to leave me alone."

"But before that you were dancing with the Germans so why do you not want to dance with our *parnyas?*"[100] answered the angry guard.

The girl still wanted to say something but obscene curses from the "long coat" and the drunken laughter of some *parnya* drowned out her words.

With pain in our hearts we remembered our girls from Gernsdorf. They were probably also living in a similar hell, because American military sentries were stationed on every road, gathering foreigners and transporting them to the camps. The majority of the camps were Polish, but there were Russian ones as well; Ukrainians and Belarusians were being sent to the latter. These camps were still being formed in order to register, feed and then transport the people to their homes. However, the French, Belgians, Italians and Dutch were already being transported. American cargo trucks were driving past our gate, decorated with greenery and various national flags. Inside they were full of young men and girls waving their hands at everyone, laughing, clapping their hands and singing their own songs. They were fortunate because they were going back to their own people in a free country. We could only sit and worry, we could only think and wait. Where will we be going and when?

Everyday the Americans brought new people to the camps and those who had come here earlier were told to get ready to travel further. A long line of cargo trucks stood outside the fence. Holding all our possessions close beside us we found our space in one vehicle and it began to move. The way pointed to the west.

The day was the April 15th, 1945. We were travelling on fine German roads. All around us spring was in bloom. The fields were turning green, displaying new growths of wheat and barley. Birds were singing and orchards were blooming, but frightening scenes of destruction, which covered all of Germany, marred all this beauty of God's creation. I remember a town called Altenkirchen through which we travelled. There was not a single whole building left standing in the town, not a single whole tree. The Americans had cleared the road with machines and along the sides lay piles of bricks, rocks, earth and glass. This was once a beautiful town, people lived in it and now... only ruins. Never before had I seen such

---
100 "parnya" is young fellow or boyfriend.

terrible destruction and never again since that time. Absolutely nothing was left of what was once a beautiful town; only ruins remained.

We were approaching *Nadrenia*[101]. This was a place of indescribable beauty. The day was sunny outside, the weather had stayed the same for several days and so the roads were covered with dust that followed us like a cloud. We are coming closer to the Rhine River, which we could see glistening in the distance. Our hearts were filled with joy because our desire was to be reunited with our brothers in Wiedenest who were somewhere close by. But in any case, we had come closer to the west.

We passed through the beautiful, slightly destroyed city of Bonn, which is the current capital of Western Germany. Then we turned onto the wide *autostrada*[102], which led to Cologne. Soon we could see the lights reflecting from the muddy waters of the mighty Rhine River. There were no bridges across the river because they were all lying in the water, reaching up into the sky with their formidable iron arms. Along the river were countless American troops as well as machinery and vehicles. Several large ships were connected together to complete a bridge to the other side, over which we slowly crossed. On the right side we could see the city of Cologne, we could see the towers of the Cologne Cathedral, but our vehicles turned to the left and we bypassed the city. Everywhere here was flat like a tabletop.

From a distance we could see many large red buildings beside the road, which were surrounded by a high stone wall, and we were driven straight to these. On a large gate the Polish eagle became visible. A white-red flag was flapping its wings and beneath it in large letters was a sign that said *Oboz Polski*[103]. A guard at the gate, wearing an English uniform, allowed our vehicles to pass through into a wide courtyard.

On one side there was an office building and everyone was told to enter, one by one, to register. The three of us entered the building, but before that we had resolved to walk a straight path and not to twist anything. We decided not to say anything untrue but to confess that we were Ukrainians, although we were citizens of Poland. That was what we decided and that was what we did.

---

101   Polish for North Rhine-Westphalia
102   Autobahn
103   Polish Camp

Behind the table sat several officials who registered everyone into large books, and handed out a document, which granted the right to live in the camp and to receive food. When we came up to the table, the first question was:

"Polish?"

"No, Ukrainian."

The eyes of the official widened and he got up to his feet.

"This camp is only for Polish."

"We are Polish citizens," we said in our defense.

"That doesn't mean anything," said the angry official. We are registering only Polish; the Ukrainians have their own camp on the other side of the city and we will transport you there immediately."

"Please sir," we again said in defense. "That is a Russian camp and we were never in Russia. We were born in Poland, we grew up in Poland, we were taken to Germany from Poland and if necessary we would like to return to Poland."

The official thought for a moment. He softened, and then went outside and discussed something with an American officer. He returned and said "*Dobzhe!*"[104] Our hearts revived.

We settled into a very fine room. From the kitchen we received a delicious supper and then lay down on the floor to rest. The camp was very active and noisy like on a large ocean pier. Large kettles of food were steaming outside and a long line of people was standing in front of it. Some were coming, others leaving. It was possible to get several helpings of soup, bread or meat. The cook was serving good American soup from a can into dishes. Some soup overflowed over the top of the dish onto the ground. There was so much soup, so much bread! Take as much as you want, as much as you need! Was this a fairytale or was it true? Lord, how hungry we were just a short time ago and now we have so much bread, as much as we want! There were no turnips or tasteless blue cabbage.

After the long journey and a delicious supper we slept very well. In the morning we walked throughout the camp looking for someone familiar but there were only strangers here. The camp was surrounded with barbed wire and it was not possible to get out anywhere from this enclosure. A

---

104 Good, or very well

guard was standing at the gate and was not allowing anyone to exit through the gate. Every hour new people were being brought into the camp. There was much noise and yelling in the camp, like *na yarmarku*[105]. There were not a sufficient number of buildings, or enough rooms and people slept all together, lying close to each other on the cement floor, covering themselves with whatever they had. There were single men, girls and entire families. The language everywhere was strictly Polish and it was not apparent whether there was even one Ukrainian soul in that sea of humanity. If there was, they were now silent, hidden and not speaking.

In one corner of the camp, the Polish boys stretched out a wire and made a passage along the ground to enter into the forest. The forest was thick with mostly spruce trees. Although the forest was riddled with bullets, it was green and smelled of resin. It was calling us to itself for freedom. We went, making our way through the barbed wire. In the forest there were several houses, which were half-destroyed; the roofs were missing, the windows and doors were broken. We went inside, and everywhere we saw the same scenes of war. Expensive portraits on the walls were destroyed, broken mirrors, kitchen dishes and torn German books were scattered everywhere. The Polish boys stuck their noses into the broken cupboards, but somebody had already been there and the cupboards were empty. There were other houses and rich villas nearby and we went there also. On the right we could see Cologne's sports stadium, resembling a Roman arena during the time of Nero. It seemed that "Urs and Lilia"[106] from Senkievich's "*Kamo Hryadeshi*"[107] stood here somewhere because close by was a fortress, which was now a ruin and the large marble stairs which lead to it were covered with broken bricks and dust. We wanted to go farther but an American military vehicle, with M.P. written in large letters on it and some military police inside, appeared in front of us. They stopped us, pointing their machine guns at us. When they saw our camp documents they put away their guns, put us into the car and drove us back to the camp. The following day soldiers arrived and set up a guard outside the fence surrounding the camp.

---

105 at the fair
106 Ursus and Lygia
107 Literally "where are you going" or Quo Vadis. Novel by Polish author Henryk Sienkiewicz

Spring had arrived in full bloom outside the camp. Not far away the clover was beginning to turn green and bees were humming, but we sat behind the wire as if we were in prison. We walked around the wide camp courtyard, gazing hungrily through the fence, desperate in our longing to get out. Up till now there was no way out of our situation.

One Sunday I went into a large room in the camp, which had been converted into a chapel and was now being used by the Polish priest to conduct services. After the service he would marry young couples. This was a unique event, which could only take place during this abnormal time of war. A poorly dressed priest stood beside a small altar that was covered with some very shiny material. Beside him stood a second person who acted as his assistant. A long line of young couples slowly approached the altar. None of them were dressed in wedding apparel or wore any jewelry. The boys were dressed in ordinary jackets and the girls wore ordinary dresses. They approached the altar, one couple at a time, knelt down, the priest spoke briefly to them, quickly sprinkled them with holy water and the ceremony was over. The married couples went outside through a side door where nobody was there to greet them. Nobody accompanied them outside or spoke any good wishes to them because everyone here was a stranger. A second couple took their place at the altar, a third, a fifth and endlessly; at times there were no less than thirty couples or perhaps more. They scattered throughout the camp and began to live their lives together as a family. Later, the majority of them left the camp single and unmarried, humiliated and with broken hearts and souls... In this manner the war not only ruined the cities but also ruined people's souls.

IN THE AMERICAN ARMY

Easter arrived in 1945 and found us in a Polish camp close to Cologne. I don't think that I have ever experienced such a sad Easter. We had enough to eat, nobody was forcing us to go to work, but a bottomless craving was eating away at our hearts. We longed not only for our country and our families, but we also longed for Gernsdorf, for Weidenest, for Schalksmuehle. That Easter I remember that I had a dream that I was back at home. I was singing together with my brothers and sisters at the service. I was singing *Christos Voskres*[108] so loudly that brother Hryn actually woke me up. I sat up on my bare mattress and the sweet dream vanished; it was only a dream. I was aware that I was still in a faraway foreign land and this awareness lay as a heavy stone on my soul.

In the evening some young Polish men came walking past our door and we overheard their conversation:

"Beside the kitchen, I heard two Ukrainians having a conversation between themselves," said one voice. "It might be necessary to find and observe them. They murdered what is not an insignificant number of our people."

"You know," said the other voice. "It would be possible to wipe them out outside the camp, but they won't let us go there. In the camp we cannot do anything because we are not in charge here. I heard that two Poles had killed a civilian German on the road, and they were arrested and taken somewhere. They might be tried by a military court."

Hearing this, I carefully hid all my personal documents. The manuscripts of the many stories I had written, I threw them into a hole with the garbage. I hesitated as I was throwing them away because it seemed that I

---

108 *Christ is Risen*

was not merely throwing away paper on which I had written with a pencil, but I was tearing my aching heart into pieces and throwing it into the hole.

From that moment on we began to make plans to escape from that camp and go somewhere else. To our good fortune, immediately after Easter, it was announced that the American army required young, strong men to do various tasks. That day Bychkowski and I signed up and on the following day we left the camp in large American vehicles. Hryn did not want to go with us and remained in the camp.

We travelled along a twisting road through the city of Bonn and then got onto the Autobahn, which ran right by the Rhine River and then turned south. The road was very straight and had not been touched or damaged by the war. The Rhine River was on the left side and on the right side there were high hills behind which, protruding like swallows' nests, could be seen small castles and various monuments. In the past these were inhabited by aristocrats, princes, *korols and csars*[109], but now they were standing empty; bombs had destroyed some of them. On the other side of the Rhine, along rocky roadsides through the hills, there were vineyards and beyond them were also red and black castles. There was such breathtaking beauty here that our eyes could not appreciate everything. The Americans were chewing gum, smacking their lips and all the time sighing: "beautiful, beautiful!"

Towards evening we came to the nice, clean town of Brohl, which was on the main road along the Rhine between Cologne and Koblentz. Formerly there were luxurious homes along this road where the rich German retreated for a time of rest and relaxation. On the riverbank were hotels and docks used for recreational boats. But now these docks were empty, there were no boats, and a company of the American army occupied the magnificent hotel rooms. And now we also would be included with them.

Bychkowski and I occupied a room on the second floor. The following day a second transport arrived, bringing another group of young men; Hryn also came with them. The three of us were together again.

In the evening I went for a walk along a path at the bottom of the hill. I noticed that our boys were already busy doing something inside an attractive, red house. I looked inside and saw that there was

---

109 Korol was a ruling monarch, Csar was a title given to any monarch

an American soldier among them. They had opened the large black cupboards and were removing shirts, shoes, towels, and men's socks. It was apparent that this was the home of some patriotic government official. He had escaped but our boys were able to gain entrance before anyone else was able to enter the premises. The American found some documents and photographic plates and without delay he turned these over for development; later he showed us the completed photographs. They were horrible! Some gallows had been set up in the yard of a concentration camp on which two people were seen hanging. Several Gestapo were holding a third person while placing a noose over his head. Beside them stood a tall Gestapo who was holding his sides and standing with his boots spread wide. He had a frightening devilish grin on his face and in his hand he held a *nahan*[110]. The Americans looked at these photographs, discussed something among themselves, paced about angrily like lions, and did not even look in the direction where the Germans were walking.

We were soon issued two sets of American military clothing, one for everyday use and one for holidays. We were also issued an American army certificate, which later would open wide doors for us everywhere. We looked at ourselves in a mirror and could not recognize ourselves. We could not believe our eyes. Yesterday we were still poor *ostarbiters* and today – American soldiers.

Our food was so plentiful that we could not describe it in words. The kitchen was located right by the Rhine. A black soldier was throwing pieces of meat, various canned goods and vegetables into a large kettle. He stirred everything together, let it cook, and then we, together with the American soldiers, approached the kitchen. We received our dinner or supper, but we could not eat even half of what was prepared. Anything that was left over the black cook dumped into the river. Never before had I seen such an abundance and wastefulness of food. It was simply too hard to believe that somewhere in the world there was such a country that had so much of everything.

What were our responsibilities? Every morning the boys woke up early and traveled by army vehicles to a nearby railway station where

---

110 A seven shot Nagent revolver

they unloaded fuel, weapons and food from the freight cars, loaded them onto high cargo trucks, which then distributed them wherever they were needed. We worked from eight in the morning until one in the afternoon. The rest of the time was free. After work the boys went for a walk in the hills, attempted to catch fish in the Rhine, or sat and warmed themselves in the sun. Each spent the time as he wished.

Since Warsaw, I still had an English New Testament with me and now I began to read it carefully. I knew many words in English and several times I would say something to the Americans in their language, which gave them the impression that I knew some English. They asked me to work in the office and I also dragged Bychkowski and Hryn along with me. We kept the lists of all our boys. We looked after all their needs, distributed to them their allocation of candy and chocolate as well as their military invasion currency[111] that could be used to purchase anything at the American military store. We never went to work at the station so we had plenty of free time, and did not know what to do with it.

One evening there arose shouting, clamour and voices calling out throughout the hotel rooms. We all ran outside, not knowing what was happening. American soldiers were embracing each other, kissing each other and loudly yelling: "Peace. Peace!" I approached our commanding officer and asked him what was happening. He embraced me so tightly that my shoulders cracked and said:

"Friend! Peace in the world! Peace!"

That evening the radio announced the news that peace had come to Japan and to Europe. Peace had found us in the small town of Brohl, close to the Rhine River.

The Americans rejoiced, observing a holiday, because for them it truly was peace. But we knew that for many nations there was no peace and among them was our nation. There was no peace for our nation and there was no peace for us either. We were not even brave enough to admit that we were Ukrainians.

---

111 Allied Military Currency (AMC) was a form of currency issued to troops during the war who were entering liberated or nearly liberated countries

After a time an American-Czech soldier joined our group and we were able to communicate with him in Czech. This was much easier for me because he would now go everywhere with me and translate when it was difficult to make myself understood to the Americans. I knew many words from the New Testament but knew nothing from their everyday language and therefore, often I could not understand them.

Once one of our friends came running to me and asked:

"Tell me, what is this 'OK'?"

I spread out my hands. I tried to remember whether I had read that word in the New Testament, but I could not recall. Then I found a similar word, "obey", but when we showed it to the American he simply waved his hand and we concluded that he did not understand us or we him. For a long time we did not know what the word "OK" meant.

Towards evening on Saturday our boys returned from work, washed up, dressed in their new clothing and vanished somewhere. After awhile the Czech soldier arrived and asked me to go with him. We walked though some beautiful orchards and there, underneath the trees, was a bar. We went inside and found that it was full of our boys who were all drinking beer. That same day, they were all taken away, told to take off their military clothing and transported back to the place from which they had been taken. Others were brought to take their place. The slightest fraternization with the Germans was not allowed.

Beautiful, fragrant days of spring passed by. We had heard that the war ended a long time ago but we did not know what was happening in the world because we did not have a radio or newspapers. We only saw open trains filled with German prisoners travelling through Brohl. There were several thousand of them in a large field surrounded with a wire fence near Koblentz. Almost everyday we saw waves of French workers travelling and singing as they returned to their own land.

Our life in Brohl was truly relaxing. We had plenty of time to rest the body but our souls were starving and needy. The Polish boys spent their entire Sundays playing cards or entertaining themselves with other things, but we could not find a place that would satisfy our greatest yearning. Many Sundays had passed since we had attended a worship service. We had no fellowship with other believers and for us this was clearly an adverse situation. We knew nothing about our brothers and sisters in Gernsdorf, Schalksmuehle or Weidenest, and they did not know anything about us. At the time, when we were living peacefully in Brohl, they were all very worried about us. Perhaps they were thinking that we were either killed somewhere on the road or had ended up in some transition camp and forcefully taken *na rodinu*[112]. Knowing that that there were many of them and that they were certainly holding large evangelical services, our yearning increased infinitely more. Many times we discussed how we might be able to find a way to our own people, but it was not possible because we were now wearing American military uniforms and we could not leave our work.

Suddenly, one day we were told that tomorrow we must be ready because our entire army division was going to be moving. The following day we were all ready. We placed all our belongings, as well as food for the trip, onto large cargo trucks. In the morning, while the sun was bathing its first rays in the Rhine, we set out on the road. That was May 22nd.

We travelled south all day. We crossed the Rhine, passed Kublentz and then turned to the east and drove through fields, forests, valleys and hills. In the afternoon we came to a town, which was almost completely untouched by the war. Along the road there were many sturdy, green linden trees and among them were two gates. Above one gate a Polish national flag was waving and above the second there was a red one. Beneath this flag there was an enormous portrait. We looked more closely – Stalin. We were horrified and turned the other way and continued further.

Our vehicles stopped beneath some linden trees and we prepared food for ourselves to eat. Later we walked outside the two gates and spoke to the guards. Behind the gates stretched long buildings. These were the camps from which people were being transported back to their homeland: to Poland and to Russia. This did not affect us and we spoke freely with everyone. Of course, we only spoke Polish.

---

112 The homeland, meaning, to the USSR

We traveled through the green fields of Germany. X identifies the author.

By evening we arrived at the town of Erfurt in the state of Thuringia. We were aware of the fact that we had travelled far from Westphalia, but having committed ourselves to this course we could not change it or do anything about it. These were dangerous times for foreigners and so we were forced to surrender to our fate as it led us down the roads of Germany.

We settled down again in what might have been a hotel or a school in which there were many nice, clean rooms. We were not there for very long because it was necessary to travel further.

Our buildings were at one end of the town. Immediately behind us were some luxurious orchards and hayfields. The days were warm, pleasant and fragrant. The lindens were blooming, the wheat was ripening and cherries were beginning to turn red. I continued to work in the office while the rest of the boys went to work. The work here was different. In the town there were large stores with various German goods which the Americans were removing and transporting somewhere else. Our boys were able to acquire some riches from this because everyday they brought to their residences something new. One day each one brought with them a photo-camera, on another day—watches, another day – new shirts and socks. Each one of them now had sacks full of goods under their beds. There was so much of everything that there was no room where to put it.

One day it was a holiday and we did not work. The boys scattered into the town and into the fields; and I also went down a path that led into a field. I looked and saw several of our boys sitting by a stream, reading something, but they did not see me. When I came right up to them, they were startled, hid the book and looked at me in alarm.

"What were you reading?" I asked.

They were quiet, glancing at one another.

"What's wrong?" I asked again, not knowing anything

"Well, we found some kind of Ukrainian book and we were reading it," said one of the boys, who always stressed the fact that he was from Lviv.

I asked them to show me the book. It was a calendar, *Zolotyy Kolos*[113]. I believe it was for the year 1938. I looked at each one of them; they were frightened and embarrassed.

"So, you are Ukrainian?" I ask again.

"No, no sir, we are Polish but we can read Ukrainian..."

I placed my hand on the shoulder of the one who was holding the book and said for the first time in Ukrainian:

"It's nothing boys, don't be afraid of me, because I am the same as you."

The boys stood around me, measuring me with their eyes and literally shining with happiness. Almost each one of them was from Halychyna. After that we no longer hid our language. It is true that in the camp and at work everyone still spoke Polish. Nobody suspected that we were Ukrainian, but now we understood each other.

In Erfurt there were many camps for foreigners where thousands of different people lived, but mostly they were recent workers from the east. These camps placed a heavy burden on the entire town and the townspeople lived in constant fear of them. People from the camps would come out of their fenced enclosure and wander through the German fields, gardens and orchards, destroying whatever they could. Everyday they were burning wooden sheds in the orchards and even houses were set on fire. A German could not even show himself on the street on a bicycle.

I recall one time when I was returning to our hotel from town, an elderly, hunched-over German was walking in front of me. Two young men came from the opposite direction and it was immediately obvious

---

113 "Golden Ear". An annual calendar-magazine published in Ukraine

that these were *nashi*[114]. When they came up to the German, they pushed him to the ground and began to beat him with their fists and feet. The German called out but they grabbed him by the neck and began to choke him. I began to run. The young men spotted the "American" and began to run away as fast as they could. I yelled at them to stop and began to chase after them but they didn't even look back. They jumped over a hedge and disappeared across a magnificent garden.

I don't know what I would have ever done if they had decided to approach me. But because they instinctively began running away I gained enough bravery and ran after them as far the fence, but there was no sign of the boys.

I helped the elderly German to get up on his feet. He thanked me and cried profusely. Considering me to be a real American soldier, he asked me to accompany him to his house, which I did.

Perhaps in the past these two young men had experienced the worst indignity and abuse from the Germans. Perhaps they had suffered repeated beatings at the hands of the Germans. But it is also possible that this old German had more than once helped these types of young men by pushing a piece of bread underneath the fence. Perhaps, he himself had been beaten by his own Gestapo for these acts of compassion to the unfortunate *ostarbiters*. This happened very frequently. It was not always clear who was innocent and who should be punished. The guilty would usually hide themselves while good and decent people often had to answer for them.

Close to our building there was a small lake with clear, warm water. There were clumps of alder trees and reeds growing around it. It was a hot day and our boys went swimming in the lake. They swam and dived in the water; but later, when they returned to their rooms, they noticed that one of their friends, a young man named Mykola, was missing. They knew that he had gone with them to the lake. They had been swimming together, his clothing had been left on the bank, but Mykola was missing.

We all rushed back to the lake. Some Germans and the American army joined us. We searched for a long time but found nothing. The lake was quiet, glistening, reflecting the sun and rippling among the reeds. We

---

114 Our own people

stood along the bank. All at once the body of Mykola floated out from underneath a bush. It was pale and gaunt as if it was made of marble.

The following day, with great sadness, we buried our friend. He was a Ukrainian from Halychyna who had come to us from a concentration camp. He had a father who was living in Canada. Many times Mykola would come to our office asking us to send a letter to his father in Canada, but the post office was not yet working and his request was left unfulfilled.

Days and weeks passed. Everyday the boys went to work; in the evening they returned bringing with them various new items. I worked everyday in the office, but most of the time I walked the streets of Erfurt feeling sad and having one great desire. We had plenty of everything for life and for the flesh, but for the soul we had nothing. Because of that yearning, almost everyday I would go to a distant field outside the town. There were some bushes growing there. Stalks of wheat intertwined with blue cornflowers[115] at the edge of the field. Quail were singing and beautiful poppies were blooming. A path, thickly overgrown with knotweed, twisted through the tall grain in the field and came out to a mound from which all of Erfurt, as well as the surrounding towns of this beautiful region, was visible. I sat there on the knotweed and dreamed endlessly, read my New Testament and prayed. Concern about the unknown was forcing my thoughts back to my home, to Gernsdorf and to Schalksmuehle.

The most stressful and worrisome thing for us was that there were no believers anywhere. For long weeks and months we were living a life that was not normal. Around us we heard only unpleasant and filthy conversations and when Sunday came, we could hear bells sounding throughout the town but we did not have anywhere to refresh our souls. The longing for our evangelical services was having a numbing effect on us. We longed to hear an evangelical song and to have fellowship with other Christians. One Sunday the three of us left early in the morning to search for German believers. It did not matter that they were Germans; we didn't understand their language, but at least we could spend an hour or two with others who shared the same faith as us. We could pray together, listen to a song and read God's Word. O how deep was our longing for the fellowship of

---

115 also called bachelor buttons

believers! We do not appreciate it when we have it but when we lose it, we regret it beyond measure.

We walked for a long time along the still deserted streets of Erfurt before we stopped beside a gate on which there was a notice written in German that evangelical services were held inside. We entered; our hearts were trembling with joyful excitement. Inside there was a long, clean sanctuary with many pews, on which people were already sitting. The organ was playing and a song was softly rising. We did not understand the words, but we knew the melody because we also sang this song: *Spasinnya Vichne Bozhy Syn*[116]. This was followed by prayer and a sermon, and after the service we were surrounded by German believers and their pastor.

"*Sprechen ze Deutch?*[117]"

"No." we answered, also speaking in German as best as we could. "We speak Polish, Ukrainian, Russian".

A lady came forward. In her eyes there were tears and much sadness.

"Then you are Polish?" she asked.

"No, we are Ukrainian. We are also Christians."

The woman began to cry. She squeezed our hand, wiping her tears.

"And I thought that you were Americans. Here you have your own brothers. Praise the Lord! Clearly God has brought you here."

Then this sister related to us that she was living with her family in a transition camp and soon they will be transported *na rodinu*.

We went with her to a camp outside the town. In the gate a guard, in a long overcoat, stood at attention. He raised his hand to his hat and then asked for our documents. We showed him our certificates. He probably did not understand anything on it, but when he saw the American military seal he opened the gate wide for us and even stood at attention. The camp was large. There were rows of black wooden buildings surrounded by barbed wire.

We walked around all the barracks and saw the worst hell and debauchery that a person could ever imagine. Several families lived in one barrack. In another young men and women all lived together in small, dirty rooms.

---

116 Ukrainian words are translated as "Eternal salvation God's Son has brought into this world", sung to the melody of "There is a Fountain Filled with Blood". In German, "*Ein heilger Born gefullt mit Blud*".

117 Do you speak German?

They sang, they yelled out with wild voices, staggering drunkenly and falling down onto the floor. The windowsills and every corner were littered with empty whiskey bottles.

In the barrack for families we found the family of the Christian woman who was now familiar to us, her father, mother, son and daughter-in-law, as well a single young girl from Kiev, sister Olya. We prayed together and read the Word of God. We saw each other for the first time in our life, but already we felt close to one another as one family. Truly, "we were once strangers, and now we are one family."

The following day I went back to that camp. I took some coffee, bread and cans of food for that family, but they were no longer there. Standing on the road, in front of the fence, was a convoy of cargo trucks. The residents of the wooden barracks were climbing up into the vehicles, carrying with them large packages, suitcases and wooden trunks.

I stood beside the guard hoping to see the family with whom I was now acquainted. Behind the wire something terrible and unbelievable was happening. Young men were carrying out dishes and smashing them against the concrete. They were bringing out mirrors, pitchers and chairs. With glee and wild laughter they were demolishing everything. Window panes were flying through the air, doors were being smashed, and wooden walls were creaking. The vandals then came out to the gate, looked at their destroyed barracks once more, and angrily spat on the ground beneath their feet. Horror filled me as I observed this scene. I turned to the guard and asked in Polish:

"Where is the family who lived in that barrack?"

"I don't know. If they are not here, they probably ran away..."

When the last of the young men climbed into the cars, the guard turned his gun so that the stock was pointing upward and with all his strength began to smash it against the cement. The gun broke in two but he still continued to smash the bent barrel several times and then threw it into a ditch. He jumped into a car and yelled at the black American driver:

"*Davay vperyod. Payechali!*[118]

The car jerked forward and the guard waved his hand at me. He must have learned Polish somewhere, because he yelled,

---

118 Go ahead. Let's go!

"*Do weidzenia pan!*"[119]

I stood at the gate by myself. Behind the gate—there was complete destruction. I went inside the fence. I could see some small trees in one corner on which pieces of paper or cloth were fluttering. I looked more closely – it was a cemetery. I saw graves and crosses. There were not more than ten; some were recent and others were overgrown with grass. I stopped beside that spot and reverently removed my cap. "Honour to you who have suffered and are now resting here!" I had a feeling that this was not the only patch of ground inside the camp, which was a cemetery, but also this whole camp. All of Thuringia[120] was a cemetery. All of Germany, and now the whole world – was one large cemetery.

A yellow-blue ribbon was attached to one cross. A small tin cross was nailed to the cross with an inscription on it that was barely visible. These words were written with an ordinary black pencil:

"Here rests Sawa Cher... (this was all that could be read because the letters had been erased by rain), born in the city of Kolodno in Kremenets district. May you rest in peace."

I felt as if something gripped me by the heart. I stood on my knees beside the grave and silently cried.

"Friend Sawa, who are you and under what circumstances did you die? You are from my homeland. You will never return to your sunny fatherland again. Perhaps there is a wife and children waiting for you..."

After that I went everyday to the familiar gravesites in the corner of the destroyed camp. I brought blue cornflowers from the field. I also brought the pain in my heart and my soul. At that time there was no better place for me to be than in the place where my unknown countryman, Sawa, was resting with eternal sleep.

The group of believers had truly escaped because we found them later in a Polish camp in Erfurt. They were aware that the residents of the camp were soon to be transported out and therefore, they together with many others, were able to get out through an opening which had been cut through the fence.

---

119 See you later, sir
120 a German state

Before long we were able to find an entire group of Ukrainians in the town who did not go to the Russian camp. They did not go to a Polish camp either but rather lived in a partially destroyed, windowless building. This became the beginning of the formation of a Ukrainian camp. They lived in great fear, starving, and without any guardianship or protection. We made the acquaintance of a navy captain, S. Shramchenko, who headed up the group. This information was relayed to our boys in the American company and they were able to provide for them sufficient amounts of whatever they needed, especially food. Capitan S. Shramchenko, shortly before his death, still wrote to me recalling our days in Erfurt.

One Sunday I went to the newly formed camp. That Sunday an Orthodox service was held in a small Protestant church. A few dozen people gathered inside the church and an elderly priest led the Divine Liturgy. A small choir consisting of five or six members sang. Turning away from the people the priest declared in a voice trembling with emotions:

"Our long-suffering Mother, our Ukraine and her people, who are living in exile, in captivity and in prisons, may the Lord God remember them in His Kingdom."

The people, especially several elderly women, crossed themselves, got down on their knees, wiping their eyes ... as the choir sang. A thin thread of smoke from the fragrant incense rose above the small altar. A single small candle was flickering and *almost-almost* going out.

I was sitting in the corner of the last bench. I was in such a wondrous state of elation that I did not know where I was. I had attended large Orthodox services countless times in Podchayiv, Kremenets, Rivno and also in Warsaw at the Cathedral of Mary Magdalene. I loved to listen to *Izhe Kheruvima*[121] by Bortinanski. My emotions would rise as I waited for "*Is polla eti, Despota*[122]" which was unsurpassed in its strength and beauty. But in all those other services, never before had I heard such singing as by those five individuals who sang without a choir director. I had heard how the Orthodox, during their services prayed for all the kings, the archbishop, the bishops and for all the clergy of the church. But here I heard,

---

121 Cherubic Hymn
122 Είς πολλά έτη, δέσποτα is translated "Many years to you, lord". The word δέσποτα (despota) corresponds to the Slavonic Church word "vladyko". An acclamation chanted in Greek in honour of a bishop

for the first time, a prayer for the long-suffering Mother, for our Ukraine, for those who were in captivity and in prisons. My heart was deeply stirred and I sincerely prayed together with my people.

After several days our boys went to work in the nearby town of Weimer. I was getting bored staying in my room and in the morning I decided to go with them to Weimer, a city known to every literary person. I would have regretted forever to have been so near Weimer and to never have seen it. Before the war, poets, writers and artists from all over Germany and even from all of Europe would come here every year to walk those same roads on which the great German poet Johann Goethe had walked. They came, not only to walk on those paths, but also to see the city, to see the house-museum where Goethe lived, where his immortal "Faust" was born. I too was now going to see the legendary Weimer for that same purpose.

The city, surprisingly, was affected very little by the war. Perhaps the Allies respected the memory of Goethe or perhaps they had other plans of their own. We came to a beautiful street lined with linden trees. Everything here was protected by the luxurious shade of trees. Roses and tulips surrounded everything. Every home looked like an enchanting charming flower, every asphalt street looked as if it had been sprayed with some type of black, shiny liquid. Beside the road there was a tall, iron gate, inside which American soldiers were standing on guard. Stretching out behind the fence were some large, red, two-storied buildings. Our vehicles drove up to a wall and stopped. We got out and went up the stairs. Lying inside, in wide halls, were piles of large rolls of pre-war manufactured goods of various kinds and colours. Entire mountains of men's woolen socks and army sweaters were in one aisle. Another aisle was filled with various types and sizes of men's boots and shoes. My eyes had never before witnessed such wealth. With all these goods it would be possible to clothe, not only all of Weimer, but all of Thuringia.

We rolled the bundles to a window and threw them down to the vehicles, where our boys sorted them. The trucks transported everything to train cars at the station and then returned back to us. This went on all day.

Towards evening we left to return to Erfurt. Our vehicle stopped beside a building and I could hear the American soldiers discussing something among themselves. I could hear them continuously repeating the name,

"Goethe, Goethe". We were standing in front of the building where Johann Goethe had lived and worked. The building had been damaged but was still whole. Once, it was wide open for tourists, but now it was closed. Together, with the Americans, we stopped in front of the stairs and went to look inside though the window. Inside it was dark. The Americans stopped chewing gum. They stood silently, deep in thought. Emotions also arose in me. I was standing in front of the home where the great Johann Goethe had lived and worked.

We continued travelling through beautiful fields to Erfurt. Our boys took with them large bundles of a various manufactured goods. They carried full sacks of shoes and sweaters. The Americans said that each one of us could take whatever we wanted. I was filled with many unforgettable memories. I had been to the city of Weimer; I saw the house where Goethe lived. These unforgettable impressions were as great riches for me.

After a while an order came that we had to leave Erfurt. Suddenly groups of fugitives and various foreigners appeared on the road. Everyone was going somewhere, traveling by wagons and motor vehicles. Everywhere there was a sense of impending fear and danger. I approached the officer in the office and asked:

"What is happening?"

"Thuringia is being turned over to the Bolsheviks[123]. Our troops have ten days to leave this town."

This news spread among our boys like a lightening bolt. We tied all our belongings together. We hurried but we did not know when or where we were going. Some of the boys began to panic. They stopped working and stood all the time in front of the office door. When were we leaving? What will happen if the Americans go and leave us behind?

Tensions rose to the very top. The day before we were in a Polish camp. While we were there the remaining residents had left for Belgium. There was not a single soul remaining in the small Ukrainian camp. The streets of Erfurt emptied. On a building, where the star-spangled American flag had always fluttered, there now protruded only an empty pole with a rope dangling from it.

---

123 Soviet Union

Our boys were all standing in front of the windows. Their belongings were lying at the gate, arranged in large piles. All the beds were made; the rooms were swept clean because that is what the Americans instructed them to do. It was necessary to leave everything as best as we could. Kazik from Warsaw wrote some nonsense messages about Stalin on pieces of paper and left all of them on the bed. Leaving the room for the final time he said:

"If they come, let them know that we were here!"

The sun was setting above the orchards. Tomorrow morning the Bolsheviks were supposed to be here but our vehicles were still not here. Our tension was reaching its limits, but the Americans were throwing a ball around in the street, chewing gum and laughing. They truly were carefree and fearless!

Then the first of the American cargo trucks came around the corner of the street. From a distance we could see the smiling black drivers as we dashed for our belongings. We looked back at the building where we had lived for a long time. We had no remorse for it. Tomorrow morning there will be new caretakers in this place. Will they be better or worse? Only the residents of Erfurt will be here to experience that.

We headed to the west, driving past the transition camps. I strained my eyes towards the spot where the wooden crosses were turning black. There was the grave of Sawa, whom I did not know, and other graves upon which I had placed cornflowers two days ago. Farewell!... Farewell!...

On both sides of the roads in Thuringia there were planted sweet cherries[124], hazelnuts, pin-cherries, sour cherries[125] and apple trees. The apples were still green but everywhere the sweet cherries were already ripe. As we drove underneath the cherry trees we would pick them. The sun was setting. A thick fog was causing a cold dew to fall on our faces.

At night we were able to rest for a short time in a dense spruce forest. We warmed up our canned food on a small portable military stove, drank some coffee and then we went farther. A crescent moon moved across the sky as if it was trying to escape from us and we were trying to catch it. Forward and forward. Occasionally we met caravans of tired fugitives. As

---
124 *chereshni* are sweet cherries
125 *vishni* are smaller and less sweet cherries

we passed them we tossed to them biscuits, small cans of army food or tins of sugar. These were all our people.

In the morning we reached an American military section that was located in some town. We had dinner there, rested for several hours, and then went farther. Luxurious German fields waved with bountiful grain. The rye had already started to turn white and the tops of the clover were beginning to curl up. Soon it will be harvest.

The sun was already setting behind the mountain when we arrived at some mounds of debris. We were told that this was the town of Giesen. Perhaps once it was a beautiful town but now it was a total ruin. Our vehicles came a station beside a hill and continued past the wreckage. We drove through some dense trees until we came to a wide green clearing surrounded by trees where the grass was taller than our knees.

We lay down to sleep wherever one found a spot; underneath the trucks, inside the trucks or right on the grass. In the morning we began to set up large canvas tents in which we would live until our group was disassembled. Up till now we had lived in hotels, in fine clean rooms, but now … in tents. But this life was interesting, truly a soldier's life. It was especially pleasant to lie in one's own tent when it was raining outside and listen to raindrops hammering loudly above our heads. Our kitchen and office were all in tents.

Immediately past the trees were hayfield; through which flowed a small stream with water, which was as clear as a tear. By the banks were clusters of green sweet flag[126]. Yellow flowers floated on the water. We would often sit by the bank of the twisting river and sing, "There's Land that is Fairer than Day". Here we often read the New Testament, especially on Sundays.

There were hayfields on the other side of the forest but with no grass growing there because, standing as far as the eye could see, there were mountains of American cardboard boxes containing various products. These were placed one on top of another, resembling buildings. The tops were covered with canvas. Between the rows of boxes were narrow aisles over which sand was spread. Each aisle was labeled with a number. In fact, this was one very large town. One section had boxes of coffee, a second had canned food, a third sugar, a fourth cigarettes. This was the warehouse

---

126 also called Acrocus calamus. The roots have medicinal properties

for the entire American army in Germany. Everyday trains would arrive to this place and our boys unloaded more goods and the mountains of boxes continued to grow.

The officers of our division, who had been with us in Brohl, were transferred elsewhere and others had arrived to take their place. The Ukrainians spoke to each other in Ukrainian, but the Polish took a very hostile stance towards this. Their attitude caught the attention of our new commanding officer, who was a very sympathetic lieutenant. He called us all together and said that each one of us can speak however they wished and desired. The Ukrainians lifted their heads up high. Ukrainian books appeared from somewhere and Ukrainian songs could now be heard in the tents. Initially the Polish were angry but in time everyone became accustomed to each other, became friends and continued to live as one transitory, wartime family.

Our greatest desire was to visit Gernsdorf. We knew that it was not very far from our present location. There was a main railway line running from Giesen to Hagen, which would take us all the way to Rüdersdorf. Day and night, the desire to visit our people, whom we had left behind, was not giving us any peace; but especially now that we were so close to them. It had been several months since we had separated from them. At that time there was still a war and shells were exploding around us. Now, there had been no war for a long time. The harvest was ripening in the fields, and freight trains were beginning to run again.

I went to the officer and requested a pass for myself and for a Belarusian with whom I had become close friends. I received the pass. I didn't walk but I ran with all my might to our tent.

"Hey, we have a pass! We can go to Gernsdorf!"

The pass allowed us to board any desired train without cost. In the event that we needed help we could report to any American army unit, which during that time was stationed in almost every town.

In the morning I together with the Belarusian Mikhas, as we called him, were already at the station and we pushed our way into an over-filled freight car. It was filled with so many people that one could not even move their shoulders. These were all German fugitives who had escaped to the

East before the advance of the Americans, and now they were returning home. Very often they had lost everything they had during the trip.

Our train was travelling very fast. It would stop at a station, new fugitives would climb on board, and others would get off, and then continue further. It went through tunnels, over glistening rivers, cutting across fields and valleys, but I was not thinking about anything, I did not see anything. There was only one longing in my soul, only one goal, and that was to reach Gernsdorf as soon as possible. Was anybody still there? Were the girls from Siegen still there? Were our people in Schalksmuehle still alive? Perhaps during all this time they had moved somewhere else. Perhaps shells had killed somebody. A long time had passed since we were here.

We arrived in Rüdersdorf, my former workplace. The train stopped. A flood of thoughts and memories enveloped me. For Mikhas everything was all strange, but not for me. I wanted to go into the field where the hand of God had held me back when I was fleeing to the shelter. I wanted to go to that ditch where I was lying, pressed against the ground as bombs were exploding around me. I wanted to go to the factory where I used to work. I wanted to see everything one more time, to experience again some thought-provoking moment. But most important – I wanted to hurry to Gernsdorf. We hurried on. We walked under the bridge where the falling bombs had wounded Barchuk. We descended down to Rüdersdorf, it was still the same path, the same trees. We had escorted our girls this way when they were leaving Gernsdorf. This was path we took as we walked together with them to work. They were not here ... I walk, think, remember. Mikhas was saying something to me, but I asked him not to interrupt my thinking. "This is my road," I said to him. "You don't know how much we suffered on it." At that moment I remembered Hryn and Bychkowski: "boys, you are there, sitting in tents, while I am on my way to Gernsdorf!" This was no ordinary matter.

From a distance I could see the cemetery, my peaceful cathedral in nature. The cross, with a bench beneath it, was becoming black. The forest was turning green. We walked on and on. There were people making hay beside the road. They were looking at us and perhaps thinking: "why are those 'Americans' going to our village?" They did not know us and we did not know them. The important thing for us was to get to Gernsdorf as fast as we can.

We were now at the first house, then the path, the bridge, and the Lutheran church. Not far, beneath the hill, I could see the dark outline of the bunker, which I once dug, with my own hands. Here was the school where we used to live, those same windows, the same doors. I felt a sharp jab in my heart and it began to beat faster. I wondered if there was anybody there?

I came up to the steps. There was a boy sitting there. It was Barchuk's Zhennya[127]. He recognized me and made a dash for the door. I could hear his childish clear voice:

"*Tatu, tatu, dyada Podworniak*[128] has come and there is even an American with him!"

Behind the door I could hear many voices and a loud commotion, but I was already on the stairs. On the porch I met Barchuk, Antonowich and all the brothers and sisters whom I had left in the spring. They were throwing themselves at me; the children were tugging my hand and jumping up to my face. I hardly recognized anyone because of the tears. Oh God, what great joy!

Late that evening I left everyone and went to my cemetery. After the joy, which I had just experienced, I was suddenly beset with an incomprehensible yearning. I remembered the distant home of my childhood, I remembered my dear mother. How blessed she would be if she could live to finally see our reunion. Day and night she waited for that reunion, even as I was waiting. Dear and unforgettable mother! How I long for you in these foreign Westphalian hills!

That evening we sat until late and talked about everything from the beginning until now. I found that the brothers and sisters in Schalksmuehle and Weidenest were all alive. They were carrying on extensive spiritual ministry in various camps. Not only were they holding large evangelical services, but also they had already held their conference, organized themselves into an association and were thinking of opening up their own Bible school. Nobody knew anything about us. They thought that we had

---

127 The boy's given name was Evhen
128 Father, father, Uncle Podworniak

become lost somewhere or had gone back to our homes. The believers had been very worried and concerned but were unable to find out anything about us, causing them to think that perhaps we were no longer among the living. We had set out on our journey during a time when everything around us was burning and being destroyed.

When it was my turn, I told them how we became "Americans". I told them that Hryn and Bychkowski were alive. That evening we prayed sincerely with deep feelings, thanking God for everything.

The following morning, Mikhas and I went to Siegen. Overflowing with all that I had learned, I returned to Bychkowski and Hryn. I felt like Joshua, who returned with delight, after searching out the Promised Land. I too was returning and bringing the best news. Our brethren were all alive. They were living together and holding large evangelical services. Conversions were taking place everywhere. There were baptisms, they had held their own conference and they were organized into an association. But we were sitting in tents. We had sufficient American bread to eat, but our souls were hungry, dying like flowers without water.

I relayed all this to my brothers in the tent, and they listened holding their breath. We firmly resolved to go to Gernsdorf, to our own people, to the group.

We took our request to the commanding officer. He listened to us and said that he could not release us because there was still much work. Soon our whole division will be disbanded and then we could go wherever we wished.

The news that we were still alive flew like a swallow to Schalksmuehle and Weidenest. Believers there thanked God that we "were dead and now we were alive, lost but now found".

After several days we were visited in Giesen by brothers Ivan Barchuk and M. Antonowich, and later by S. Yankowski and S. Kaplich. They could not enter our tents but we were able to meet them in the beautiful green hayfields. We sat for a long time beside the glistening stream and in a meadow among the trees. There we prayed and experienced immeasurable blessings. During that time there were no distinctions among us as Ukrainians, Russians, or Slavic, but we were all brothers in Christ. Our hearts were wide open before one other, and the recent horrors through which we had passed were still fresh for everyone. Later all this would be forgotten and in many instances we would look for various destructive reasons to close our hearts and become as strangers to one another.

At last the long awaited day came when we were told that our entire army unit was being disbanded. We were given rations for the road and issued a special pass. Carrying our canvas duffel bags we went to the station. In the distance, past the hayfields we saw our tents and the shining stream. For some reason it was sad to leave our truly restful and carefree life. We did not know what was waiting for us, but we were looking ahead with hope and faith. Therefore, we left with courage and joy.

We arrived in Gernsdorf on Friday and on Sunday a large group of our acquaintances from Weidenest and Schalksmuehle came to meet us. The group included Tarasiuk, Harbuziuk, Siery, Polischuk, Kaplich and Ostapchuk. Several sisters from Schalksmuehle also came with them. We began with a worship service and then we went as one large group to the forest and the hayfields near the stream. We gathered flowers and we shared our past experiences with each other. We sang; the guitars of brothers Bychkowski and Polischuk became alive. Our voices and our hearts were refreshed. Our music and resounding evangelical songs swept over the green Westphalian hills until late. Do you remember them brothers and sisters? Those of you who were there and sang?

Our guests left the following day but we stayed in our former Gernsdorf. It was now a completely different life from what it was formerly. There were no more air raids by American airplanes. There was no more working in the factory. But all our people were not here. Our former evangelical services were not here. Because of that we still had a longing and hope to be part of a group. We clearly knew that only Schalksmuehle would be able to fully satisfy us.

One day we went to the nearby town of Siegen where, before the war, a large number of our people lived and worked and where there was a large group of Christian girls from Greater Ukraine. But Siegen was not the same place that it used to be. Our people were still there but they were no longer working in factories. They were living in camps, which served as large collecting points, waiting for transportation to go back home. A large number had already left but the majority was still living here. We had access to them but not as before. Many of the girls from Greater Ukraine were already designated to leave but they were looking for ways to stay behind and avoid going home, but there was no way out for them. Not yet knowing what our fate will be, we also could not help them in any way. At the stations and everywhere in the town, posters were hung announcing, "all former citizens of the Soviet Union must return *na rodinu* ". The Germans did not have the authority to shelter them and the Polish camps were not allowed to accept them either. Those poor people did not have the smallest legal right to live in a foreign land. Many of them were hiding in forests and ditches, searching for kind people who would be able to help them to get into a Polish camp. They were being tracked on the streets in the towns and at train stations. German police would arrest them as some kind of criminal. Many of them went to the transition camps with tears and despair but some were able to escape into Polish camps and were rescued.

The long-awaited day came and gradually we began leaving our dear Gernsdorf. During this time various camps were being organized everywhere and foreigners were not allowed to remain in the villages. In the villages there was nothing to eat. Therefore all foreigners, who had not returned home, gathered in various camps, which were under British military control, and there everyone was given sufficient food and shelter.

One day our group finally arrived in Schalksmuehle. It was a great joy to see the town for which our hearts had always yearned. It was located among high hills surrounded by forests. It almost seemed that the town had been deliberately set there by someone's hand. The barracks of our believers were small and black like the earth. There was a flowing stream, a railroad track, as well as a hotel, which was now occupied by our acquaintances.

On Sunday a large service was held in a spacious Protestant church. The choir sang. We were asked to say or sing something. Bychkowski and I sang *Khto b Meni Dav Kryla*[129]. After the service was over we talked with each other, became acquainted with many new believers and then we went with the youth to the forest where there was a beautiful lake with a large dam. The songs of our young people could again be heard on the green

---

[129] "Who would give me wings", words by S. Bychkowski, music by J.S. Flaris. Published in *Ridna Pisna*, No. 119

bank, and together with the swallows, were carried on the surface of the clear water.

We found out that our believers had already formally organized themselves as an association of believers. The first conference of our members was called on June 27, 1945 in Schalksmuehle. This conference did not make many resolutions or policies, but rather selected an organizing committee to call a bigger conference, which also took place in Schalksmuehle on July 4. That was the date that marked the beginning of our future ministry known as the Slavic Evangelical-Baptist Union of Germany. The members of the committee consisted of the following people: W. Husaruk, president; P. Gordeiv, vice-president; Z. Reczun-Panko, treasurer; S. Nischik, secretary.

While in Schalksmuehle we discovered that through the American military chaplains our association had already made contact with its counterpart association in America and Canada. On the day following the surrender, our brethren in Germany had already received the first letter from brother I. Neprash. All of this lifted our spirit. Our brethren in the free world knew about us and therefore there was no reason for us to be afraid.

Our believers in Schalksmuehle were hungry. They used every possible means to find food, as more and more believers arrived everyday. The barracks were small. Not only was there no room to live, but also there was not even a place to sit down. The senior brothers did some research and found that a large Polish camp was being organized in the town of Ludensheid and all of us decided to go there.

Large American military vehicles arrived. We settled under the canvas cover and set out on a new course. The black barracks beside the hill in Schalksmuehle, with their small windows and rusty tin chimneys, were left empty. Here our believers had crowded together and had suffered much for long enough. Here they endured many hardships and joy, but now the time had come to leave those barracks, to travel farther, carrying with them only various memories in their hearts and souls.

The large trucks drove past the station, the stream, and the tall church and began to accelerate. Farewell Schalksmuehle!

LUDENSHEID

The town of Ludensheid was situated among the wonderful hills of Westphalia, which were profusely covered with green pines and hazelnut bushes. The town was as tidy as the kitchen of a good homemaker and had not been damaged by the war. The streets were swept clean, glistening, and nobody here would even throw a match onto the sidewalk. There were many churches in the town, mostly Protestant ones. There were many stores that were now closed because there was nothing to purchase.

Outside the town, beneath a forest of young spruces, stood some enormous grey barracks to which we were transported. English and Polish flags were waving at the gate. There was also an armed English guard standing there. The guard let our vehicles pass through and we entered a wide courtyard.

There was real confusion inside the camp. Many people had already arrived and large cargo trucks filled with foreigners continued to arrive. They were all being unloaded in the courtyard and then they had to search the entire camp for a place for themselves. We also were unloaded and scattered like sheep among the long buildings. We began running, looking for better rooms but they were all demolished inside with broken windows or broken doors. Wherever there were undamaged rooms, these were already occupied by other people.

The general appearance of the Polish camp in Ludensheid

I recall that I walked together with brother Z. Reczun-Panko searching for empty rooms. Unable to find suitable ones we ran to the farthest building with the number **3** above the door. Other believers followed us, and then still others, and soon we occupied the entire third block. Eventually all the believers, who had already found a room for themselves in other buildings, also moved here and that same day we settled into every room of the third block. Our life as refugees began in this building. A life filled with various incidents and experiences about which one could write an entire large book.

First of all we began to bring our building to a proper condition. The older brothers noticed that the single men, single girls or those without children had found better or more convenient rooms for themselves while families with small children had to settle for smaller, crowded rooms. It was therefore necessary to make a better distribution of rooms, and so immediately a so-called "building committee" was formed which would be responsible to fairly allocate rooms for everyone. This became a reality as within a family, without complaining and without any unnecessary problems. If a large space was not necessary for someone, they willingly gave it away to another family. We, single young men, initially found for ourselves a very fine room, but later we had to surrender it to others, because we could see that families with children had to have much more spacious accommodations.

The Third Block in Ludensheid where all believers settled

By the next day our third block was washed, cleaned and we all had a room. The families were separate, the young men were separate and the girls were separate. Everyone was separated but at the same time we were all together because we were living in the same building. In other buildings in the camp there were arguments and fighting to get better accommodation. The Polish camp-police, which was already organized, and several English soldiers had to get involved to settle arguments, but among us, thank God, everything was quiet.

On the second or third day after we had all "settled in" we gathered for our first evangelical service. In our block there was a large, bright assembly room, which from the outset, we dedicated for worship services. And now we gathered together in this room. We sang, prayed and listened to the preaching of the Word of God and afterwards we had a lengthy discussion. It was necessary to get our lives in order, to think about our spiritual ministry in this place, as well as about everything else. Brother P. Gordeiv was elected to represent our group before the camp administration and brother F. Lewchuk was chosen as the pastor of the congregation; he would be responsible for our spiritual life. The secretary and treasurer of the group was brother Z. Reczun-Panko, and the director of the choir was S. Bychkowski. In addition there were various other committees created to deal with all of our needs and problems. Everything was anticipated in advance and everything was organized very well. The camp authority treated our block with respect and used it as an example for others. Our organized life continued in this manner. During this time our congregation had approximately two hundred and fifty members, not counting the children. Later when we left Ludensheid it was more, but not significantly more, because even though the congregation increased because of new conversions, there were also a fair number of members who left to go to other camps, especially to camps in the American zone.

Some of our brethren worked with the camp administration, others worked in the kitchen, in various offices and in the school. Some of them knew English and the English would often call on them when there was a need for an interpreter. Because of this our third block earned much respect for itself in the camp.

Services took place almost every day. During the week there were prayer meetings, special Bible lessons and on Sunday there was a service for everybody with the singing of the choir and a sermon from the Word of God. We had many preachers among us and all of them took turns preaching under the guidance of the church committee. S. Bychkowski conducted the church choir and brother Ivan Polischuk conducted the men's choir. In the beginning our services took place in our block but soon the room was too small and could not accommodate even a portion of the listeners, so the camp administration gave us a better, much larger room in a different block. These services were attended by all of our believers as well as by many who had never heard an evangelical sermon in their life. There were conversions, and then baptisms which were now held in different Protestant churches in Ludensheid.

The camp in Ludensheid was Polish under the control of the occupying English army. But the entire administration, under the leadership of a camp commander, was Polish. These were good people who knew the fate and the difficult situation of former Soviet citizens and therefore accepted many of them into the camp. The greatest number of those who were coming to our services were from this group and the largest number of conversions were also from among them.

News of the large group of believers in Ludensheid spread throughout all of Western Germany. Now, wherever there were any believers in camps in other towns, they tried at all costs to come to us. And so everyday new brothers and sisters arrived. Among them were old acquaintances, some of them we had known before the war. There arrived unknown people and there arrived elderly, highly esteemed former preachers. In this way our congregation continued to grow every day. The believers in Western Germany said that Ludensheid was truly "Jerusalem" and so they also longed to come to that "Jerusalem" and be present there in person.

Spiritual leaders of the Slavic Evangelical-Baptist Union of Germany:
Seated from left to right: S. Nischik, Z. Reczun-Panko, P. Gordeiv, W. Husaruk, P. Kaplienko, W. Gutsche, H. Boltniev, L. Galustyan, and I. Barchuk.

Soon all the students from the Bible School in Weidenest also came to Ludensheid. Many girls from the nearby camps came and our third block could not accommodate everybody. The believers dispersed among the other buildings, but we still saw each other every day in the kitchen where we all assembled together for food. We also saw each other at the services and the special outings, which the young people arranged.

Our large group of believers was not only known in Germany but news of it also spread beyond the borders of Germany. Various American and English army chaplains began to visit us. They preached at our services. We had our own interpreters, which also added more recognition and respect within the entire camp for our block. These official chaplains always reported, first of all to the camp leadership, who would often accompany them to our services. The camp commander was a Polish captain, but he truly was our friend.

During this time various courses were organized in the camp, which were attended mostly by the residents of our block. There were actual schools to teach the children, although they were all in Polish. There were courses to learn English and even a sewing course for the girls, which was taught by sister M. Ivanova and brother P. Kalinka. In spite of the fact that many of our young men and girls were studying something, there was still much free time left over which we took advantage of by reading books and going on outings in the beautiful hills of Westphalia. These were beautiful sunny days. These were unforgettable years of our youth.

Our food was very meager and whoever could not subsidize their food was truly at the point of starvation. Every day we received from the kitchen, coffee for breakfast, coffee for supper and some type of sparse soup for dinner. We stood in long lines outside the kitchen and waited for our inadequate portions. But although there was nothing to eat, nobody was forcing us to do any work. We had no responsibilities and lived on a very rigid diet like in some recreational resort.

The Slavic Evangelical Baptist Union had already been organized among the refugees for a long time. It coordinated all the spiritual ministries, not only in Ludensheid, but also in the other refugee camps. The main centre of this Union was now in our block and therefore it was here that long meetings often took place, discussing various plans and searching for ways to make our situation known to the believers in Canada and the USA. The postal service did not yet exist for us during that time; therefore communication was possible only through the English or American military chaplains.

In the camp there was also a Polish Catholic priest who as usual demanded that his faithful keep as far away from us as possible, but he was not successful. We were too influential so he was unable to turn the people against us without any cause. Most importantly, the camp commander was not a Catholic fanatic and he treated us with much respect.

I remember one time when there was a funeral in the camp of a young Polish man who died in some kind of incident. The men's choir from our congregation was invited to the funeral and at the graveside where we sang evangelical songs. The priest stood and listened with his head bowed low.

Our congregation continued its refugee life, our spiritual ministry expanded and God visibly blessed our work. Almost at every service there were new people, new conversions and new prayers. Among the believers there was peace and unity and a true Christian love. Believers from all of pre-war Poland were gathered in the camp. At one time they belonged to various religious organizations, but the war had removed these human borders and differences and now we were only brothers in Christ, one large Christian family. There were also no differences among the different language groups. There were among us Polish, Russian, Belarusian; but the majority were Ukrainians. During the services the songs and the sermons were in Polish because this was the nature of the camp. However, if someone did not understand Polish, they preached or prayed in their own language. Everyone was free, each one felt as if they were in their own home within the congregation.

But this did not last long. And I now want to describe the saddest page of my memoirs. As once in the quiet Garden of Eden, a serpent came and stirred up disagreement within our congregation.

Some kind of Polish national holiday was being observed within the camp. I think it was the anniversary of their victory over Germany. A large assembly of dignitaries was to be present in the large camp auditorium with appropriate speakers and songs. Although our camp had approximately eight thousand people, there was not a single choir among them, except us. The camp authority therefore invited our church men's choir to sing at this elite gathering.

The large auditorium was filled to the rafters with people. We arrived and took our assigned seats on the platform. The assembly began. After an opening statement by the commander of the camp, our choir beautifully sang the Polish national hymn, *Jeszcze Polska Nie Zginela*[130]. The entire auditorium stood to its feet, the military all stood at attention. This was followed by a short address by a major and then our choir sang the Polish patriotic song, *Nie Rzucim Ziemi Skad Nasz Rod*.[131]

After the assembly several Polish individuals came up to us, some military people thanked us. But for some reason we were not satisfied with the result because we knew that this was not our place.

That evening as we were sitting in our common room, one of the brothers, a member of the men's choir said:

"I wonder what would happen if we went as a choir to some Ukrainian nationalistic festival and sang *Shche Ne Vmerla Ukrayina*[132]."

This question fell as a spark upon our hearts. Up till now we had not thought about this. Nobody had raised this question before because there was no reason or need. But now it stood before us in its entirety. Truly what would happen?

A silence fell among us. Then one of the brothers said:

"I think that we should not attend either a Polish celebration or a Ukrainian one. Our choir is not worldly, but belongs to the church. Singing worldly songs does not become us. There are so many untruths in those songs; as if we are a Polish nation, a Polish people who would go and fight for a Polish state and if necessary we would sacrifice our last drop of blood for the Polish state. But this is not the way it is! First of all we are not Polish, but Ukrainians. But most important we are Christians and we are not preparing to fight or to shed our blood for any other cause. Enough already about brothers killing brothers."

"That is true! That is true!"

That same evening we made a firm decision that we will not attend any more such assemblies and we will no longer sing worldly Polish songs.

Eventually another assembly took place in the camp, and again our choir was invited, but we declined to attend. Then several brothers from

---

[130] "Poland is Not Yet Lost" which is the first line of Dabrowski's Mazurka,
[131] "We will not forsake the land of our ancestors". First line from "*Rota*" meaning Oath, by Maria Konopnicka
[132] "Ukraine has not yet perished", the complete line actually has the idea of "Ukraine's glory has not died nor her freedom: National anthem of Ukraine.

the congregation, especially several uninformed Belarusians, turned angrily against us:

"You see, they want to build Ukraine here", they said.

And thus a spark of disagreement was cast within the family of the God's children who had been blessed up to this time. If until now Russian or Ukrainian offended no one, from now on this was not the case. Ukrainians began to defend their language and Russians and Belarusians loudly began to grumble saying that "Ukraine never existed, does not exist and never will."

Initially this misunderstanding was just a small spark but in time it gained a wider dimension, spreading into other camps. The consequence of this was the formation of the Ukrainian Evangelical-Baptist Church in Germany, which carried out its ministry completely separate from the Slavic Union.

I do not wish to say anything further about this because those wounds are still fresh for many and have not healed. I don't want this to darken my very best memories, my very best pages of a time when all Ukrainian, Polish, Russian and Belarusian believers were one blessed Christian family. I am saying, with the greatest certainty, that Ukrainian believers were the least to blame. Those who, without any reason, began to despise the Ukrainian language were responsible for any future friction and for any nationalistic disagreement, and because of this they also despised those who spoke that language.

Autumn painted the Westphalian hills with gold. It was especially beautiful when the brilliant sun was shining and the wind rustled the yellow leaves. There was such wonderful solitude and beauty in the forest during these times. I don't think that there is such a beautiful autumn anywhere as in Westphalia. Flocks of sheep were grazing in the fields, squirrels and long-tailed magpies were jumping in the trees, streams, as clear as a tear, were flowing between the hills. Excellent roads glistened as they wound among the bushes.

We walked among the hills, picked nuts, and looked for mushrooms and *pidpenky*[133]. We were not doing this for sport or recreation, but because we were truly hungry.

---

133 Honey mushroom

Christmas arrived. There were so many memories and so much sadness. This was already the second Christmas in a foreign land. Families were preparing for the holidays but we were all alone, feeling melancholy, and not having any reason to prepare for anyone.

Towards evening we received a slightly larger portion of food from the kitchen as well as an American care package, which was to be shared among several people. Inside there was a can of fish, some dried prunes, raisins, coffee and something else which I do not now remember. We shared this among ourselves but there was very little of anything for each person.

Outside our windows, Christmas Eve welcomed us with the birth of Christ. A heavy stone of sadness and longing for my family lay on my soul. How are they celebrating this holiday over there? If only someone would tell me that they are still alive and are thinking of me.

I took my portion from the American package and went outside. That evening I wanted to find someone who was more poor than me and give it to them. That was the feeling I had which for some reason comes to a person especially at Christmas time. It seemed that if they give something to someone who has less, then they are doing it for their own family wherever they are.

Behind the fence of our block stood some black wooden barracks where Germans lived, primarily women with children, who were fugitives from Eastern Germany. The snow beside the barracks was always crowded with children who were all very poor. "I will go to them," I thought, "and give them some dried prunes and nuts."

So I went down a pathway.

Coming to a group of children I pulled out the nuts, waved at them with my hand and said:

"*Komme, komme her...*"[134]

The children saw me coming to them and began to yell and scream as they rushed to the doors of their barracks. I began to feel sorry for myself because even the children were terrified of me when my heart was filled with sincere love and compassion for them. It was not their fault because many times Polish residents of the camp attacked them and therefore they were afraid of all people from inside the camp.

---

134 Come, come here

After a trip through Western Germany
From left to right: O. Harbuziuk, M. Podworniak, I. Tarasiuk

That evening I went by myself into the snowy forest and walked for a long time among the green pines. Beside a road near the forest there was a grave of some German soldier who was killed here two years ago but now the grave was covered with snow and only a small part of the cross was sticking out. I stood by the grave and then walked by myself into the forest. It seemed to me that never before in my life had I felt so sad as on this Christmas Eve.

The next day I had a desire to go all the way to the town of Dingolfing in the American occupied zone where brother A. Nichiporuk lived. The trains were already running but they were only freight trains. I barely managed to force my way into one car, which was already filled with people. Outside it was night and snowing. Suddenly one of the Germans lit a candle, set it down on the floor, and everyone stood around it. Someone began singing "Silent Night" and our car truly became a cathedral with a Christian service. The Germans stood there respectfully and worried. Among them were several prisoners of war who were returning home. All of them were going somewhere, looking for something and not having a real Christmas. It's a known fact that Christmas is not celebrated in any country of the world as solemnly as in Germany.

That Christmas Eve I saw a scene, which I will never forget. One elderly lady recognized her own son among the prisoners. With a loud joyful cry she fell up on his chest and could not utter a word for a long time. She cried and her son cried. The candle flickered with a yellow light, which jumped around over the dark heads of the people. During that time such joyful scenes were repeated at every station of post-war Germany, but this scene I especially remembered. I was sitting in the corner of the car looking out at the darkness of the night through cracks in the wall and experiencing my own thoughts: when will I be reunited with my own mother in a similar way? How blessed I would be then!

WITH A GOSPEL SONG

Pastor Boleslaw Gotze was well known among our people from before the war. He was travelling and holding evangelical services throughout the towns of Western Germany, especially in the towns of Westphalia. During this time he also visited our camp. When he heard the singing of our choir he suggested that we accompany him and sing during his services. We agreed and brother Ivan Polischuk announced choir practices. Every evening we held rehearsals. We learned Ukrainian and German songs and when the announced time came we set out on our trip. There were not many of us but we were well prepared, parts were assigned and we sang beautifully.

Pastor B. Gotze

Today I do not remember all the towns that we visited with pastor B. Gotze because we visited so many of them. When we arrived at the different places we saw that large posters had already been hung up in prominent locations announcing the services, featuring pastor B. Gotze and the singing of the Ukrainian Evangelical choir. In the evening, a hall or a church would be filled with German listeners. Brother B. Gotze would preach and we would sing. It was mostly the elderly who attended these services because the German youth had not yet all returned from the front. After the service the German Christians invited us to their home for the night. They became acquainted with us and inquired about our previous ministry among our people.

Initially we tried singing in German, even though we did not understand everything that we sang, but brother B. Gotze said:

"Brothers, sing in Ukrainian ... Let the German Christians hear your wonderful melodies."

And so we sang. We did not merely sing simple songs like, *Oy Kudy Pidu Shche Ya*[135], but we also sang concert pieces such as *Hospodnya Zemlya*[136], *Yak Harni na Horakh Stopy*[137] and others. God blessed our singing and the messages by Pastor B. Gotze. We realized that we can serve the Lord through song, and now the field was wide-open field for this ministry.

Soon afterwards we made a similar journey with brother L. Galustyan. We learned a whole series of songs and set out into all of Westphalia. There were many believers there, especially the so-called Free Brethren, who graciously opened the doors of their churches to us. Brother Galustyan preached deep and meaningful sermons, we sang and the German believers were captivated and moved. Sometimes, one service had not yet concluded when we would be approached by an elderly German brother from another evangelical congregation and asked if we could also come to their church, which we did. Everyday there were new people, new places, new churches and a new gospel message.

However our primary goal was not to merely travel among the German churches. We knew that the Germans, especially in Westphalia, had many

---

135 "Oh Where Will I Go" *Ridna Pisnya*. No. 67
136 "The Lord's Earth", *Ridna Pisnya*, No. 83
137 "How Beautiful on the Mountain are the Feet", *Ridna Pisnya*, No.71

fine preachers, they had large congregations and choirs. A Bible-based culture was evident in every aspect of their life. Our desire was to carry a gospel song to our own nation, which during this time, was scattered throughout many camps. Each one of these camps was under the administration of the occupying English army and was wide open to the preaching the gospel message. This truly was the most appropriate time not to stay in place but to venture out into the vast field of spiritual ministry. So we went.

Brother W. Husaruk came to our camp and when he heard our singing he met with some of the elder brethren from our congregation and suggested that brother Ivan Polischuk organize a men's choir, which could go the various refugee camps with a gospel song and a message from the Word. Brother W. Husaruk's suggestion sounded very practical and essential and fell upon everyone's heart. Brother Ivan Polischuk selected the voices and choir practices were announced for every evening. I was also included in this initial men's choir. We added songs from other Slavic languages to our repertoire because we knew that we would be required to go to various refugee camps. In addition to evangelical songs, we also prepared a series of Christian poems. We found brother A. Sus, who was not only a good bass singer, but also recited poetry extremely well. But we also knew that songs and poetry would not be sufficient for our ministry because the most important thing we needed was also to present the gospel message. For this purpose God gave us brother Ivan Barchuk.

Although during this time the refugee camps were open to the preaching of the gospel message, that opportunity would soon close. Each camp had its own administration, which was concerned that their people would not only have enough to eat but that nobody disrupted the peace in their camp. Therefore, without a special pass it was not possible for an organized group to enter the camp. It was necessary to obtain a special pass from the occupying military authority, which we were able to easily obtain from the administration in our camp.

We set out on our first trip. We came to a large Belarusian camp, its long black barracks were located at the bottom of a hill. I don't now remember which town this was; I believe it was Goslar. An English soldier stopped us at the gate. When we showed him our pass, he opened the gate wide and waved us through with his hand.

We made quite a spectacle of ourselves before the entire camp as we stood in a wide courtyard with bundles on our backs. Curious people came out of every barrack, staring at us as if upon a supernatural wonder. They devoured us with their eyes and bombarded us with questions:

"Who are you? Where did you come from?"

Ukrainian Missionary Choir before their first tour
From left to right: I. Barchuk, W. Siery, V. Kucenko, M. Podworniak, T. Siery, I. Polischuk, J. Stebelsky, L. Efimowich, O. Machnik, E. Kucenko and S. Nischik

When they found out that we wanted to hold a gospel concert in their camp they rushed back to their barracks and after a few moments the entire large camp was aware that there would be a concert that evening.

The commander of the camp showed us to a large concert theatre, which had a high stage with a large curtain that fell in waves all the way to the floor. In addition, the commander instructed the camp police to go to each barrack and announce that today there would be a gospel concert in the camp. His only question was what would be the cost of admission to the concert. When we told him that admission was going to be free, he was very amazed.

Although it was called a Belarusian camp, it turned out that in this camp there were many Ukrainians and therefore we selected songs in Ukrainian and one song in Belarusian.

That evening we came to the theatre half an hour early but we could hardly make our way to the stage. The large hall was completely filled to capacity with people who had come to our first gospel concert. At first we were terrified and looked at each other. One of the brothers said:

"It is not important that so many people have come, but what will we give them? With what will they leave from this concert? Will we be able to accomplish our purpose?"

Before the concert, we prayed behind the curtain and encouraged one another. And then we began.

We began with *Otche Nash*[138], and then brother A. Sus recited the poem, "The Great Teacher" by O. Konysky, then another song, another poem -- *Ridna Xata*[139]; item followed item and then a sermon at the conclusion by brother I. Barchuk. I will never forget that first concert. Sixteen years have passed since that day, but I can still feel the emotion in my heart as if I can see them again: bold brother A. Sus, brother Ivan Polischuk standing in front of us with his guitar, the hall was filled with people, every spot was filled. They were all standing on their feet and no one was even moving. They were grasping at every word although they did not know who we were or to what organization or church we belonged. Many of them had come to the concert thinking that they will hear traditional Ukrainian songs; perhaps they will see dances or something else. Instead there was a small group of young men who were singing about Jesus. Standing among the people were Orthodox and Catholic priests, who were also listening with the greatest attention to everything that we presented to them.

The concert ended. We came down from the stage but we were unable to reach the door. The people surrounded us, pressing our hands and thanking us. There were tears of emotions in their eyes and we were

---

138 The Lord's Prayer
139 Native House

experiencing the same emotions. God had blessed our first steps. Praise Him! Let us go forward!

The following evening we were in a different place, in a different camp that was also Belarusian. Its small barracks, surround by mature trees, were situated on a hillside. There we found a Christian family and in the evening we had a wonderful gospel concert. A very large number of people attended. Many of them heard a live sermon from God's Word for the first time in their life.

I recall that after the concert we were surrounded by people in a long hallway who were thanking us and asking us questions. "Where are you from? Who are you?" We were then approached by a young Belarusian intellectual who immediately began to speak:

"It is very bad that our camp allowed you to come in here."

"Why?" we asked.

"Because you were sent here by a Soviet Repatriation Commission," he replied sternly.

"On what basis can you say that?" we uneasily asked him.

"Because in your songs you were calling for people to return home. But we ... we are people of Western Belarus. We used to be Polish citizens and we do not wish to return home. We do not need your agitation," he concluded emphatically.

"What song are you talking about?" we asked. "Here are our songbooks, show us."

"This one... Wait, how did it go..." The Belarusian struggled to remember. "Oh now I remember: 'Oh, return to your native home.'" In our repertoire there was a song for the men's choir, *Ti Pokinuv Otsya, v Hrisnhi Svit Pishov*[140], which had the following chorus:

> '"O return, to your native home!
> You are lost in a foreign land...
> Hear the tender call of the Father,
> O come back, my son, come back."

A large group of people surrounded us. They had been listening to our concert with the greatest interest, but now they were sensing that perhaps a

---

140 You have left the father and gone into a sinful world", *Ridna Pisnya*, No. 53

Repatriation Commission had sent us to them. They stood there frowning and becoming angry. Brother Barchuk picked up the songbook and came up to a light. The crowd surrounded him on all sides. He read the entire song in a loud voice and then, to convince these people, he was forced to speak another sermon. He added to that which had not been said during the concert. He convinced them. The faces of the people became more gentle, their hearts softened and they began nodding their heads as a sign of their agreement. The young Belarusian intellectual also understood and shook hands with each one of us.

During this trip we met brother W. Husaruk as well as his son Evhen. Together we visited a large Ukrainian camp in Gottingen. This camp did not have wooden barracks but it was in large, red, brick buildings. Nearby, there was also a large Polish camp but we went to the Ukrainian one first. We were welcomed very graciously and shown to a large auditorium. Our gospel concert was announced over the camp radio, which was broadcast through loudspeakers in all the buildings. In the evening, as we expected, the hall was filled to capacity with people. The majority of the people were from Greater Ukraine, but some were also some from Volyn, Halychyna and Belarus. The commander of the camp was an elderly, intellectual person who spoke very little to us and we had the impression that he was annoyed for some reason. He sat in the front row facing the stage and looked at us intently and listened carefully to each item. We sang, recited poetry, Evhen Husaruk played beautifully on his violin. The listeners were affected and stirred to the depths of their soul, especially when brother A. Sus recited the poem *Ridna Xata*. Many people cried from heartfelt emotions. At that moment their hearts were prepared and ready to listen to the words of a concluding gospel message. Both brothers W. Husaruk and Ivan Barchuk spoke short sermons.

When our concert had ended we wanted to come down from the stage, but all at once the commander of the camp raised his hand and with a loud and menacing voice called out to us:

"Please do not come down from the stage!"

Each of us felt a twinge in our heart as it began to beat faster. We had not told him that we were Baptists because he had not asked us about that. But now he understood that our gospel concert was not an ordinary concert but it was truly a service with the preaching of the gospel and prayer. Therefore we waited, expecting that this angry commander would soon come up onto the stage and apologize to the camp residents for allowing us into the camp, disparage our presentation, then he would remove us from the stage and throw us out of the camp. But fortunately our foreboding was not realized.

Ukrainian Missionary Choir preparing to go on their trip

The commanders came up to us, turned to face the crowd and as far as I can remember he said the following words:

"My dear camp-residents. For many months we have been living here in our refugee camp. From this stage we have heard many songs and many speeches, but such dear and living words from home that we heard today have never been spoken here. Do you agree with me?"

"Yes, yes, sir," called out many voices.

The commandant turned to us, walked up to each one, sincerely shook our hand and with a radiant, satisfied face said:

"My dear countrymen, on behalf of our entire camp, we sincerely thank you for your holy and living words. May God help you to sow that cherished word with which you came to us. This is exactly what we needed in this foreign land. We will never forget your concert. Thank you, sincerely thank you!"

The people all rose to their feet and we saw that today we were exceedingly victorious here. That evening inspired us over and over to continue our journey because we were convinced that at this time the harvest was truly ripe among the refugees. The opportunity that we had at that moment to preach the gospel happens once in hundreds of years. Our people had recently suffered difficult wartime misfortunes. All those sufferings were still fresh, and now they were gathered into large barracks where they sat and waited for someone to come to them with a familiar song and an encouraging living word. God had chosen us to be alive during such a time. He brought us here, so how could we waste such a golden moment?

The following day we repeated the same gospel concert in the neighbouring Polish camp, and from there we went to other places and to other camps. Wherever we went we saw that the field was very large for spiritual ministry among the refugees. In every camp we held large gospel concerts and wherever there were groups of believers we had evangelical services for them where we also observed the Lord's Supper, especially in those places where our preachers seldom visited.

During that first trip we were also accompanied by brothers W. Helech and A. Mulko who helped us in every way.

When we returned to Ludensheid we gave a report to our congregation about our ministry. We told them our impressions and our observations. Our report awakened a desire among many of the younger brothers to also do something for the Lord. After a short time another group of singers was organized in Ludensheid, which completed a missionary journey among the various camps. I was not a part of that group therefore I don't know which camps they visited and what success and blessings they had. I believe that they travelled through the entire American zone. They had good singers among them and their trip was also successful and effective.

That was 1946, the first year after the end of the war and many of the camps were already well organized. In general the people in the camps spent their daily lives just sitting without any activity and therefore they were glad to come to our concerts or services. In Ludensheid there were many individuals who had been involved in Christian ministry and now the majority of them, either by themselves or several of them together, ventured out on long missionary journeys, preaching the Gospel. Often they were hungry, cold, and tired, placing themselves in various dangers during these abnormal postwar times. But they did not pay attention to any of these things. I really wanted to include the names of those fervent workers but I will not do that because I don't know if that is what they would have wanted. I am convinced that God knows about them and at the right time they will receive their reward for their labor. Their work brought much fruit.

Regretfully among them were other brothers, some of whom had once been involved in the ministry, but who had forgotten their high calling. Instead of now working for the Lord, when there was such a golden opportunity, they went into *torhivlyu*[141]. The period which followed the end of the war was noted for speculators in the black market and several of our brothers also became involved in that "mission". They also went on long trips, laden with various dangling trinkets, and were immersed up to their heads in the mammon of this world. But thank God that there were not too many of these. They had no respect among our brethren and therefore I do not have anything further to say about them.

Our services in Ludensheid continued to be lively and well attended. Almost every Sunday, someone would return from a missionary trip and bring reports about the other camps or about the organization of a new church. They informed us about where the believers were and how many of them there were. Our men's choir decided to get ready for another missionary trip, but this time to go, not only throughout Westphalia and the nearby provinces of Western Germany, but to go farther all the way to the American occupied zone and to distant northern Germany.

The brethren recommended that we re-organize the choir and add ladies' voices. This is what we did. The result was a double quartet with

---

141 trade

brother Ivan Polishchuk as the director. We began to prepare intensely for our missionary journey. Every evening our lively songs would resonate throughout the third block, recitations and other items were rehearsed. Unfortunately, brother A. Sus, who was a good reciter of poetry, would be unable to accompany us. In his place we had sister Olya Machnik, who was not only a good singer but was equally good at reciting poems about the Christian faith. We exceedingly regretted that brother S. Bychkowski could not go with us on this trip, but he was the choir director of the Ludensheid congregation. His responsibilities there prevented him from being released from the church for any great length of time. We learned that brothers Ivan Barchuk and Stephen Nischik wanted to go with us. Brother Barchuk would go as a preacher alongside the choir and brother Nischik would be the organizer of our performances and gospel concerts. It must be said that both of them carried out their responsibilities very well.

The long awaited day of our departure came at last. Many believers gathered on the stairs of the third block and sent us on our journey with prayer and good wishes. On our back, each one of us carried a heavy backpack, which contained our songbooks, food and a change of clothes. It was pouring rain outside, and the sky was covered with grey clouds.

The train yard was very crowded with people and we barely squeezed into the dirty freight cars. It was cold outside because it was still early spring, the final days before Easter.

We travelled for a very long time. Sometimes we would wait for hours at a damaged station as crowds of people swarmed outside our train. The braver ones tried to climb onto the top of the cars and when the police chased them away they pushed against the closed doors or clung to the stairs. Some crawled with their luggage between the cars, trying to find a comfortable spot where the cars were connected together, but the police found them and chased them away. In our car it was so tight that we all stood on our feet and were unable to even move our hand.

Then the train began to move. It huffed, expelling black smoke and ashes on us. It rushed through tunnels and emerged again onto wide plains. At every station where we stopped it was the same scene. There were thousands of people with bundles and small children. These were all various fugitives who tried to escape during the air raids and from the front, but now they were returning to their ruined towns and villages. They had been sitting for days and nights at the station, sleeping on dirty floors inside the destroyed waiting rooms and waiting a *long-long* time for their train. Among those in the pitiful crowd were many German soldiers. They wore their faded military uniforms without any type of identification, not even a button. Some of them were limping on long crutches; some of them had only one leg or one arm. These were all recent soldiers of the "invincible" German army who were now returning to their homes from prison camps or from hospitals. Nobody was paying any attention to them; nobody had any sympathy for them. They had to sleep on the floor. They had to push their way into the over-crowded freight cars. Their crutches were not awakening any sympathy in anyone because every German town and every home was now on crutches. All of Germany was now standing wounded, waiting at destroyed stations in post-war Europe.

Brother S. Nischik with his family.
He was the organizer of the concerts for the Ukrainian Missionary choir.

Up until now, for some reason, I was under the impression that the Jewish and German nations were the most tolerable towards their own people and would not abuse their brother under any circumstances, but now these convictions crumbled. Many times I saw as Jewish civilian police would force people from the ghetto to go to work or unmercifully beat weak elderly men and women with a stick. They were all equally unfortunate people of the same faith. Now I saw a German invalid, a soldier with one leg, who was trying to reach a handrail on the train car so that he could somehow push his way inside. But other healthy and strong Germans pushed him down and crawled over his head as he fell to the ground. Beside the cars also stood a mother with children, perhaps they were orphans because their father did not return from the front. Nobody paid any attention to her cries. The war makes people heartless and inhuman, resembling animals who care only about themselves.

Once people learned how to push their way into trains or trolley cars, this become a way of life in the large cities. Later, when transportation became more normal, people would continue to push against each other even though there were empty seats in the cars.

We arrived in Munich. Once this was a large, beautiful city with many church domes, museums, and parks. But now on this cold morning, we encountered piles of rubble with the odour of disorder. Formerly, this was the centre of Hitler's conspiracy against the entire world. Various conferences were held here which tried to keep the world from a Second World War. But all of this turned into destruction and Munich was now lying in ruins. We came to those ruins with a word of eternal peace, which a person could find only in Jesus Christ. We did not yet know how we would be received here. We did know that in Munich and in the surrounding area there were dozens of various Slavic camps, the majority of which were Ukrainian and it was to these that we desired to go with a gospel song.

We made our way through the damaged streets to brother Kosenko's home where our arrival was expected. There we found good friends and we were able to rest and make plans for tomorrow and the day after.

The following day we joined the local Baptist congregation for a worship service and communion. Many believers came from the neighbouring camps, as well as those who lived in private homes in the city. It was Good Friday and the mood of the believers was very solemn.

The next day we had a rehearsal to prepare for the Easter celebrations. The weather had cleared up outside and it turned warm in one day. We went out to observe some sites of the city. It was especially interesting for us to see the town hall where there was a large clock, which indicated the current hour by chiming the corresponding number of times, and playing music that could be heard throughout the whole city. At twelve o'clock, noon, doors beside the clock opened up and twelve large figures came out and walked grandly around the clock tower, posturing solemnly to the onlookers who were standing below. Then, one by one, they withdrew through the door that closed immediately after them. During the march beautiful music played and many interested spectators, especially American soldiers, gathered beside the town hall. They probably didn't have anything like it in New York or Chicago. They clicked their photographic cameras and sighed in amazement. Germans can make such wonderful things. They were also responsible for that which now caused Munich to lie in ruins.

In the morning, just as the sun rose above the trees, we were already up on our feet. We gathered in the small room of brother Kosenko's home and greeted the holy Easter morning. Brother S. Nischik read from the Bible about the resurrection of Jesus. We sang *Christos Voskres*[142] three times and prayed, thanking God that He had also risen in our hearts.

Each one of us had received a small piece of black bread on which some margarine was thinly spread. After this meager breakfast we traveled to the town of Karsfeld where an Easter service was announced in a Ukrainian camp.

We arrived in Karsfeld, which had one of the largest Ukrainian camps in the American zone. The camp had a happy, festive appearance. The youth were wearing embroidered shirts and the children were endlessly ringing a large bell, which hung near the camp church. The elderly were sitting everywhere beneath the barracks, conversing, perhaps remembering how they once celebrated Easter at home.

---

142 Christ is Risen

Group of believers in Karsfeld after the service

A small group of our believers lived in this camp and we had a blessed Easter service for them to which they invited other people. We sang Easter songs and encouraged them with the news of the risen Lord. The local believers were strengthened by our visit.

Having some free time, I walked around the camp hoping to find someone from my villages. I was told that there was an elderly woman from Volyn living in one room and I went there. I caught her just as she was about to go to the main kitchen to get dinner. We became acquainted. She was from the town of Shumsk in the Kremenec region[143]. She told me her painful story, how the Germans captured her only son in a field and took him into forced labor somewhere in Germany. The poor mother could not endure her grief and attached herself to a transport going to Germany, with the hope of finding her son. Up until now she had not found him because Germany was very large and nobody knew where he went. The elderly mother tearfully asked me, that when I went to the other camps, to look for her son. I later looked for him but was not able to find any trace of him.

---

143 Mountain in the Carpathian Mountains on the Ukrainian-Polish border

In the afternoon we returned to Munich, because our service had already been announced there. Among the large number of people who came there were many believers, but there were also those who had never heard a live evangelical sermon. Much to our joy and delight a Negro American army chaplain also came to the service. Some of our singers saw a person with a black face for the first time in their life. He preached and brother S. Nischik translated his words into Ukrainian.

The following day we again had a service in Munich which was attended by a very large number of people. The same chaplain also came but this time he came with his assistant. They were amazed with our singing and we were again fascinated by the chaplain's playing on the harmonium[144].

We spent the entire week in Munich, holding blessed services every day. Several new people came forward during the services to surrender their lives to God.

From Munich we went to Ingolstadt. There was less devastation in this city than in Munich but there were still many ruins here. Outside the city there were some mounds covered with grass and some wall-like structures that were surrounded by water. Inside the moss-covered walls, there was a large and well-organized Ukrainian camp. The camp administration hosted us very cordially, and released to us a clean and spacious hall for our services. We had a service that same day and several hundred people came and listened with the greatest interest to the Word of God and evangelical songs. When the service ended, people surrounded us on all sides requesting that we give them a Ukrainian Bible. Unfortunately we did not have many Bibles with us, and those that we had, we gave away within several minutes. We were forced to send one brother back to Munich to bring more Bibles, which we had received just the day before from America through the American military chaplains. Besides Bibles, we also distributed large amounts of other Christian literature in Ingolstadt.

After the service we were interested to walk among the high mounds, which remained as a witness of a former military defense. There were massive trees growing on the mounds that were surrounded by water, held in by various embankments and ridges. We were told that hundreds of years ago, when the German kings fought against each other, this spot was

---

144 a reed organ

one the strongest defenses of that time. And now as we walked upon those fortifications our thoughts raced into the distant past and inadvertently we compared it to the terrible present. People fought in the past and they were still fighting now, because people's hatred is always the same. In the same city we also saw an ancient Catholic cathedral, which we were told, was built by this same king in honour of the victory he had over his enemies. The church, which was made of bricks, was now turning black and crumbling from age. It once cost countless sums of money, and perhaps hundreds or thousands lives of the king's prisoners to construct the walls and mounds. Truly how terrible the world was back then when people came at each other with a sword and a cross. The Catholic Church encouraged them in this warfare and blessed the shedding of people's blood. But did that only happen back then?

The following day we had another service in the camp and one in a German Baptist church in the town. In the camp of Ingolstadt lived several families of believers: Stepanenko, Osipowich and others who held their regular services there.

From Ingolstadt we travelled to Augsburg, I believe this was the largest Ukrainian camp in the American zone. It was located in a large, brick, multi-storied building where the German army had been stationed at one time. We held a large service in Haustetten[145] where we met brother L. Galustyan who had arrived from Fulda. So many people came that everyone could not be accommodated inside the hall and some of them stood outside and listened beneath open windows.

The following day our sisters were hoping to be able to rest for a while because they were getting tired from all the performances. But a messenger came from the town of Neu-Ulm and told us that the believers there were already waiting for our arrival. So we went.

Towards evening we arrived in Ulm. We hurried through the ruins of the city to the Ukrainian camp, which was located in attractive army barracks beside a green park. At the gate stood police, wearing white helmets on which was written *Ukrayiner*[146], who did not allow us past the gate. We felt that things were not the same here as in other camps. For some reason

---

145 A suburb of Augsburg
146 Ukrainian

there seemed to be more security and a tighter control. Up until now we had dealt with the German police, with Americans, English and Polish, but for the first time we met Ukrainians, that is with our own people, and we came up against a brick wall.

While we waited, an official from the local UNRRA[147] was called. He looked at our documents, opened the gate wide and said in English:

"Please enter! You are allowed to be here."

We walked through the gate. A wide campground opened up before us surrounded by long multi-storied buildings. There were many people everywhere. It almost resembled some kind of marketplace. Only Ukrainian could be heard in the camp. Various posters and announcements were hanging everywhere and immediately it became evident that this large, well-built camp was organized like a former *Sich Zaporizhian*[148].

We entered the home of a family of believers while brother Nischik immediately went to the camp administration to request the use of the camp hall for the concert. The administration released to us a large hall in a building very close to the gate. An announcement was made over the camp radio that in the evening there will be a concert by the Ukrainian Missionary choir that had arrived from the American zone.

We arrived at the hall at the announced time and found that many people were already there. Some stood against the walls, some sat on the benches waiting for the concert. Some stood outside on the stairs but when they saw us approaching they immediately began to go inside and take their places.

We sang a song and during the singing we noticed that a Greek-Catholic priest ran into the hall and began persuading people who were near the door to leave the hall. The people became confused, some began to leave, and others continued to sit on the benches. Some returned from the entrance way because the priest, whose face had become very red, was passionately saying something to them. Suddenly several young men ran into the hall. They stood by the entrance and began to cough loudly and stomp their feet. The commander of the camp, who was in attendance, stood up and loudly said:

---

147 United Nations Relief and Rehabilitation Administration
148 A fortress of the Zaporozhian Cossacks

"Gentlemen, please don't cause any disturbance here, please conduct yourself like civilized people. If you do not like it, please leave! This concert is authorized by UNRRA and you have no authority to cancel it."

The agitators would not listen to the commander. Several more young men rushed in to support the others and together they pushed their way forward as one angry group and loudly shouted:

"Away, from our camp you cursed heretics! Get out with your propaganda, and if you do not leave, we will drag you out ... Get out sectarians!"

Our song stopped, our arms slumped and our hearts fell. This was the first time that we had encountered such a spectacle. Therefore, we only stood on the stage like defenseless sheep and looked at one another. The windows in the hall were all wide open into some kind of a garden and we, men, could escape but what would happen to our ladies? The angry crowd by the door became larger, more disorderly and riled up like a storm. The commander of the camp, seeing that the situation might turn out bad, called out through the window to the police at the gate. Several policemen ran in, took their rifles off their shoulders, and began to force the agitators out the door. The hall was filled with much shouting and noise. The police continued to push the troublemakers with their rifles, forcing them outside as they yelled into the whole hall:

"You just wait *sectanti*[149]," they shouted, waving their fists at us. "When we get back to Ukraine, we will show you! Not one of you will be left, you cursed heretics."

Finally the police were able to force them out and closed the door. We were left all alone inside the hall. Beside us was the commander of the camp, the local believers and a small group of peaceful people who came to our concert. The crowd continued to boil outside, banging the door with their fists as various voices shouted out:

"Get out of the camp, *sectanti!*....Get out, heretics!"

The entire heavily populated camp gathered in front of the building. There were women, children, young and old, because everyone wanted to come and see the unusual scene. The rioters spread out into the crowd and now the people were arguing amongst themselves. Some were for us and some were against us. We wanted to go out among the people and tell

---

[149] sectarians

them that we were the same kind of Ukrainians as they were, that we were also refugees living on the mercy of UNRRA. However, the commander asked us not to leave the hall. It truly was dangerous to leave because, as we found out later, the angry young people, encouraged by their priest, had gathered in groups and armed with rocks were waiting for us to come out.

When the crowd had somewhat dispersed, the commander called several policemen who walked in front and behind us. In this way they escorted us outside the gate, leading us all the way to the town. The commander also walked beside us, constantly apologizing:

"It was not our fault that this happened, gentlemen. I have never seen such savages before. Where did they grow up? Who brought them up? Our Ukraine would be a poor place if these savages would take over the leadership. It is an embarrassment before the foreigners among whom we are currently living!"

Brother Ivan Polischuk,
Director of the Ukrainian Mission Choir

We had absolutely no complaint against this commander because he was an intelligent person from Greater Ukraine and the antics of the Greek-Catholic devotees were foreign to him, as they were to us.

In the evening we found ourselves in a foreign German town and did not know where to go. But fortunately local believers, who also left the camp with us, invited us to the home of some German believers in Ulm. That evening we were able to hold our service together with the Germans. We sang many songs for them, and through a translator, we spoke short testimonies and felt that we were at home here. God performed a wonderful miracle in that distant strangers, whom we had met for the first time in our life, had become one family through the redeeming blood of Jesus.

We sat with these good German believers until late into the night, talking about everything. Sisters came from the Ukrainian camp, bringing potatoes, tea, and milk and prepared a fellowship meal for everyone. Seated around a wide round table, an elderly German brother prayed with us with tears in his eyes. I will never forget that supper, but especially one very cheerful sister from the Ukrainian camp who spoke with the German believers in half-Ukrainian and half-German and the Germans somehow understood her. For example, when we were already seated at the table, and the German hostess was still busy at the stove, this sister took her by the hand, dragged her to the table and spoke *very-very* quickly:

"Schwester Rosa, *bitte essen kartopli pokamict warm!*"... That is, "sister Rosa, please eat the potatoes while they are hot."

The hostess smiled and sat down. We also enjoyed much laughter in spite of our unsuccessful concert.

We went to sleep late that evening, settling down on benches or on the floor. Fresh air from the orchard was coming into our room through the windows that were wide open. It took a long time for me to fall asleep because something was troubling me in my soul about what we had experienced in the camp several hours ago. I recalled my journeys in pre-war Halychyna, but especially a Baptist funeral at which I was present in the village of Tysiv, near the town of Bolekhiv. We walked in a long procession through the entire village to the cemetery, singing funeral songs. We walked past the gates of the property owners of Tysiv. The people came to the road, stood at their front gates, smoking pipes, but nobody would remove their hat as we walked past them with the body of the deceased. I was truly amazed by this because at home in Volyn, regardless of whose funeral it was, the citizens of Volyn would stand when the body of a deceased was carried past them, take off their hat and hide their cigarette or throw it away. When we returned from the cemetery, the leader of the local congregation accompanied me to the station in Bolekhiv and I said to him:

"You know brother, where I come from the people are not like that. There, every villager will remove his hat when a funeral procession goes by."

The brother shook his head, looked at me and sighed deeply. Then he said:

"My dear brother, that is still not so bad that they only stood with their hats on and smoked. It's a good thing that they were not throwing rocks at us. That has also happened. Then they are frightening, truly like animals." He became quiet for a few seconds. We walked by a hill. On the right we could see the white tops of the Carpathian Mountains. Then he spoke further:

"When our first child died, the poor thing lay there for three days because it was not possible to bury it. The people, who were stirred up by their priest, stood with sticks in the streets near the cemetery gate and would not allow us to even come close. They began throwing stones and sticks and later, when the Polish police from Bolekhiv arrived, the people were dispersed and we were able to bury the child. Later we gathered at the home of the brother and sister whose child had died. We sat and grieved. The mother was crying and we were trying to comfort her, when suddenly the door opened wide and *bukh*[150], the casket of the child was thrown through the door. The mother screamed, we were all frightened, the door closed and several men ran away from the house and out through the gate. We sat the whole night by the casket with the child. The following day the police from the head of the village came again and we had a second funeral. Such were the times! They had managed to dig up the grave, brought the child and threw it across the threshold into the house. Now it is still good that they only stand with their hats on. At least they are not throwing stones and for that we praise God."

---

150 boom

Those early memories, tied together with what I had witnessed in the camp, took my sleep away. Truly what would happen if, God forbid, those followers of the Catholic faith returned to Ukraine and took over the leadership there? How many non-Catholics would have to lay down their lives? How many tears and how much bloodshed would there be?

We spent the night with the German believers and the following morning we left again for Augsburg from where we planned to return to our camp in Ludensheid. We had a wonderful service in Haustetten and on Sunday we repeated the same service at the Ukrainian camp in Augsberg. At that time the printing of the translated songbook, *Pisni Khrystyyan*,[151] was completed and all the believers sang from the new songbooks.

The next day we got ready to leave for our own camp because our sisters were tired, but we were unable to leave. A messenger came from the Ukrainian camp in Ulm with a message that we had to go there without any delay. It became apparent that the local UNRRA found out about all that had happened. It forbade the people there to leave the camp for a time. They took away some of their food, and commanded that those responsible for the riot be identified. They also sent someone to go after us to make sure that we would return. Aside from UNRRA, the prevailing majority of the residents in the camp was not in agreement with the Catholic intimidation and begged us to come to them without delay.

We returned to Ulm. We were not even asked to show a pass at the gate, they already knew who we were. The commander of the camp met us with a beaming face and a joyful heart. They again released the large hall to us and we held there, not a concert, but a large and blessed evangelical service, which was also attended by the German believers from the town at whose house we had recently spent the night. *Shwester* Rosa came, representatives from UNRRA came as well as an American military chaplain. He preached in English and brother Nischik translated into Ukrainian. The large room was packed with people. There was not a trace from the recent storm. After the service many people came to us, apologizing for what had happened, but we had nothing against those good people because we knew that it was not their fault.

---

151 Christian Songs

Brother Ivan Barchuk,
preacher with the Ukrainian Missionary Choir

We spent the night in Ulm and the following day we left to return to Ludensheid. Our train flew like an arrow across the green fields of Germany but we did not have a chance to enjoy the beauty of those fields. The train car was so crowded that we had to stand all night and all day. The people were so close together that it was not possible to even move a hand. The worst part was when we had to transfer from one train to another. It was often necessary to stand for long hours and when the train arrived and two people got off, twenty people pushed forward to take their place. They crawled over each other's heads, pushing their way through windows, dragging one another by the hands or by their feet as the American soldiers photographed such scenes and laughed until they were crying.

I recall one time when we stood for almost the entire night in a large crowd at a damaged station waiting for the train. The station was without a roof and without any lights. The night was cool and it was dark everywhere. The people were like the sea, we all stood waiting, no one was yet allowed onto the platform. We were crammed together, shoulder to shoulder, head to head, like herrings in a barrel. Everyone was carrying a bundle on their back. The ropes were irritating, cutting into the flesh. Beside me stood a thin, emaciated German soldier with an unshaven face. He seemed to be returning from a prisoner camp.

When the conductor appeared early in the morning and walked past the iron fence the people became agitated. Everyone prepared to advance as soon as the gate opened, to push through the fence as quickly as possible, because everyone would not be able to board the train and it would be necessary to wait for the next one. I could see that the German soldier beside me was becoming restless as he adjusted his dirty backpack. Seeing that he was getting ready to get in front of me aroused that evil human "I" in me. Apparently Satan was whispering to me: "Look, perhaps that German had murdered hundreds of people, this terrible trouble has come upon the world through them and here again he wants to be in front. You must not allow him to go first. You go …" When the gate opened I elbowed my way forward. I became angry and slightly pushed the German and got in front of him. But this tired soldier was more courteous and better than me. He only looked at me and silently stepped behind me. My face was covered with shame. My conscience awakened and I was ready to crawl underground from shame. I am a Christian but I had acted so unchristian-like. Who knows, perhaps he was a Christian also and had never harmed anyone in his life.

I moved slowly with the crowd. I could feel the ground shaking beneath me. The prisoner was walking behind me. When we were past the gate I saw now, for the first time, that he had only one leg and was leaning on a crutch with his right arm. My conscience overwhelmed me and I wanted to throw myself at this unfortunate soldier, to hug him and beg his forgiveness for my wrongdoing and my unchristian conduct. We had stood alongside each other for almost the entire night, waiting to get onto the platform. I was on two legs, and he … on one. If I am so tired, how much more tired is he. Lord, forgive me that I am so ungracious to my neighbour!

The train had not yet arrived and I saw that the soldier had walked to one side and was leaning against a wall, with his backpack placed beside him. I went up to him.

"Do you speak Polish, Russian?" I asked.

"No," replied the German.

I thought it was very unfortunate that I could not communicate with him, but a Christian man, who was standing nearby, was able to help. He came up to me and asked in broken Russian:

"What do you want from him? I can help you."

"Tell him," I replied, "that I want to sincerely apologize. He knows the reason why. I was not aware that he was a cripple. I am very sorry and I am begging for his forgiveness."

The soldier extended his hand to me and I could see a tear in his eye. I gave him a large can of American food, a package of white crackers and rushed to board the arriving train. I got inside the car and the train began to move. I could feel as a large and heavy stone had rolled off my heart.

From that time, as much as I was able, I always tried to let someone else go in front of me. Let him go ... I will not be wronged in the least. But I will have peace in my heart.

Again we travelled through the beautiful, green landscapes of Westphalia. We were all sincerely grateful to God for the completed journey and for all that we had seen and experienced. We were grateful to all the brothers and sisters whom we had met, but especially to gracious UNRRA which helped us everywhere.

UNRRA – this is an English acronym for "United Nations Relief and Rehabilitation Administration". In Ukrainian it was known as *Uprava Dopomohi i Reabilitatsia Ob'yednix Natsiy*. This was a large international-aid organization, which was created to assist post-war refugees in Europe. This organization had enormous financial assets and a large number of personnel in all of post-war Europe. It had its own hospitals, stores with food and clothing and now all the camps in the American, English and French zones of Western Germany were under its guardianship. We were also under its custody. Since this humanitarian organization was created by Protestants, the majority of its officials were also Protestants. Because of this we had free access to all the camps. Ukrainian Catholics also lived under the guardianship of this

Christian organization, ate the bread which they received from an American Protestant organizations but hated Protestants with the same angry hatred that Catholics had during the Middle Ages.

******

We were back in our third block in dear Ludensheid. Inside were all our brothers and sisters - our entire large Christian family. How pleasant it was to feel the warmth of our rooms, and sense the warm hearts of our people!

After we rested for a few days the believers arranged a special evening service during which we related our experiences on our journey. Together everyone thanked God for everything.

Sunday School at Ludensheid, later in Frille

The congregation of refugees in Ludensheid had increased again. Believers from all of Western Germany were trying to transfer here, considering it a great fortune to be able to live in our "Jerusalem". Many had already been transferred and there was no longer room for everyone in the third block. Believers were dispersed throughout the other blocks. Our elder brothers were trying to halt that great migration because why should we be gathering together in one camp while closing our evangelical services in other camps? No, we had to be in all places. It was necessary to shine our Christian light everywhere and to plant the seeds of evangelical truth in all the camps. Our brothers, who were preachers, slowly began to leave our camp and transfer to other camps, especially into the American zone. Because of that decision, the spiritual ministry revived and new congregations, containing new believers, were organized.

The Union committee encouraged all preachers of the Word of God to travel to those places where there was a need. This matter was continually discussed during meetings of the committee and written about in the Union publications. For example in a magazine for May-June, 1947, the following appeal was made: "There is a great felt need for spiritual workers, but especially for Ukrainian preachers to work in Kiel, Heidenau, Bathorn, Godenau, Goslar, Gottingen and other places. This appeal is to brothers who are free to leave their current location and move to work. It is never too late to do this".

During that time we were already organized as a strong Slavic Union. Every month our newsletter went out, informing believers about our life and highlighting important events. We could see that the ministry among the refugees was gaining a wider scope and venturing forward with bold steps. Our preachers were travelling throughout all Germany, holding evangelistic services and performing baptisms and our family was growing with each day. The services in Ludensheid were also increasing and the hall could no longer accommodate all the people. Baptism services were taking place. The German Baptists in Ludensheid gladly released their churches to us for our growing services.

In our congregation in Ludensheid there were many young men and women, which resulted in wedding celebrations. The first such joyful celebration was the wedding of brother Wasyl Siery and sister Tania, both were singers in our travelling choir. When there were no weddings we, single men, did not feel our singleness as deeply, but now it was beginning to gnaw strongly at us and pursue us. Brothers Polischuk, Bychkowski and others, including myself, began to look around if something would also "catch our eye"[152]. This *shchos*[153] certainly caught our eyes and our hearts. We found partners for ourselves and decided to get married in this foreign land. But this was easy to say, but to bring it to a reality was quite difficult.

---

152 Literally "to dust our eye"
153 "*щось*", something

First of all, neither UNRRA nor the civil authorities recognized a church ceremony by itself. It was necessary to have a civil marriage, that is, confirmed by a German court. This required that one have a birth certificate and other documents which none of us had. We went to various German administrations in Ludensheid as well as to other towns, but everywhere we received the same firm answer. It was necessary to have a birth certificate. But in the meanwhile we decided to again venture out on another missionary trip with the hope that somewhere on the journey we would be able to find a good German court that would help us. Although this was not our main goal, nevertheless, we kept it in our minds.

After we completed the first trip, our choir did not stop singing. We saw that people were hungry to hear an evangelical song in their own language, many of whom had never heard one therefore. We considered it sinful to sit idly in the camp and waste precious time when all around us there was so much spiritual work to be done. Before long we began to prepare for a second mission journey. With more experience, this time we were planning a longer trip with a larger repertoire, as well as a reserve of physical and spiritual strength.

During the previous trip we had encountered numerous inconveniences. Countless times we were completely exhausted and hungry. This time we wanted to ensure in advance a food supply, transportation and everything else that we would need. We went to the local camp administration with our problem and to our great amazement and joy the camp administration promised to give us an American cargo truck which would drive us to the next camp, issue food for everyone, as well as give us the proper documents so that we would be admitted into every camp, provided with food, and if necessary provided with further transportation to wherever we needed to go next. Truly this was a great help! Anything more we could neither expect nor desire.

The day came for the Ukrainian Missionary choir to leave on its second trip. Many believers gathered on the steps of the third block to see us off and express their best wishes for the road. All of us had large backpacks on our backs and wore heavy leather shoes. Our hearts were filled with joy because we were able to do something on the mission field among the refugees.

An army vehicle with a large canvas top was standing by the gate and we approached it. A cold drizzle was falling. The sky was frowning and it seemed that the grey clouds, sailing above the hills, were touching the tops of the tall evergreens. But the wind and rain did not frighten us because we are now under cover. We could hear it softly tapping against the canvas and splashing on the asphalt road. We were gone...

The Westphalian roads ran alongside the hills, snaking through the spruce forest, making sharp curves, descending down and then going up again. Our vehicle hurried along these roads, moving ahead and ahead, farther and farther. After several hours of this twisted driving, some of us became sick, tied bandanas around our heads and were holding ourselves so that we would not *poyikhaty do Ryhy*[154] But we could not hold it for very long. We asked our good driver if he would stop, even for a short time, because we had to get out of our *buda*[155] and get some fresh air.

Ukrainian Missionary Choir before their second trip.
From left to right: I. Polischuk, L. Efimovich, I. Barchuk, E. Kucenko, J. Stebelski, M. Podworniak, T. Siery, W. Siery, V. Kucenko and O. Machnik

---
154 "Go to Riga"; ie. throw up. *Rihaty* is Ukrainian for "to vomit"
155 Shelter or enclosure

We arrived in Warburg at three o'clock in the afternoon. Our vehicle left us at the train station and returned to Ludensheid. We settled down and waited as brother S. Nischik went into town to look for transportation. After a short time he returned with the good news that an American military vehicle would soon come and take us further. Therefore, our documents were helping us and opening up doors. After about half an hour, the vehicle arrived and we headed in the direction of the city of Kassel. Rain kept falling all day.

Towards evening we arrived at a camp in Munchenhof. Beside a thick spruce forest stood some long wooden barracks pressed one against another. This was a camp for elderly Russian emigrants who had gathered together from all of western Germany. Among them also was a group of believers. The barracks were poor, faded from the sun and surrounded by a forest on one side and mud on the other. French prisoners lived there once, but now various refugees occupied the barracks.

Our vehicle had not yet come to a stop at the camp gate, when some wonderful sisters from the camp, who were aware of our arrival, had already appeared. They led us to their barracks and there we saw how miserable their life was. The rooms were small, divided with old blankets or some torn military canvas. There was one corner for each family. In the corner stood a water pail, a gas stove, a wooden table, some kind of bench with crooked legs, and against the wall was a wide, wooden bed. The people were squeezed together, experiencing discomfort. There were two guards and camp police at the camp gate, standing there day and night and not allowing any repatriation commission to even approach the gate.

That evening the camp administration issued food to us for several days. We thought that we would be able to rest from the trip that evening and hold a concert on the following day. However, the local believers as well as the administration of the camp asked us to have a concert that same evening. They released to us a large theatre auditorium with many seats and a fine stage. Messengers went out throughout the camp and the administration made an announcement over the loudspeaker that there will be a concert today. This was our first performance. We would see how it would go.

At the announced time we arrived at the auditorium and found it filled with people of all ages. Trembling with excitement, as well as being overtired from the trip, we barely made our way to the front and hid behind the curtain. From there we walked onto the stage where the camp director awaited us. He sincerely greeted us and introduced us to the residents as the Ukrainian Missionary Choir, which was travelling among the camps. We immediately could sense a good atmosphere and gained confidence. Before us was a sea of heads, hundreds of hungry souls, hundreds of unfamiliar faces. At the beginning we sang *Otche Nash*[156] and the people all rose to their feet. Following this we sang again, recited poems and brother Barchuk had a sermon. After the sermon our program continued and at the conclusion brother S. Nischik still spoke a final word. We were later told that there were over one thousand people inside the auditorium, but throughout the entire program no one left or even moved. The people sat, listened and sighed reverently. They had never had a concert like this before.

After the concert, we went down into the auditorium, greeted the people and became acquainted with them. It was evident that the people here were not old emigrants, but there were many Ukrainians, recent *ostarbiters,* as well as people from Polish-Belarus.

The next day we explored the camp and the surrounding area. The camp was interesting, resembling a Cossack enclosure. White smoke was rising from each barrack. Small piglets were warming themselves in the sun beneath the buildings and chickens were scratching the ground. Ropes were strung from one barrack to the next on which laundry was drying. In a few places, tied to a pole, there was a cow or a horse standing. There were wagons filled with straw for the cattle. The people who lived here had their own cows, horses, geese, ducks and rabbits. One barrack had a wooden cross on it and we were told that this was an Orthodox church.

That day we visited an old palace in a nearby forest where a German king once lived. An elderly German conducted us through luxurious rooms, showing us the former glory of Germany and explaining everything to us. There were beautiful paintings and carvings everywhere. In one room stood a bed in which the brother of Napoleon once slept. Everything that

---

156 The Lord's Prayer

was standing here had withstood a long period of time and the war had not touched it. The castle was standing in a thick forest where no bomb had fallen. Everything was whole and unharmed. Germany was rich in museums and historical memorials and wherever we had an opportunity we visited these old memorials.

We returned to the camp through the dense forest. A light rain was beginning to fall. Above a nearby rafter there appeared a multi-coloured rainbow. What a miracle! In Ukraine, there were now severe blizzards and here on February 5th... a rainbow.

In the afternoon we held a service in the camp for the local believers. This was similar to our services at home. Women, children and men sat on long benches. We all sang together, sharing true fellowship and joy.

In the evening we had a service in the camp auditorium. It was pouring rain outside and not too many people attended; however, all the local believers and over one hundred outsiders were present.

Congregation of Ev.- Baptist refugees in the camp "Lysenko" in Hanover, during the time of a visit by the Ukrainian Missionary Choir.
Seated from left to right are brothers: I. Barchuk, S. Nischik, P. Hnilitski, J. Repetski, and F. Kaplun

The following day, leaving the camp in Munchenhof, we set out further on our journey. In the morning we arrived at the station and boarded a train, which was going to Fulda. There were not too many people on the train because this was not a main railroad so we occupied one empty compartment. When the train began to move we began to sing a song, which soared freely like a bird throughout the entire train. In Germany this was allowed only for an organized singing group that was travelling. Therefore we also sang. A young man was walking along the corridor. When he heard our singing he stopped and listened to our songs and conversations through the partially open doors of the compartment. I went out to him.

"Do you understand our language?" I asked him.

"Yes, I understand," replied the young man. "Personally, I am Polish. But before the war we lived in Volyn and so I understand Ukrainian."

I gave him a Polish Christian tract. The youth took it, looked at me and I could see that he had tears in his eyes.

"Are you a believer?" he asked.

"Yes, a believer," I replied. "We were in the camp at Munchenhof and now we are going to Fulda. We are holding evangelical services and gospel concerts. And where are you going?"

The young man burst into silent weeping and leaned against the door. I took him by the hand and led him into our compartment. We did not know what had happened to him. He sat down on the bench, as tears flowed down his face.

Brother S. Nischik sat down beside him.

"What is the matter with you? Can you tell me? Why are you crying?"

After a while the young man came to his senses. Looking at us, with eyes full of tears, he said:

"You are – brothers and sisters! Oh, how happy I am! It has been three years since I saw any believers. In our camp there are only three believers: My mother and I, and one other Ukrainian sister. For three years we have not attended any service. We did not have communion and because of that it has been very difficult for us. Mother will be very happy when I tell her. We thought that in all of Germany there were only three believers, but there are so many of you here." He greeted each one of us as he wiped the tears from his eyes.

At the next station our new-found brother transferred to a different train, and we continued farther.

Towards evening we came to the town of Fulda. It was already late. Brother Shweitzaris, who joined our group in Munchenhof, was also with us and now he was our guide to a Polish camp. We walked among the ruins of the town; around us it was dark and cold. Brother Shweitzaris walked in front and we followed him in a single file. In this manner we came to a large Polish camp where several Belarus Christian families lived. A guard wearing a Polish military uniform was standing at the gate. Above the gate hung the Polish national flag. Beyond the fence, through the fog, we could see some tall buildings. It was evident that the camp was large and active.

The guard, upon seeing such a large group, was not certain if he was allowed to let us in. He telephoned to his superior and then he led us into the guardhouse and told us to wait there. After a short time the commander of the camp arrived. He examined our documents and told us that we could stay as long as we wanted. Our papers stated that we were under the protection of UNRRA, as was also the Polish camp in Fulda.

We went to look for our people and found all of them while they were still at their prayer meeting. The brothers and sisters were happy to see us. We still sang several songs at the service that evening before we went to get some rest. The believers had plenty of problems with us because they did not have enough room to accommodate everyone for the night. But being practical people we set up long benches and chairs, laid straw on the floor and we all had a place to sleep.

The next day we held a choir practice while brother Nischik went throughout the camp to complete plans for the evening concert as well as to make arrangements for food for several days. The local UNRRA provided us with food and the camp administration released a large theatre hall for our use. We found out that there were Ukrainians as well as Belarusians in the camp so we prepared our program to include all Slavic languages.

The concert was scheduled for 7 o'clock in the evening but several minutes before seven every seat in the large hall was already filled with people. We entered onto the stage through a side door and instinctively felt that today we will have a great victory in this place. We were not mistaken. We had a time of prayer backstage and then took our places as the large curtain parted in the middle. Our song flowed forth as the audience became benumbed with anticipation. A second song followed, then a recitation, another song and a sermon. Nobody in the auditorium even moved. Everyone listened as if it was something they had never heard before in their life. Among those in attendance were many Polish military people, many Germans from the town who had heard about our arrival and had come, as well as many employees of UNRRA.

That evening we sang 15 gospel songs in Ukrainian, Polish, Russian and Belarusian. We gave an opportunity for every nationality that was in attendance to hear a gospel song in their own language. The audience was so delighted with our concert that they chose from amongst themselves one man who stationed himself at the door and everyone who came out would throw some money into a hat. In this manner they collected 294 German marks for us. We realized that we had to keep a record of our finances. I was chosen as treasurer and the money was entrusted to me and our cash supply increased with every town. When we returned from that trip to our Ludensheid, we brought with us several hundred German marks, which were left over after all our expenses, had been paid. We transferred all that money into the general Union account.

We spent another night in Fulda and in the morning we hurried through the almost empty streets of the town to the station. We boarded the train to Ansbach and travelled for the entire day. Our sisters were becoming somewhat tired but they kept the promise that they had made before we left, that they would not complain or have any regrets.

There was no Ukrainian camp in Ansbach but there was a large Latvian camp. In the town many of our believers were living in private homes where they also held their own services; therefore, we had to hurry from to one group to the other.

We still arrived on time for the service and were able to greatly encourage the local believers with our visit, taking part in preaching the Word of God as well as in song.

After the service we hurried to the Latvian camp. Our sisters were using the last of their strength, but they continued to walk. We arrived at the Latvian camp. The buildings were large and undamaged by the war. It had many windows that allowed much light to enter. We found out that the camp commander was not at home and because of the late hour it would not be possible to hold a gospel concert that evening. We were only able to have a service with the local Latvian believers.

We arrived at a large, clean hall. Within a short time many people found out about our arrival and came to the service. The majority of the people who came were elderly and could understand Russian. The young people did not understand and therefore the sermons by brothers Nischik and Barchuk were translated into Latvian by brother Zinger. We sang in Ukrainian and Polish. After the service the gracious Latvian sisters prepared a tea. Again we were convinced that in Jesus Christ there was no distinction among nations. We could all be one family when we have the love of Christ in our hearts.

An Evangelical refugee funeral service in Augsburg

In Germany, the Latvian Baptists were organized as the Latvian Baptist Association and the Estonian Baptists were organized as a similar nationalistic association. But I believe that in comparison to us, there were much fewer of them.

In the morning we were again at the station and again we were on the train for a whole day. We had to transfer many times and wait for a long time at different stations. Finally we boarded the train that would take us to Augsburg. Outside it was rain mixed with snow, but inside the train it was warm. It was also warm in our hearts and souls.

It was Saturday and towards evening we arrived in Augsburg. We went without notice to the home of brother Nazarenko who was greatly delighted by our arrival. At the same time perhaps he was somewhat worried about where he would find space for us to sleep. But somehow everything would work out. There were long benches and a floor and there would be space to sleep.

On Sunday we had a blessed worship service in the home of brother Nazarenko that was attended by many believers from Augsburg and its surroundings. That evening a gospel concert was announced in Haustetten. Many believers also came to this concert as well many outsiders because prior to the concert we had hung up large announcements in prominent places.

The following day we explored the historical city of Augsburg. Afterwards we were invited to the Latvian camp, "Baltic", where a farewell service was being held for American military chaplains. Many people attended and the hall was filled to capacity. There were many American military personnel present as well as many other listeners. The service was conducted in Latvian. We did not understand their language but they understood our songs and thanked us sincerely.

We returned to the hospitable home of brother Nazarenko late that evening.

The next day we had a choir rehearsal while brother Nischik rushed around all day to different officials settling various matters on our behalf. The central office of UNRRA told him that we would not be given any food if we stayed in private accommodations. We would have to go into the city and spend the night in a building for which UNRRA was responsible. We went into the city. We were given dinner in a large German school and after dinner we returned to the home of brother Nazarenko because an evening service was again scheduled in Haustetten. The service took place in a large dining hall and there were many more people in attendance than we expected. Almost the entire camp administration attended, employees of UNRRA came and the large hall was filled to its capacity. We selected the best songs, poems and narrations from our repertoire. Brothers Nischik and Barchuk preached. The people were very satisfied and invited us to come again.

The following day we had to go into the city where the main UNRRA centre was located and where we were given a room and sufficient food. In the same building there also lived many French, Belgians, Dutch, Latvians and Russians. We held a choir practice there and in the evening a gospel concert was announced at a Ukrainian camp in Augsburg. The camp was large and possibly the largest in the entire American zone. We arrived in the evening and saw that announcements about our concert had been hung everywhere.

We entered the enormous theatrical auditorium and saw that there were not very many people there, not more than a hundred, which was almost nothing for such a large room. As we started our concert more people began to arrive, but not too many. It became evident that the power of Catholic activity was also at work here, making every effort in advance to prevent people from coming. Only a few Greek-Catholics came, but there were people from Greater Ukraine, Volyn and Polisia. People who could still think and decide for themselves what they should do. An American military chaplain was present and spoke a short word and our choir presented the rest of the program. Brother I. Barchuk concluded with a strong sermon.

After the service we were invited to the home of one family for the evening and it was very late when we returned to the central UNRRA building. Meanwhile, so many people had arrived from somewhere to the UNRRA building that it became impossible to even turn around. There were various nations, different nationalities, truly an international mass of people. We went to the head of the UNRRA and requested that we would be permitted to hold an evangelical service for all these people. The commander granted our request. The following day we were shown a large room where we held a service. So many people came that the room could not accommodate everyone. The service continued for over two hours and we had a song and a word in every Slavic language. In attendance were Latvians, Polish, Hungarians, Yugoslavians as well as Ukrainians, Belarusians and Russians. After the service many people came up to us, thanking us for the word and the song.

Within this large multi-national gathering we met believers who had come here from Berlin after the war. They told us many things about the spiritual ministry by Ukrainian evangelicals, which had been started there in 1940 by the first Ukrainian emigrants. Later when the Germans began bringing young people into forced labor from Greater Ukraine to Berlin and surroundings, the spiritual work increased to such a great extent that in the Ukrainian Evangelical Baptist Church on Friederich Street[157] over 500 people were converted to the Lord. And possibly this congregation was the only Evangelical Baptist Ukrainian congregation in post-war Western Europe.

First pioneers of the Ukr. Ev, Baptist Church in Berlin, 1940.
Seated from left to right: F. Lucyk, Sushko, Dr. L. Zhapko-Potopowich, Kiffer, S. Nischik, Iv. Uhryn

---

157 Friedrichstraße

Sunday found us again at the Ukrainian camp in Haussatten. In the morning we had a service, which was attended by very many new listeners. After the service we had to hurry to a second Ukrainian camp where our service was announced for the afternoon. Outside it was raining and snowing. We walked across the entire city with our backpacks on our backs, but nobody paid any attention to us because everyone in Germany was walking in a similar manner.

We arrived at the camp, which was surrounded by a high fence. The guard at the gate let us in, because he knew beforehand about our arrival to the camp. We were shown to the hall for the service and found that there were already over 50 people inside. With every moment more and more new people arrived. When we began the service with the song, *Khryste Prebud Ty z Namy*[158], every seat in the hall was taken. Mainly elderly people who were refugees from all parts of Ukraine came to this service. They listened with great attention to the preaching of the gospel and later thanked us as they became acquainted with us.

We returned to the central UNRRA building late in the evening and began preparations to travel further. One brother-doctor hosted us with supper, and in the morning, while it was still dark; we were already walking to the train station. The city was still sleeping. Snow and rain continued falling on us, but we continued on, not paying any attention to the weather. For some reason everyone was feeling lively and cheerful.

After twelve o'clock in the afternoon the train arrived in Ingolstadt, where believers were impatiently waiting for us. Ingolstadt was a beautiful old city with many historical monuments. It spread out on both sides of the Danube River but the city was now in disarray and reduced to ruins. Nor far from the Danube an old fort was visible above which a yellow-blue flag was flying. This was the location of a large Ukrainian camp.

The family of brother Dennis Stepaniuk welcomed us sincerely and joyfully. We settled down for a rest while brother Nischik went to the local authorities to find out whether we could hold a gospel concert in the camp. After a while he returned and told us that the camp administration was allowing us to use the large theatre hall and our concert would be held

---

158 Christ Be With Us

tonight. We prepared large announcements and hung them in conspicuous places in the camp and began to prepare for the performance.

The camp in Ingolstadt was unique. We had never encountered any like it until that moment. Every day, towards evening there was held a so-called *zbirka*, which all the residents of the camp attended. The women stood separate from the men while the commander of the camp loudly read the world news, the camp chronicle, various announcement and then everyone sang the Ukrainian national anthem and returned to their barracks. Today brother Polischuk and I went to the *zbirka* to hear if the commander would announce our arrival. There were several hundred people there who stood in complete silence as the commander read: "Today the Ukrainian Evangelical Choir from the English occupied zone has visited our camp. At eight o'clock this evening they will present their concert in the theatre hall. Those who wish can come and listen. Admission is free".

Before eight o'clock we arrived at the theatre and saw that it was completely filled. The entire camp leadership as well as UNRRA employees were seated in the front rows. We prayed behind the curtain before we stepped out onto the stage and sang the beautiful song, *Hospodi Bozhe Nash*[159] . The people all seemed to hold their breath as they rose to their feet. Brother Barchuk spoke an opening word before we continued with our program. People were moved to tears. The majority of them were hearing an evangelical song and message for the very first time.

The next day it was raining and we did not have an opportunity to look around the town. We were forced to sit inside the camp, preparing for the evening service. The theatre auditorium was being used for some kind of gathering so the camp leadership gave us a different room, which was also large and very nice. Our service that evening was a blessed one to which many people came. Among those in attendance were two Americans; one was a Baptist chaplain and the other was a major in the American army. They both spoke a short word that was translated into Ukrainian by brother Nischik.

In Ingolstadt, we sang, not only in the Ukrainian camp, but we were also invited to sing for the American soldiers at a German church. After the service a man came up and introduced himself to us. He spoke Ukrainian

---

159 "Lord, our God", *Ridna Pisnya*, No. 84

very well and told us that he himself was a German. He had lived in Brody before the war but now was living in Ingolstadt and had come to listen to our singing. When he saw our group he unexpectedly asked:

"Are you all married, travelling as families, or are you still single?"

"Some of us are married, and some are single," we answered. "This friend of ours," we said about brother W. Siery, "has had a church wedding, but did not have a civil one. We are also engaged and would like to have a civil ceremony but we do not have our birth certificates and without them nobody wants to perform that ceremony for us."

The unknown man looked at us and said:

"If you wish, I can help you."

"Really? We would be very grateful to you."

"All of you come and see me before ten o'clock tomorrow. Here is my address." He gave us his business card.

The following day we went into the city, but we did not have the slightest faith that this unknown man would be able to help us. We thought that perhaps he was some kind of con artist, perhaps some kind of swindler who was trying to get money from us. But we went. We arrived at the given address and found that it was the address of a German court. We asked for the name that we were looking for and the man whom we met yesterday was called into the corridor. He led us to a large room, which was especially dedicated for conducting a civil wedding and set the entire personnel of the court into motion. Employees rushed about, bringing in some type of papers, writing out birth certificates, and recording our names in a large book.

"Do you have witnesses?" our acquaintance asked us.

"No we do not, but we can bring someone from the camp."

"That will take too long," he said, "but you can sign for each other."

After several moments we received official German marriage certificates. Our acquaintance shook our hands and wished for us the best in life. We thanked him sincerely. And so now we were married and unmarried.

We discovered that this unexpected benefactor, who performed for us a very great service, was the head judge in Ingolstadt.

With wonderful feelings we returned to the Ukrainian camp. Even though it was pouring rain outside, it seemed to us that this was the finest, sunniest weather that we had ever experienced in out lives. We had in our pockets, close to our hearts, fresh marriage documents. Our lives as single men had come to an end and we could hardly believe that we were married. All of this happened so suddenly and unexpectedly. Here in Ingolstadt our lives as single men had come to an end. It was stamped with a large German stamp. What had happened could never be reversed; it was stamped for all of life. This was a very major event for us!

Ukrainian Missionary Choir during their second trip.
Seated from left to right: V. Podworniak, T. Siery, I. Polischuk, J. Polischuk, O. Machnik
Standing from left to right: W. Siery, M. Podworniak, S. Nischik, L. Efimovich, E. Kucenko, I. Barchuk

From Ingolstadt we travelled to Munich where believers were waiting for us. We only spent the night there because the next day we left for Karsfeld where a service was scheduled in the Ukrainian camp. A large number of young people from Munich accompanied us and we arrived in the camp as a large group. Reserved for us was the former Ukrainian Autocephalous Orthodox Church where we held a large service. Many people came because our announcements had been hung everywhere in the camp.

After the service we returned to Munich. A fierce storm arose outside which was toppling the burnt walls of buildings. Traffic had slowed down on many streets but we were able to arrive at the comfortable home of one brother and the storm was no longer frightening for us.

The next day was Sunday. We held our services in a German Baptist church. There was one service for Ukrainians and one for the German believers at which we sang in Ukrainian and German. The German believers warmly welcomed us.

The service had not yet ended when a large vehicle, which was especially sent for us from the nearby international camp, was already standing in front of the house of prayer. Our service for the evening had been announced there in advance. In a few minutes we arrived. The camp was very large, almost like an entire town. We met Polish, Ukrainians, Serbs, Russians, Czechs, Latvians, Estonians, Uzbeks and others. Our program that evening was therefore varied. We were in a large theatrical auditorium that had long rows of seats. A large number of people came and every seat was filled. We ministered in word and song as usual and God blessed the service. We felt and saw this with our own eyes. We learned that this was the first evangelical service, which was ever held in that gigantic camp.

After the service a vehicle from UNRRA came for us again and drove us back to the city. We were all physically tired, but refreshed in our spirits.

In the morning we received a telegram from brother A. Nichiporuk from Dingolfing that everything in their camp was ready for us and everyone was already waiting for our arrival. And we went.

Dingolfing was a small and very clean town. The camp for refugees was located in an old wooden barrack outside the town. There was nobody there from our people, except the family of brother and sister Nichiporuk. We had misgivings about whether we would be favourably received, but our doubts later dissipated like smoke. Up till now we had not been received so graciously anywhere as in that place. We were given a large hall for our services. The commander of the camp welcomed us and told us that officially the camp was Polish but there were also Ukrainians, Belarusians and Russians in the camp and they were all expecting words from us in their own language.

We had a very large service there in the evening. Almost every one of the residents of the camp came, along with their commander, local UNRRA employees and the local Orthodox priest. After the service the people did not want to disperse, they asked us to sing more songs, recite more poems and preach.

The following day the camp prepared a dinner for us in the large dining room, which was also attended by the entire administration and employees of the camp. There were many people seated beside the long tables, but everyone's attention was on us. The commander of the camp and a representative from UNRRA spoke. They thanked us for visiting their camp, and wished success for us in our further ministry. That camp with its fine people and the sincere treatment that we received at the camp from the local UNRRA during that time has remained in my memory. There were many people in the large kitchen, and the cook, in a white apron, stood beside a kettle and poured good Ukrainian borscht for everyone.

We had several hours of free time during the day so we went into the town. It was small but very clean. Not even one bomb had been dropped here during the war. On a hill outside the town there was a cemetery and we went there. I had never seen such a cemetery anywhere before. It was surrounded by a high brick wall, which was whitewashed on the outside with lime. The cemetery was clean and beautiful like the room of a good housekeeper. There was a bunch of flowers on each grave. A pathway, sprinkled with fine yellow sand, led to every grave. Each grave had a gravestone or a simple cross on it and on several graves lamps was burning. Two elderly Germans continuously walked about with large brooms, shovels and watering cans and took care of the cemetery as if it was some great historical place.

While we were in Dingolfing we received invitations to visit other similar camps but we did not have time. It was necessary to return to Munich where a baptism service was announced for Sunday.

We were back in Munich. Again we went to the hospitable home of brother Kosenko, but this time we realized that there would not only be any space to spend the night but even to place one foot. Believers arrived from all Bavaria and the home of brother Kosenko was like an overcrowded station. A song was flowing, *Dorohiyi Khvylyny Nam Boh Daruvav*[160] and one brother said:

"These moments are precious for us, but for brother Kosenko, they are unhappy because where will he put us all to sleep?"

That evening we found ourselves with a real problem. Regardless of how we were arranged, it was not possible to assign a place for everyone to sleep. People lay down on benches, on chairs and on the floor. I remember one brother sat down on the stairs, leaned his head against the wall and stayed that way all night. Two other brothers found some kind of shed outside, where pigeons lived, and slept there. Oh what a night this was, impossible to forget! Brother Kosenko, as our host, walked about troubled and always asked:

"*Nu yak brati, dobre?*[161] Perhaps someone needs something to place under their head?"

"Good, good, we don't need anything," somebody's voice called out. "You also go to sleep."

Did brother Kosenko sleep that night? I do not know even today. I think he sat somewhere all night or walked about.

The following day we were so very tired that we could barely stand on our feet. We felt that we did not sleep at all but had been standing somewhere at a train station, waiting for a train. But there was no time to think about resting.

We all hurried to a large public pool in the town where the baptism[162] was to be held. The large building where the pool was located was not damaged by the war and the pool was filled with clean, rippling water. Many people had gathered. The celebration began with the song, *Nedaleko za Rikoyu*[163], but the singing did not have the same sense of celebration for us that we once felt on the banks of the rivers in Halychyna or Volyn. There we had spacious hayfields and boundless expanses of fields and our song flowed *far-far* away. But here it was like a bird in a cage, bouncing off the

---

160 Precious moments God has given to us
161 Well brothers, is it good?
162 The author used the expression "holy baptism by faith" which frequently was used to describe the act of baptism.
163 "Not far away, across the River" sung to the melody of "Shall we gather at the River"

solid walls of the swimming pool and falling helplessly into the water. The song was unable to find anywhere to escape into the wide-open spaces.

Those, who would make a covenant with the Lord today, entered from a side room. There were exactly twenty of them, mainly young people. Brother S. Nischik had a short word for them, our choir sang several songs, and then brother Kosenko performed the act of baptism.

After this we all went to a German Baptist house of worship where there was the acceptance of new members to the church, followed by the Lord's Supper. When we arrived the building was already full of people who had come from the different neighbouring camps as well as from the city of Munich. Our service was again large and blessed.

In the evening we were again at the home of brother Kosenko. There were two small rooms and a kitchen in his house but altogether there were exactly fifty-three of us! It was again possible to sing *Dorohiyi Khvylyny Nam* but nobody sang because everyone was only thinking about rest. That night was also difficult for us, but somehow we survived it. In the morning we left for Augsburg. Along the way we dreamt that in Augsburg we would be able to rest. When we arrived we learned that today there would be a farewell evening for an American chaplain, which was being arranged by the Ukrainians of Augsburg and our choir was invited to sing there. Therefore, there were no longer any thoughts about resting.

The large hall in Augsburg was filled to the walls with people. There were many young American soldiers present and among them was chaplain Harrison who was leaving to go to another place and the evening was dedicated to him. There were many speakers, we sang many times and at the conclusion there was a farewell speech by the chaplain, which was translated by brother Nischik.

After the service there was a fellowship supper at the home of one brother. Chaplain Harrison was also there with us. It also became an unofficial farewell service for us—tomorrow we were leaving Augsburg and Munich and going farther to southern Germany.

We spent our final night in Augsberg and from there we went to Füssen which was located beneath high mountains not far from Tyrol. Along the way brother D. Yasko joined us.

First Ukr. Ev.-Baptist Church in Munich in the summer of 1947. The picture was taken during the time when the church was visited by brother K. Hrikman.

At the station in Füssen we were met by local believers who invited us to their camp, which was located in a large building outside the town. We were well received because they already knew about our arrival and even supper was already prepared and waiting for us on the table.

In the morning we went to view the neighbourhood. There was much to see here. Everywhere there were tall snow-covered mountains, streams glistened at the foot of the mountains and flowers were beginning to bloom. If it was still cold in northern Germany during this time, it was already a true spring here. The sun was flooding all of nature with its rays, casting its golden rays on the shining streams, which were flowing everywhere from the mountains, and kissing us as if to welcome each one with spring. Our group walked along a narrow path up the high mountain. Along the road we saw shrines of different sizes in which there were many Catholic marble figures, mostly of former popes wearing tall hats and with serious, terrifying faces. Devout Catholics stopped beside each shrine to pray then continued up the mountain. At the very top of the mountain stood a tall cross. Beside it there was a bench and many low bushes that had not turned green yet. We stood there and looked at the white mountains of the Alps that stretched out to the south. They were covered with snow and shone as if they were carved from marble. The mountains seemed to be so near that one could shake hands with them but they were still *far-far* from us. The mountain air here was clean and healthy. It seemed to a person that he was just a tiny bug among those mountains. What a wonderful world! We sat down on the bench beneath the cross. We sang a song which soared above the mountains and hid somewhere in the chasms. It escaped and did not return to us again.

We returned to the camp because our service was scheduled for two o'clock in the afternoon. The residents of the camp were able to learn about the service through the announcements that we hung up in prominent places.

The theatre hall was very large here, but only a few people came. We discovered that there were many people here who were not friendly towards us. They managed to forewarn others and stopped them from coming to the service. We began the service and by the end of the service more people had arrived. In the evening we announced a second service in the same hall, which was attended by much more people. The camp commander set up a microphone in the hall, which broadcast our program throughout the entire large camp. It could be heard in all the corridors, in the public square and in any room where the people had their own radio.

When we returned from the service to the home of the believers where we were staying, we found many people there. They asked us to sing for them again and to read more from the Word of God. So we had one more service and were forced to repeat almost every item from our program.

We went to sleep late that evening but by four o'clock in the morning we were already rushing to the station. Our road now led back to Munich, and after that to our home, to our dear Ludenscheid ...

It was dark and cold outside and we are completely exhausted as we waited for our train at the damaged train station in Munich. Our train arrived but inside there was no room to sit or even to stand. It was still more than two hours before the train would depart, as more and more people continued to arrive. They crawled through windows, pushed through the doors, clung to the exits and between the train cars. We, with our large backpacks, were also making every effort to push through so that we could at least get into the corridors of the cars.

Brother Ivan Uhryn
conducted much ministry in the city of Munich and surroundings

We left Munich. It was not clear if we would ever come here again; therefore, it would be in order to say something about this large and now international city and about the spiritual work here. Munich – the capital of Bavaria, was greatly damaged during the war. Some areas of the city were completely ruined and there were still many human corpses buried under the ruins. During the time of the war we saw as hundreds of American and English airplanes flew over Rüdersdorf to southern Germany and now we could see the results of what the airplanes had sowed in many places of Bavaria. Countless camps for all nations and nationalities were set up within Munich itself and its surroundings, and one could now hear various languages on the streets of Munich. The majority of the camps here were Ukrainian. The majority was from our nation. All of them were living under very harsh conditions. Some were living in barracks, some in private German homes; some were in damaged buildings living like rats. There were many brethren who were preaching the Word of God to these people. On June 16,1946, the First Ukrainian Evangelical Baptist Church, organized by brother Ivan Uhryn, was registered in the *Bavarskomy Ministerstvi*.[164] Believers came from other camps to Munich, 68 of whom were added to that congregation. From 1946 to January 1950, 98 people were baptized and became members. The Ukrainian-Evangelical Baptist church in Munich had 165 members and it became the mother-church of all other Ukrainian Evangelical-Baptist Churches in Western Germany. Brother Ivan Uhryn ministered to a great extent in the Ukrainian evangelical field in Munich and surroundings. Later brothers S. Nischik, M. Tesluk, A. Mulko and others also actively ministered there.

In Munich there was also a large Slavic Baptist congregation that included Russians, Ukrainians, Belarusians and other nations.

*****

The train began to move. The police pulled anyone who was hanging onto the sides of the doors down, but we were already inside. We were standing among people who were so tightly packed together that it was not possible to even move a hand or foot. A cold wind was blowing through broken windows and we were becoming overcome by sleepiness and unbearable fatigue. It was especially difficult for our sisters who did not have a place to sit down and did not have any strength to stand.

We suffered in this manner all the way to Frankfurt where we transferred to a train, which went to Dillingen-Siegen-Hagen-Ludensheid. To our good fortune we had a place to sit down on that train and look out through the window at the beautiful scenery of Germany. We travelled through Rüdersdorf, which was so well known, to me and brother Barchuk. Through the window we saw the factory where we had worked and waved at it.

---

164 Bavarian Ministry

**Baptism in the city swimming pool in Munich in 1949,
which was performed by brother Ivan Uhryn**

We travelled through our unforgettable Siegen and saw through the window of our compartment the quiet streets of the town where we had walked during the war. There was the wide, dark opening into the bunker under the mountain where we had once hidden. It had long, deep passages which continued under the entire mountain, and until now, there has not been a bomb in the world that could destroy that mountain. This opening was now deserted, but as we travelled past it, we were reminded of many things. Siegen was especially memorable to brother and sister Siery because they had lived there during the war while we only went there occasionally.

Towards evening we arrived in Altona from which we travelled by car to Ludensheid. It was a quiet evening outside and our hearts were also quiet and peaceful. In the distance we could see the third block and inside there was much light. We wanted to get to our own people as soon as possible. We had yearned for them and they for us. Carrying our backpacks and all our feelings and experiences, we climbed the stair. Finally we were home. Thank you Lord!

Our large congregation announced a service for the following day during which time we related the things we had seen and experienced on the road. We thanked God for everything.

In Ludensheid we had many good times and anxious moments. We experienced many different Christian celebrations, one of which was the large wedding of four young couples, members of our congregation. Believers came from many camps, from far and near to attend this wedding. The large third block could not accommodate all the guests. The long corridors were decorated with greenery and flowers, the floors and stairs were washed until they gleamed. Four couples were to be married: brothers S. Bychkowski, I. Polischuk, P. Yunka and M. Podworniak. Beside each couple stood a different preacher: P. Hordiev, M. Dubowy, I. Pidhoretsky and I. Barchuk. None of the young couples had a father or mother, or any brothers or sisters present from their own family. But there was a large family of believers who were there, their brothers and sisters in Christ and because of that they were fortunate beyond measure. Thy felt that today everyone loved them even more than at any other time before. From the early morning people were looking at them differently and smiling. Today, everyone had something to tell them, to do something for them and be helpful in some way. All the believers and everyone who had gathered showed this with their actions. They contributed whatever they had and prepared a large wedding reception. Tables, covered with refugee food, were set up in the long corridors and seated at the table were *people-people* ... Songs were flowing; there were speeches and musical numbers by our small orchestra. And we, that is the married couples, deeply felt, that in spite of some small nationalistic misunderstandings, in spite of some sparks of adversity, we were nevertheless related in Christ Jesus. We were especially convinced of this during the large wedding in Ludensheid. And so thank you to all the brothers and sisters who helped to arrange that wedding.

The Ludensheid congregation during the wedding celebration

Our travelling choir was not idle but continued to sing at various celebrations in our own church and travel to other Slavic and German evangelical congregations. I recall that we also travelled to Weidenest for the funeral of sister Spalek, the wife of a well-known Polish Baptist preacher.

Frequently the youth from our congregation held social events in the hills and green plains of Westphalia. One time we completed a trip to a place, which was well known throughout all of Westphalia, and perhaps throughout all of Germany, the famous town of Attendorn. This town was situated by a small mountain stream and surrounded on both sides by beautiful fields of grass and green spruce trees. The train stopped beneath a very high hill beside an elegant station with elaborate corridors and wide wooden benches. There were many chairs, tables and booths outside the station. Once countless tourists came to this place, not only from Germany but also from all of Europe, and those chairs would be filled with people. But now there was nobody there except our Ludensheid youth. We gathered by the hill beside some closed iron doors; we stood there and waited.

A tall German arrived. He smiled at us and opened the door with a large key. He informed us that we were going to enter a deep cave[165] underneath the hill, and therefore if anyone had a jacket they should put it on because it will be cold underground. We descended the stairs, going deeper and deeper. The German walked in front and we followed him. The stairs ended but we continued farther and farther, always deeper and deeper, like going down a hill. We were in a deep underground cave. Water was continuously trickling on both sides of wet walls. Above our heads pale electric bulbs were blinking, illuminating large piles of rocks. The silence here was truly that of an underground cavern. Out path suddenly turned to the right, we walked around a protruding rock and there before our eyes opened up the underground kingdom of Attendorn. We were affected to the bottom of our soul and awestruck beyond measure. We stood beneath a wet wall as the German showed and explained to us this wonder of nature. A large room was formed by itself, as water fell drop by drop from above creating an absolute wonder. Water trickled down for many years, for countless centuries. Because it was cold here, it solidified, becoming hard as a rock, creating wonderful figures, statues and complete castles. They were white as if they were formed from the best marble. In several places they were greenish and grey. Electric light bulbs, which were strung behind us, cast various colours on that amazing site. Over here was a figure that resembled a king on his throne and over there opened up a wide curtain with long folds and various intersecting twists. Some stalactites were especially lit up; resembling real flames ... these were called "hell". There were different flames with varied colours, which formed various impressions in the soul.

The German led us around those underground palaces and showed us a small lake. We stood behind a metal barrier where we were able to see to the bottom of the lake. We saw some types of stones, but we did not see a single fish, a single snail or a single water bug. There was not a single life form in the underground cave. The water in the lake did not even move but remained still and motionless like everything in this underground kingdom. The water was as transparent and clear as a tear. We could see the bottom as clearly as the palm of our hand but our guide told us that this lake was very deep.

---

165 Atta Cave

We continued farther. We went past the lake, past the illuminated white figures; we saw other wonders of nature and then gradually began to ascend to the top. We felt a dread and fear in our soul. Around us were only rocks and deep underground tunnels. What would happen if all of that suddenly collapsed? But it was better not to think about that, only to get to the top as soon as possible! ...To the sun, to some air...

We continued to ascend to the top, on the right wall an electric light bulb was flickering. Because it was frequently burning it produced a small amount of heat and light and thin strands of moss had begun to grow beside it. Life had made its way even here in the underground.

When we reached the top, each of us breathed more freely. We looked back at the entrance, which led into the underground cave, and also involuntarily we looked up at the enormous mountain, from underneath which we had just come out. The mountain was *high-high* and we were underneath it by the same distance!

In a small shack we bought some postcards of Attendorn landscapes. We purchased some small booklets, which described how and when the cave was opened, who developed it and how many thousands of people have visited it, etc.

We returned to Ludensheid filled with wondrous impressions from what we had seen.

FRILLE

After the wedding we did not remain in Ludensheid for very long. One day we received an announcement that a Belgian army was coming here to take up permanent residency and we would have to move to a different Polish camp. None of us knew where we were going, no one protested, nobody could choose a different place because we were all helpless people under the protection of UNNRA and so we silently accepted everything. If we had to leave, then we would go.

Refugee believers at the station in Ludensheid before their departure

One morning our luggage was all ready and large army vehicles stood beside the buildings. They transported us to the station where empty train cars were already waiting for us. Many German believers from Ludensheid, with whom we had enjoyed Christian fellowship, came to see us off. The small Ludensheid station and the platform were filled with people. Some were already seated in the cars; others were looking for a place, loading their luggage on board. But we believers stayed together as group. We had decided that when we arrived at the new place to stay together as group, and ask that we not be separated. Only when we were together would we be able to help each other if there was a need.

We travelled all day. Through the open windows we said farewell to the green hills of Westphalia because who knew if it would be possible for us to ever return here. It was sunny and warm outside. The hills were waving at us with the tops of the evergreens. We went through different towns and villages. Sometimes we stood and waited for longer periods of time at destroyed stations, drank coffee and then continued farther. Each car had its own people with a leader assigned to each group. We travelled as a completely separate group from the third block. We also had our own leaders and nothing else mattered to us.

Somewhere past Bielefeld, the Wesphalian hills ended. Our train passed a large monument, which was standing on a hill and pointing with its hand and then we came out onto a flat plain. Up until now we had seen only hills, rocks, spruce trees and rivers in Westphalia. Now we could see level fields that were densely seeded with green onions. On both sides of the railway tracks, as far as the eye could see, there were onions and we could also smell them inside the train cars! Beside the forest the Weser River glistened and a city became visible. We were told that it was Minden, which was not far from, was Lahde, the new place where we were being sent.

Towards evening we were brought to Lahde. The sun was setting as we began to look out from the train windows. Empty autos were already waiting. There were representatives from UNRRA and many Polish policemen. The police allocated the people into the cars, throwing their bundles and suitcases onto a pile. However, our brothers said that we would guard the belongings from our group by ourselves. The commander of the camp recoiled and said in a loud voice:

"I am the commander of the camp here and it will be as I said."

Our brothers went up to the UNRRA representative. The commander saw that they were talking in English and calmed down. We placed our belongings together on a pile, selected several brothers to guard them overnight, and went by car to Frille which was two or three miles from Lahde.

**Towards evening we were brought to the small station in Lahde.
In the front are brother and sister Trostianchuk**

Frille was a nice German town, surrounded by productive fields, and located very close to the Weser River. As we travelled towards the town we expected to find some kind of wooden barracks there, but we were mistaken. This was a type of Polish camp, which we had never seen before. The English occupying forces had sent all the Germans, with their livestock and household goods, out of the town and settled Polish people in the empty homes. Besides Frille, the Germans were also evicted from their homes in the towns of Weitersheim, parts of Lahde and other towns. The reason why the English occupiers did this was not clear. It was reported that perhaps during the war there was a German concentration camp in this area where many different people were tortured and that the local citizens had helped Hitler to abuse those camp residents. For that reason these town people were now being punished. If this was true, then there could not have been a more fitting punishment for those towns. The Polish settled in the German houses but after a short time brought them to complete ruin. They destroyed the orchards, gardens, fences and buildings. Towards the end they even began to burn down the properties but the English occupiers put an end to this lawlessness.

The vehicles brought us to Frille and dropped us off in a large town square beside some kind of school. Later we were taken to different homes. Each family, depending on the number of people, was given a house. Single men shared one room with several other individuals; single young women were also housed separately. All the believers could not be accommodated in Frille and therefore some were transferred to neighbouring Weitersheim. And in this way our life as refugees began in a new place. At first this life seemed strange, because in Ludensheid we all lived in the same building. We saw each other every day, we met in the corridors; but now we were scattered throughout the whole town. Our living conditions of being in a house in the town now resembled a more normal human lifestyle. The only regret was that the real owners of those houses were somewhere in different towns, living in crowded conditions and mistreated; but we would not have to answer for that.

In Ludensheid there was a common kitchen for all the residents of the camp. Every morning and evening we all went to the kitchen, stood in a long line and received our breakfast, dinner and supper. It was not the same in Frille. It was necessary to go to the store and again stand in a line. We were given food, which was unprepared, and now it was necessary to cook it at home. Immediately, our food became much worse than it was in Ludensheid. For example, bread that was made from corn meal, was not fresh. When it was cut open, then what looked like thin strands from a spider web were pulled from it. Instead of whole milk we were given skim milk, even for small children.

As in Ludensheid, so also in Frille, we first of all thought about where we would "set up an altar" to God, where we would gather for our worship services. In Frille there was a large Lutheran church with thick bushes planted around it. It resembled a Catholic church. It was given for our use. When we arrived for our first worship service we were awestruck that we would be holding our services in this large, magnificent building. There were massive black pews for seating, a place for the choir and a place for the preacher. We continually held our services in this church until we left the place. During this time our choir was very large. Every singer from the former travelling choir joined the choir and the permanent director was brother S. Bychkowski. If only you had been there to hear how our songs resounded in this church; especially songs like: *Nad Rodinoy Nashey*[166] and *Chwałę daj Panu*[167] and others. We had a sufficient number of preachers who took turns preaching. We had many new listeners, and eventually the Word of God, which was sown, produced an abundant harvest. In this large Polish camp, which spread out into several towns, there were also many Ukrainians and Belarusians. The word spread about our services and new visitors were present at every service. Later there were conversions as well as baptisms, which took place in Frille by the old mill as well as in the Weser River. Many people gathered at these celebrations. Some came simply out of curiosity and others were eager to hear the preaching of the gospel. These baptisms reminded us of the pre-war ministry in our native land which were now being resumed in a foreign land.

On the way to a baptism in Frille

---

166 Над Родиной нашей восходит заря (Over Our Homeland a Star has Risen), composed by Adam Herman Ivanovich, 1889-1945, a Russian Baptist composer and choir director

167 "Praise the Lord (O my soul)". Polish translation by Pawel Sikora (1906) of "Lobe denn Herren, a meine Seele" by J.D. Hermschmidt (1714)

In addition to our service in Frille we also had a regular service in the neighbouring village of Weitersheim that took place in a school. All of the believers who lived in the village came to this service and there were always many new listeners. Later, with the approval of the congregation, we opened regular services in Papinghausen[168] under the leadership of Brother Barchuk that were conducted only in Ukrainian. These two services took place every Sunday in the afternoon. There were also occasional evangelical services in Polish at Lahde.

Initially the services in Frille were in Polish only, but later the brethren began to preach in Russian as well as in Ukrainian. I discovered that there were many Orthodox Ukrainian and Belarusians in the camp who were holding their own Orthodox services in the attic of a large building. I attended those service several times and was impressed by the extreme poverty of their worship setting. There was a small altar covered with a white cloth on which several candles were burning. A very elderly priest conducted the service in Slavonic. On one side behind the priest was a cantor who was singing with a trembling voice and was being helped by several young men and women.

Baptism candidates in Frille. In the centre is Brother H. Boltniev

---

168 The name "Ponihausen" found in the text is probably an error. Gloria Perekrest, daughter of Ivan Barchuk, writes: "the name of the village was Papinghausen. The reason my dad started services there was that we transferred there because it became a Ukrainian camp. The services were during the week and we still went to the regular services on Sunday.

I remember, I believe it was in the year 1930, when the Romanian Prime Minister,[169] Metropolitan Miron, who was using force to persecute Protestants in his country, came to Warsaw. At the Orthodox cathedral in the Praga district of Warsaw, Metropolitan Miron participated in a service that was attended by many people. Countless candles were burning; various priests squirmed in their glistening robes. A wonderful choir sang, many Polish policemen circulated around the cathedral, guarding the prime minister-metropolitan. The people stood on the sidewalks because there was no room inside the cathedral. The metropolitan-prime minister was met at the door of the cathedral by the Warsaw metropolitan, Dionysius, and together they entered the cathedral. People climbed up onto the fence and into trees just to be able to see that splendid ceremony and grand service, at least from a distance.

I was in the cathedral during that time, close to where various foreign diplomats in long black frocks were standing, together with Polish dignitaries who had come from across the border. The singing of the choir, mingled with the smoke of fragrant incense, spread throughout the cathedral. Gold glistened from the restored icons, flags and crosses. But all of these shiny, lifeless forms did not touch my soul in the least. The small Orthodox service in the attic of the old building in Frille made a significantly greater impression on me.

The main centre of ministry among the refugees moved from Ludensheid to Frille. Almost the entire committee of the Slavic Union now lived here and therefore very often the meetings of the committee took place here. All the leading brethren would come from the other camps and we would always have new speakers and larger services. Not long ago the eyes of the refugee believers in Germany had been focused on Ludensheid, but now it was on Frille. Everybody wanted to live here, and if not to live here permanently, then to be present at least once at such a large gathering. Various believers came and visited us.

---

169 Patriarch Miron of Romania and Metropolitan of the Orthodox church was also prime minister of Romania

Brother S. Bychkowski,
director of the church choir in Ludensheid and later in Frille.

During this time various courses were being offered in many camps, especially courses in choir directing. There was also a great need for Bible courses and such courses were made available in Frille. These were not ordinary short-term courses, but this became a true Bible School. Brother V. Gotze came as a teacher to Frille. Many younger brothers came from other camps and the Bible School began its instruction. This was a major achievement for our mutual ministry among the refugees, because many brothers, wherever they are now, former students of that Bible School, are still working today to a greater or smaller extent in God's field. The Bible School began its work while still in Ludensheid and later transferred to Frille where it grew and was renewed with new students.

The large number of believers was very favourable for ministry in Frille, as well as in other camps in the American and English zones, where there arose a great need for spiritual workers. The brethren from the church committees, as well as the Union committee, proposed that the preaching brethren not remain in Frille, but would move to other camps. There were many who listened to this good advice and left for other camps. Because of them, new groups of believers were organized into larger and smaller congregations.

VISITORS FROM ACROSS THE BORDER

News about our life and spiritual work in Germany spread far across the ocean. Immediately after the end of the war, through the military alliance of chaplains, we made contact with our fellow believers in America, Canada, England and other countries. While we were in Frille, the post office began operating and we could freely correspond by letter with the entire Western world.

Before long we were visited by prominent brothers from across the border and from across the ocean. If I am not mistaken Dr. Louis, the general secretary of The World Baptist Association, first visited us. He travelled through the entire list of refugee camps. He also visited our services. He attended the multitudinous gatherings, which were organized, on the occasion of his arrival. One such large gathering was held in Hanover where Dr. Louis and Dr. Bella were welcomed on behalf of the various refugee representatives. Dr. Louis observed our refugee life, appraised our circumstances, saw our large organization and the extent of our ministry and was deeply impressed by all of it. We too were very much satisfied with his reaction but felt that it was not enough. It seemed that Dr. Louis, even if he wanted to, as a foreigner would not fully understand us and would not be able to form the appropriate conclusions regarding our life. Our desire was that someone from our own nation would come to us from across the ocean, "bone from our bone and blood from our blood". This desire was fulfilled in a short time.

Evangelical service in Hanover on the occasion of the arrival of Dr. Louis

One Sunday it was announced that brother K. Hrikmann was coming to visit us from Belgium. The following Sunday we truly had the joy of welcoming this dear guest among us. We all assembled in a large Protestant church, our wonderful choir sang and brother K. Hrikmann was deeply moved by everything that he saw. He saw that the opportunities that we had at the present time for Christian ministry would never again be possible. And he said to us from an overflowing heart:

"Brothers and sisters, the kind of opportunity that you have today for ministry in Christ's field, will never again be possible. God has called you here and therefore cherish this time. Soon you will depart from here, going into the entire world, and what you had here will only be a memory."

Brother K. Hrikmann, together with his wife, visited us.

After visiting our "Jerusalem", brother K. Hrikmann visited other camps and saw the same scene everywhere... a tremendous ministry among the refugees.

The Bible School in Frille.
Seated from the left: H. Boltniev, L. Galustyan, V. Gotze and P. Hordiev

Shortly afterwards, brother P. Deyneka from the United States in North America, who was well-known among the Slavic brethren, visited postwar Europe, which included Germany and our Frille. He also brought us a word of comfort and encouragement. Many services were held in Frille and Weitersheim. Brother P. Deyneka was greatly impressed by our organization and the harmony in our ministry. But, no less than brother K. Hrikmann, he was deeply moved by our material poverty. From a material side, it was a most difficult time for us to live. With every day our food was cut back and any additional rations were reduced. In some families a true hunger was beginning to stare them in the face. Those who somehow could obtain something for themselves, trade for something with the Germans in the surrounding villages, or beg from someone, somehow managed to get ahead. But whoever lived only on that which was provided from the kitchen suffered from hunger. We could only listen to the words of comfort from our visitors from across the ocean, although this was very precious for us. We asked them if they would be able to organize for us some kind of material help from across the border. The brothers wrote down our requests in their notebooks, departed from us as we impatiently waited for their response.

After the service in Weitersheim, during the time when brother P. Deyneka visited the congregation.

I remember that I accompanied brother Deyneka to Lahde, and then returned by myself, walking across the hayfields to Frille. We all knew this path very well, because we often went to Lahde to the post office or to get different products. Among the shrubs and vines flowed a stream and beyond the stream there were flat fields and a deep silence. This was one place that reminded me of Horyn in my native land. As I walked and contemplated, I saw a large group of people coming towards me. Each one of them was carrying a large shiny shovel on his shoulder. They resembled an army carrying rifles. They walked past the bushes and then walked out onto the road that led to Lahde. I learned from a Polish acquaintance that these people were going to a field in Lahde where corpses from concentration camps were buried during the war. Some kind of American military commission had now arrived and the graves were going to be opened. They were searching among the corpses for the body of an English military flyer who, before the very end of the war, had been shot down in the area and they thought he was buried here. I followed after the people.

After we passed Lahde, we saw in a field, a cemetery surrounded with a wire fence where there were uneven graves, which were overgrown with grass. English soldiers were already standing there, wearing long rubber gloves and masks. The people began to dig the green graves and soon opened up a large common grave. I had never seen such a scene before in my life, as I stood there numb before the large opening. An English soldier, in large rubber boots, entered the hole, and tried to lift the head of a corpse which was lying face-down on top of other corpses. The front of the head had already decomposed and fell onto the shoulders of another corpse. A horrible, partially decomposed skull stared up at us from the hole. The people beside the hole gasped in horror and took a step backwards. The soldier walked upon the bodies as if he was walking on sheaves of straw. He was looking through some kind of glass, searching for any remains of decomposed clothing. This was a terrible scene, which I shall never forget! The hole was very wide and filled to the top with decomposing corpses. They were laying one on top of another in the same position in which some angry person threw them in. One was face up, one was on its side, others were face down, and others were twisted with their heads under their feet. But what affected us most was when we saw two corpses, which were lying face down, at the top of the pile with their hands tied behind their backs with wire. This is how they were hung or shot, and still bound they were thrown into the hole.

The commission searched for a long time but was unable to find anything and a command was given to fill up the hole. Who was lying there? Who were these people? Nobody knew. It was related that there were quite a few larger and smaller concentration camps in the surrounding area from which corpses were brought and buried as if they were merely some kind of cattle. It was futile to try to find someone here because the cemetery was very large. The graves, which were all mass graves, were all overgrown with grass and were very numerous.

Not far from the cemetery there was an asphalt road going to Lahde. Apple trees, pear trees and other fruit trees were planted on both sides of the road. The road split just before Lahde, creating a wide intersection on which stood a bronze monument. It was a bust of either Beethoven or Bach; I don't remember now which one. It was facing in the direction of the blackened, excavated cemetery and it seemed to me that its bronze face had become more black. Oh Germany! All your past glory and culture has been greatly blemished by genocide and till the end of time nobody will remove from you these terrible blemishes.

I continued to Frille, broken in heart and soul. An elderly German was doing something in the field and my Polish acquaintance, who was walking with me, said:

"If I had permission, I would go to him, slice him up alive, poke his eyes out and I would be satisfied with that..."

"Good," I said, "but what if he was not guilty?"

My acquaintance did not say anything. I was also quiet. It seemed to us that everything around us was silent. What can be said? Where can one now find the real ones who were guilty of this terrible genocide? They were all hidden in the darkest places. They erased all traces of their evil deeds behind them, they changed their names, they changed their appearances and were living somewhere in large cities afraid of their shadows. To a large extent, the innocent residents of German cities were bearing the blame. Such was the unwritten law of those dreadful times of war.

One Sunday we found out that Dr. Rushbrooke, the president of the World Baptist Alliance, was coming to us from England. We began to make preparations for that event. Brother Bychkowski announced extra choir practices for the programs. We *zubryly*[170] each song several times, desiring that this time our singing would be such as never before. And it seemed to me that it truly was what we had hoped for. That was made possible by the tall Lutheran church, which had exceptionally good acoustics, as well as the focus and preparedness of all the singers. Elderly Dr. Rushbrooke actually got to his feet and looked upward to where our choir was standing. The church was completely filled with people because the Polish learned that the "most senior Baptist" had arrived and they came to see and to hear what he would say. Disturbing rumours were being spread within the camp that Dr. Rushbrroke was already making a list and soon all Baptists would be leaving for America. Because of this, new people began coming to our services, but when they realized that none of us were leaving to America, they stopped coming.

---

170 Crammed by memorization

Dr. Rusbrooke in Frille
From left to right: S. Nischik, a Baptist pastor from London, W. Helech, Dr. Rushbrooke,
H. Boltniev, P. Kaplienko, H. Hordiev, Z. Reczun-Panko and Efimowich

After the large service all our elder brothers, together with the church committee, had meetings with Dr. Rushbrooke. We told him our needs, our hurts, and our requests to our brothers across the border. Dr Rushbrooke listened to us, sympathized with us, comforted us, and told us to patiently wait, because soon we will be receiving material help and after that will come emigration. We waited. We waited patiently but for some brothers this patience wore off. They went to different places, worried, listened to various rumours about emigration and were prepared to travel to the end of the world if only they could leave immediately. They were ready to register to go to Brazil, to distant Venezuela or whoever would receive them, if only they could leave the abnormal life in the camps. Again and again, we all witnessed the fact that although we were mature believers, we had wonderful services, we called ourselves evangelical Christians or Baptists, but we had very little real faith. If God had sustained us until now, then why should we not trust Him fully again? Trusting God was difficult for many. We did not yet know ourselves fully; we did not understand our human nature or our frail faith. Quite a few of the refugee believers did not even consider that once they were across the ocean they would quickly forget their current need which was to break out of hungry Germany, but they would soon desire a new car, a new house, even finer than those of older Americans and Canadians. They would get involved in competing for higher wages; plunging headlong into materialism and forgetting everything that God had done for them in the past. In Frille, nobody thought about that but unfortunately that is what happened to many of them.

Dr. Rusbrooke saw our organized ministry, saw our needs, and especially our physical needs and left us with the best thoughts and empathy.

The head of the Ukrainian Evangelical Association of North America, pastor Wasyl Kuziw, also visited our congregations in Frille and Weitersheim. In addition to our congregation he also visited other camps, especially the Ukrainian ones in the American zones. He attended our Evangelical-Baptist services; he became acquainted with our ministry and held large evangelical services in the camps, which were also attended by our believers. Pastor Kuziw came to Germany as a representative of the YMCA. He had much influence in this well-known international organization. He had many connections with Protestants throughout the world, and therefore was able to organize quite a few evangelical Reformed pastors, who had worked in Poland before the war. Various Orthodox and Catholic intelligentsia were also drawn to him. Large choirs, conducted by well-known refugee conductors, sang during his services, but there were always people there who *ne shukali Isusa, a chliba kusa*[171]. They took advantage of the generosity of Pastor W. Kuziw, taking advantage of his popularity in UNNRA, within the American military authority as well as among American Protestants. Pastor W. Kuziw helped many of them, but later they abandoned him and were never grateful to him. Not only they, but many former, pre-war evangelical Reformed pastors, for whom pastor W. Kuziw did many good things, they later paid him back with dark ingratitude. And if anyone in life had experienced ingratitude from people for the good he did, it was pastor W. Kuziw, a person with a wide heart.

All of our guests from across the border saw our life, saw our needs and accurately understood them.

---

171 "Were not looking for Jesus, but for a piece of bread". Possibly a reference to John 6:26.

Pastor W. Kuziw in the American Zone with Ukrainian Evangelical Reformed pastors

HELP FROM ACROSS THE BORDER

Our guests from across the border left us but evidently they told about us wherever it was necessary. They touched the hearts of those across the ocean who had the same faith as we did and help came quickly. Soon the civil postal system began to operate again and we received our first letters from across the ocean. Up till now we had carried on correspondence by letters with our brethren across the ocean through the American or English military chaplaincy, but it was very limited and irregular. Now we would go every day to the German civil post office in Lahde where we had a mailbox for our Slavic Union, and there arrived letters, magazines and parcels containing food products. How delightful and pleasant it was to receive those first news from our pre-war acquaintances and fellow-workers in God's field from across the ocean! It was especially enjoyable to receive Christian magazines. The war in Europe had destroyed our spiritual literary ministry. Not a single evangelical periodical was being published, and therefore we truly were hungry for the printed evangelical word. When we received our first copies of *Chrystianski Visnyk*[172] and *Seyattelya Istyni*[173], we could hardly believe that there was still such a country in the world where our magazines and spiritual literature continued to be produced.

---

172 Christian Herald
173 Sower of the Truth

Refugee congregation in Frille

Later we found that in the USA, our pre-war publication, *Pislanetz Prawdy*[174], was again being published by its former editor, Brother L. Zhapko-Potopowich. The first issue of the new *Pislanetz Prawdy* came to the Lysenko camp and when the brothers from Frille found out about that, they sent me, together with another brother, to bring the issue to them. The road to Hanover was long. We searched for a long time among all the believers in all the camps before we found the first issue of *Pislanetz Prawdy*. It was being circulated from person to person, from barrack to barrack. Eventually we found it and in the evening we began the trip to bring it to our camp in Frille, as if it was some kind of relic. During the trip we read it from beginning to end and then from the end to the beginning. We did not read it; we literally devoured it with a hungry heart and soul. It seemed that it had come to us, not from Chester,[175] a place unknown to us, but from our native land, from Lviv…

Besides the Christian periodicals, we soon began to receive parcels containing food from across the ocean. They arrived in an organized manner to our Union in Germany and then distributed to the believers in all the camps. In every camp, where there was a congregation, brethren were assigned who were responsible for an equitable distribution of the

---

174 Messenger of Truth
175 The magazine was first published in Chester, Pennsylvania

parcels. For example, in the larger congregations the following brothers were responsible for the distribution of parcels: Frille and Weitershaim – H. Boltniev, P. Hordiev and M. Podworniak; Hanover - Z. Reczun-Panko, F. Kaplun and I. Maykut; Holzminden –P. Rutsky and D. Bolsunowski; Lintorf – J. Volkovich, I. Piddhoretsky and Il. Kubryn; Lubeck –I. Holonko and Ivan Mankowski; Munich – D. Yasko and S. Nischik. In the smaller camps, the leaders of the group were responsible for the distribution of parcels. This was a very delicate and responsible work which encountered various problems, various human characteristics and whims, but I don't remember any major misunderstanding or complaint occurring anywhere.

Brother Nikodim Lukianchuk greatly helped the refugees in Germany

Organized material assistance was coming from the World Baptist Society, from brother Neprash, from the Baptist Society in Denmark, from the Russian-Ukrainian Association in USA, from the Ukrainian Mission Bible Society in the USA and Canada, from brother P. Deyneka and others.

Quite a few Evangelical-Baptist congregations in USA and Canada sent care parcels to individual addresses known to them and in this manner they rescued their fellow-believers, if not from real starvation, at least from severe malnutrition.

Ukrainian believers in Munich receive the first New Testaments, distributed by bothers S. Nischik and M. Tesluk

I recall the first care parcel that I received. It was from brother W. Bura of Detroit and contained canned meat and sardines. The parcel came exactly at a time when we truly had nothing to eat. After that, parcels began to arrive more frequently, almost every week. I received them very often and therefore, to all the brothers and sisters who personally sent me that help, a sincere and heartfelt thank you!

At this time a special thank-you must be expressed to brother N. Lukianchuk for all of his help. While we were still travelling with the missionary choir in the American zone, during the time when there was still no contact between Europe and America by mail, brother Lukianchuk searched through various military chaplains for ways to help us. Later when normal correspondence opened up, he committed all his zeal and energy to helping the refugees. Refugee believers in Germany received hundreds of parcels from him, and later also received affidavits to depart to the USA.

Our refugee life during our stay in Frille was characterized by a series of different events, but especially it was known for the vibrant spiritual ministry in the camps within the American and English zones. Many brothers who preached, heeding the good counsel of the Union committee, left our large congregation to live permanently in other camps, but especially in those camps where there was a need for spiritual workers. Those who stayed behind in Frille were also not idle – everyone tried to do something for our mutual benefit, for the Lord and for their neighbours. From time to time we organized groups consisting of several brothers who took with them rations for two-three days and went on short missionary trips to those camps where there were small groups of believers, but where there was not a full-time minister. Many times we travelled from here to the city of Hanover where the Ukrainian camp called Lysenko was located, one of the largest in the American zone. There was a large congregation of our people in the camp; brothers J. Repetsky, and F. Kaplun ministered there, and later, brothers Z. Reczun-Panko and Iv. Polischuk transferred there. We travelled to the camp in Haidenau, which was close to Hamburg, where a fine congregation also existed. Later we travelled to Cologne where there were several camps with many believers in well-organized churches. Brothers H. Domashovetz, Iv. Pidhoretsky. Il. Kubryn, J. Wolkowich and others fervently ministered in Cologne-Mulheim and Lintorf.

When believers first arrived in Cologne-Mulheim, there were only a few of them, but later this congregation increased up to seventy members. The first preacher in the congregation was brother H. Domashovetz, his assistant was brother Ivan Pidhoretsky. Later when brother Domashovetz moved permanently to the American zone, the leader of the congregation was brother Ivan Pidhoretsky, and his assistant was brother Ilya Kubryn. All of these brethren, who were longtime former ministers in Halychyna, continued to minister in Germany with unwavering strength and commitment and God continued to bless their work.

Far to the north, close to Belgium, was the Bathorn camp where many of our people lived; there was also a congregation of believers. There was much spiritual work to do because the refugees were scattered throughout all of Germany.

I recall one very unique camp in Haidenau, not far from Hamburg, which we visited several times. The people lived in large, metal barracks that resembled a large barrel. During the winter it was very cold in these *bochkakh*[176] and during the summer it was very hot. We held our evangelical services in such a large *botchtsi* because it was large and accommodated several dozen[177] listeners.

Truly our life as refugees was very interesting, full of various incidents and experiences. The history of the beginning of the individual Evangelical-Baptist congregations in the countless camps was also interesting, but I don't know if we would ever be able to describe the entire refugee history. Perhaps that would not be possible because many of us have forgotten it a long time ago, immersed in American and Canadian prosperity...

Z. Reczun-Panko
treasurer of the Slavic Union

---

176 barrels
177 The word used here is *decyatki*, or multiples of ten

During that time the Slavic Union was at its highest level of organization in terms of strength and activity. An information letter was printed regularly every month. The Union had its own account for which brother Z. Reczun-Panko was the long-time treasurer. Everyone contributed their donations to the account from which many spiritual workers from the entire association received financial assistance for their travelling expenses. The Bible School carried out its teaching ministry; conferences were called for spiritual growth and to discuss business matters. The most attended event was our conference in Lubeck, which was held on September 5-8, 1946; during this time our travelling choir sang for the final time. An even bigger conference was held the following year in the city of Hanover.

During this period we also travelled to the most northerly part of Germany, the city of Kiel. Our choir visited several camps there, where our people lived. The barracks there were large, spreading out on a wide hill. Beneath the hill glistened the blue North Sea on which there were always countless fishing boats with white sails. There was also an evangelical congregation in that camp.

The Slavic Union had forty-one active missionary workers at that time. An article, printed in the Union periodical for the month of July, 1946, clearly described their work where the following was printed: "The Gracious Lord has blessed our work everywhere. We can joyfully report on baptisms which took place in several localities: in Bergdorf, 7 people were baptized; in the Hanover area -15; in Ludensheid – 35; in Cologne – 4; in Kiel – 1; in the Munich area – 48; in the Kesel area - 17".

From 1946, similar successes were happening in all the camps until the time when we departed from German soil.

While still in Ludensheid, we could see ominous black clouds looming on the bright horizon of our refugee life. It began as small friction and misunderstandings between Ukrainian believers and the so-called "Slavs" and followed us in various aspects of our work to Frille; they appeared and disappeared again and this continued until the conference in Lubeck. Peace-loving individuals on both sides continually tried to put out the sparks of mistrust, disagreements and malice, but there were also those among us who stirred the flames, adding fuel to the fire, looking for guilty parties on only one side, but in fact, there were guilty ones on both sides. The conference in Lubeck was unable to extinguish that fire, but rather made it even worse.

A portion of the delegates and guests at the conference in Lubeck

I tried very hard to bypass this sad page of my memoirs, but it was not possible because all of this happened within our Christian family. All of us endured this, all of us refugees were saddened by it, and therefore to omit this episode in our life was not possible.

Nineteen Ukrainian preacher-delegates from the different camps, as well as several Belarusian brothers, made a proposal to the conference to separate the ministry of the Slavic Union into autonomous groups; that is, Russian, Polish, Ukrainian and Belarusian. The Slavic Union would be made up from those four groups. The proposal was to maintain the Slavic Union, but it would be divided by nationality and the preachers from each nationality would be responsible for their own ministry. We would continue to be one association, we would gather for a combined conference at which each group would report on their work, etc.

This proposal did not appeal to some brethren from the Union committee, they strongly opposed it and considered it as division among believers. They preached a number of sermons about the unity of believers, and all of this had a great affect on the delegates at the conference. After a vote, the proposal of the Ukrainian believers was not accepted. Not only was the proposal not accepted, but the whole situation seemed to suggest that the Ukrainians, not only wanted to leave the Slavic Union, but also wanted to create division in the Union. In reality, this was not the case. The only reason to create a new group was to energize the ministry and make it more successful.

We returned from the conference in Lubeck with a weight upon our hearts. Ukrainians, Russians, Belarusians and Polish were all travelling in the same train cars, going to the same camp, but instinctively we felt that some kind of wall had been created between us, some type of intolerance was developing among us. No one did anything intentional to reinforce this, but it grew by itself, casting an ominous shadow on the Christian unity that we enjoyed until now. Several specifically selected preachers committed themselves to speak about the matter and without any reason attacked Ukrainian delegates, urging the conference to beware of those *prozvodyashchikh razdeleniye*[178]

As usual on Sunday there was a large service in Frille at the Lutheran church and a similar service was held in the afternoon in Weitersheim. Our choir sang majestically, the brethren preached and it seemed that there was no trace of the unnecessary misunderstanding in Lubeck. But that was only the way it appeared; in reality the misunderstanding in Lubeck had only started, it had only been sown. Now it spread to all the camps, it fell upon every heart where it either withered or grew; it all depended upon which heart it had fallen.

This division was especially evident at the conference in Hanover. Delegates came from all of Germany: Ukrainians, Belarusians, Russians and Polish. At once it was noticed that two camps existed here, two trains of thought and two directions. For some reason Ukrainians were frowned upon which caused them to consolidate and stick together.

Soon after the conference there was a baptism service in our congregation. This time it took place in the Weser River. We all stood together in a large group on the steep riverbank. Our song flowed above the river, our prayers rose up and in spite of everything, each one of us thought and was

---

[178] Russian for "creators of division"

deeply convinced that for believers there was nothing better than to live in one group. This was the command of our Lord and all sincere believers in Germany strived to fulfill this commandment. Unfortunately the command was not fulfilled the way it was intended. The ones responsible before God for this will not be those peace-loving believers who tried to make peace but rather the individuals who didn't care about peace and unity; individuals who learned nothing from their long wandering.

A portion of the delegates at the conference in Hanover

LITERATURE-PUBLICATION MINISTRY

Brother H. Domashovetz,
member of the Board of editors of the magazine *Doroha Prawdy*

Although the conference in Lubeck rejected the proposal to organize into nationalistic divisions, it did promote a very good resolution: to publish a magazine in each of the Slavic languages. The conference appointed a board of editors for each magazine, whose task it was to initiate the work. A similar of board of editors was appointed for the Ukrainian magazine, which included the following brothers: M. Podworniak, H. Domashovetz and I. Tarasiuk. It was my fate to become editor-in-chief.

I recall that one day our board of editors gathered in Frille for a meeting. We invited several other Ukrainian brothers for advice and discussed how to get the work started. During that time there were already various magazines and newspapers in many of the refugee camps; all of them were published periodically and we also decided to publish the first issue of our magazine in a foreign land in a similar style. On each question in our discussions we encountered very difficult obstacles but our great zeal for this work filled us with hope. We decided to publish a magazine, but now we had to come up with and agree upon a name for it. I thought, thought but nothing came out. All the suggested names had either existed in the past or exist today in the free world, and none of them suited our situation. We needed a name that reflected our current life and would speak for itself right from the start. Finally brother H. Domashovetz literally rose to his feet and said:

"Brothers, the best name for our periodical will be: *Doroha Prawdy*[179] which will be abbreviated as D.P. Are we not all D.P.'s? Let our publication have the same name."

We all accepted the name suggested by brother Domashovetz; we named our periodical *Doroha Prawdy* and went to work. Brother S. Bychkowski allowed us to use his typewriter, one of the brothers obtained a cyclostyle matrix[180] and we began to transfer the articles, poems and other material onto stencils for the first issue. The work was difficult, we were doing this work for the first time in our life, but we made progress and impatiently waited for the first refugee periodical to come out.

When the material had all been assembled we then realized that we did not have any paper. Fortunately brother I. Tarasiuk had as many as two

---

179 The Way of Truth
180 a type of duplicating machine in which ink was forced through a stencil onto the paper.

pairs of shoes; he agreed to sell one pair of shoes and with the money buy some paper. Soon we received the paper and the first issue of our refugee evangelical magazine, *Doroha Prawdy*, for the month of November, 1946, came out into the world. It was very poor, characterless and meager, exactly like its editors and readers.

The civil post office was already in operation, so we mailed our magazine throughout all of Germany and also sent it across the ocean. From that moment we went farther and farther ahead in our effort. I walked across beautiful German fields many times every month from Frille to Weitersheim where brother Bychkowski lived, hammered on his typewriter and then returned home, organizing everything in my mind, meditating, thinking and re-thinking, because the greatest responsibility for this work fell upon me. I gave up all my time, all my rest, and God gave me strength, patience and everything else. Our periodical was published regularly. Besides the editor, other brothers took part in the work, especially S. Bychkowski, W. Siery, F. Lucyk, I. Barchuk and others. God greatly blessed the publication of the magazine because this was the only Ukrainian evangelical magazine in all of Germany, which came out regularly until the time of the departure to the USA of the last editor, brother O. Harbuziuk.

The magazine *Doroha Prawdy* was initially printed under the so-called "manuscript rights"[181] on a cyclostyle; the print was very unclear and its external appearance was poor. After my departure to Canada, the magazine was turned over to brothers O. Harbuziuk and H. Domashovetz, who changed its format and printed it using "true fonts".[182] In this manner *Doroha Prawdy* matched the finest Ukrainian religious magazines, which were being published in Germany during that time. It fulfilled its great mandate for the glory of God and the benefit of our brotherhood. Later the magazine *Doroha Prawdy* became the voice of the Ukrainian-Evangelical Baptist Church in Germany.

During that postwar time in Germany there were quite a few newspapers and magazines published, but almost all of them were published

---

181 An article published by the author who automatically owns the copyright for that article.

182 A method of typesetting where molten metal was injected into a mold which had the shape of the character. The linotype was an example of typecasting machine used for printing small magazines and newspapers during that time.

according to "manuscript rights" on a cyclostyle, and were very poor in their outward appearance and technical format. When the magazine, *Doroha Prawdy*, was published using true type fonts it then resembled other foreign religious magazines, which were being published in Germany and was authorized by the American military authority.

Brother Ilarion Tarasiuk,
member of the editorial board of the magazine *Doroha Prawdy*

Alongside the publication of the magazine *Doroha Prawdy*, a small publishing group was formed and with some hard and cooperative work we were able to publish several books. We published a collection of Christmas poems called "Star of Bethlehem"[183], a poetical dialogue by brother G. Domashovetz called "Duel"[184], a small booklet by S.B. entitled "Unity"[185], a small booklet by brother I. Barchuk, "Mother of God"[186] as well as several booklets by brother F. Sitarz: "The Church of Christ is not an Organization but an Organism" and other books. This small publication effort was the beginning of an entire range of publications, which our Ukrainian brotherhood was able to produce in Germany. This time we were not using an ordinary cyclostyle, but rather using "true fonts". Brother S. Bychkowski published a songbook with notes called "Melodiyi Skytaltsya"[187] (on a cyclostyle). Under the editorship of H. Domashovetz, two thousand copies of the book "The Articles of Faith of the Ukrainian Evangelical-Baptist Church" were published; brother S. Bychkowski published a second songbook with notes called *Ridna Pisnya na Chuzheni*; two editions of *Pisnyi Christiyan*, a songbook without notes, were also published ; a novel by N. Lukianchuk, *V Odnomu Seli*; the research of professor T. Hrebinka, *Pro Katolistki Dogmatism*; a collection of poetry by H. Domashovetz, *Z Burchlivix Dniv*[188]; and a very valuable publication, the New Testament in a small format. In addition H. Domashovetz published another two of his works, "The Ukrainian Evangelical Movement" and "Religion or Faith." L. Bykowski managed the publishing house in Germany.

Regarding publications from among all the Slavic refugee groups, the Ukrainian believers were the most active group. The printed evangelical word spread throughout all of Western Germany, creating for our brotherhood a wide recognition, but above all, it was awakening sinful souls

---

183 *Zirka Vyflyemska*
184 *Dvoby*
185 *odnist*
186 *Bozha Mati"*
187 Melodies of the Refugee
188 Publications mentioned are; "A Native Song in a Foreign land" by S. Bychkowski; songbook, "Christian Songs"; a novel, "In One Village" by N. Lukianchuk; "About Catholic Dogma" by Prof. T. Hrebinka; a collection of poems "From Tumultous Days" by H. Domashovetz.

to a new life in Jesus Christ. This was the most important goal of each author, the goal of our entire brotherhood and the goal of our small publishing group.

I believe that after the Lubeck conference, only one issue of a Russian evangelical periodical was published, as well as several issues of the Polish magazine, *Slowo Prawdy*[189], a pre-war Baptist magazine published in Poland. I don't remember the exact date, but I believe that *Slowo Prawdy* was printed for the final time on March-April, 1947 and after that it was not published.

I don't know if there was any attempt to publish a magazine in Belarusian. I believe that the Belarusian board of editors did not produce even a single issue; however, there was a Belarusian page in the Union periodical.

In 1946, while still in Ludensheid, a Polish songbook called *Piesni Pielgrzyma*[190] was published, and in 1947 in the American zone, a fine Russian songbook, entitled *Pesni Skitaltsya*[191], was published, which was very essential for the Russian believers.

Thus as we went through our refugee life we cared, not only for the oral proclamation of the gospel, but also for the printing and distribution of spiritual literature. During this time significant progress was made in this matter, especially by the Ukrainian Association.

The inadequate publishers of the magazine *Doroha Prawdy* found accommodation in my home. On the other side of the wall lived brothers W. Gotze and L. Galustyan, teachers at the Bible School; therefore, everyday we would have many visitors. Behind the house there was a German garden, beyond the garden there glistened a narrow stream. These were memorable times!

---

189 A Word of Truth
190 Songs of the Pilgrim
191 Songs of the Refugees

**Brother O. Harbuziuk,
the final editor of the magazine *Doroha Prawdy***

It is in order to point out that brother Nikodim Lukianchuk from America made a large financial donation for the publication of Ukrainian Christian literature but especially for the publication of the magazine, *Doroha Prawdy*, during the time when the magazine was being printed using "true fonts" in the city of Kronberg.

The Evangelical-Baptist Association was not the only one publishing Ukrainian Christian literature, there was also notable work being done by Ukrainian evangelical Reformed pastor, W. Borowski. It must be said that he made contact with America through the military chaplaincy even before us, and at the beginning we could only obtain Ukrainian books, magazines and Bibles from across the ocean through him. In Germany, pastor

W. Borowski was involved in *Biblioteka Ukrayinskoho Yevanhelyka*[192] and published a whole series of useful works on the cyclostyle.

The Slavic Union, and later the Ukrainian Evangelical–Baptist Church, was sincerely committed to the publication and distribution of Christian literature. In every issue of our periodicals the need for Christian literature was always emphasized. For example, the Union magazine for April-May, 1947 wrote: "Let us remember that we must spread Christian literature among unsaved people. This is our holy obligation. Literature accomplishes a very large amount of missionary work..."

The Slavic Union had a sufficient amount of Christian literature in the Russian language because all the missions abroad, who worked among Slavic nations, cared about this need. But regarding Ukrainian literature, we had to care about it ourselves. It is true that later when there was normal contact by mail with our brothers in the USA and Canada, Christian literature in Ukrainian began to arrive. A large amount of assistance came from the great promoter of the printed evangelical word, the late brother Joseph Shkula.

Work on the magazine, *Doroha Prawdy*.
From left to right: F. Lucyk, I. Tarasiuk, M. Podworniak

---

192 Library of Ukrainian Evangelicals

The former Wernigerode society, *Switlo na Skhodi*[193], was a great help in the publication of Ukrainian Christian literature. It now operated in the city of Stuttgart. Our acquaintance, brother Dyck lived there, and because of his efforts this society re-issued several former pamphlets by professor W. Marcinowki, which had a large impact on its readers. Several works by brother I. Barchuk were also published; notable among them were a collection of sayings in Russian in three volume called *Iskry Uma*[194], *Dlya Koho Isnuye Svit*[195] and others.

The society *Svitlo na Shkodi* had extensive contacts with all Protestants in Western Europe. Because of its long time traditions it was closely linked with the spiritual work among the Ukrainian people and therefore sincerely assisted us with Christian literature which they published themselves as well as searched for it for us in other places. One time we received from this society fifteen hundred copies of Dr. I. Ohienko's translation of the New Testament, and there were many such occasions.

A special recognition must be given to the Slavic Mission in Czechoslovakia which did much to distribute the Word of God among all refugees during the war as well as afterwards. It often reviewed the translation by professor Dr. Ivan Ohienko and distributed many thousands copies of it among our people. This mission printed Christian literature in Russian; it published a Russian evangelical songbook, a Bible History and a calendar for daily readings of the Word of God. All this spiritual bread began circulating among all the camps. Ukrainians were especially grateful to that Society for the publication of a Ukrainian New Testament in several editions.

The main promoter for the distribution of Christian literature was brother Stepan Osadchiy, who visited every camp countless times, especially in the English zone, and handed out Christian literature wherever he went.

It was very difficult to print anything in Germany during that time because there was a lack of paper. Not only could the refugees not obtain any paper anywhere, but also the Germans did not have any either. If there

---

193 Light in the East
194 Sparks of the mind
195 For Whom does the World Exist

was any paper it was in the custody of the occupying allied military authority, and to obtain any was very difficult. For example when the society *Svitlo as Shkodi* wished to print Christian literature, the following information was printed in our Association magazine for January-February, 1947: "It is with joy that we announce that the society, *Svitlo na Shkodi* desires to begin printing holy Scripture, Christian books and tracts. The committee decided to support this initiative and to help the society in its enormous undertaking. First of all, at the request of the society, we need to systematically organize the collection of used paper, old magazines, paper boxes from parcels and send everything to the society who will receive half a kilogram of clean paper for every kilogram of used paper. To organize this important and useful effort, we are requesting that without delay individuals be appointed in every congregation and every group, wherever our believers live, who would collect and send the paper. Please send the names of those who will be collecting used paper to brother Ivan Barchuk, but for parcels containing used paper, send these to Stuttgart to the name of brother F. Dyck."

This was the post-war situation in the publication of Christian literature.

The committee of the Slavic Union was deeply interested in Christian literature. They decided to organize an Association library, which would be located wherever there was a Bible School. Brother I. Tarasiuk was appointed as the librarian and he fervently began collecting various books for the library. Unfortunately this work did not have much success because brother I. Tarasiuk soon left for England. Secondly, there were very few books among our believers. They all came to Germany without anything and were not able to acquire anything here. For the majority of them, if they had any books, they lost them all in the whirlpool of wartime events. For these reasons, it was not possible to acquire a larger library.

We distributed Christian literature mainly in those camps where there were no believers. This was the channel, which opened the way to becoming acquainted with people who had never heard about us.

I remember that during the trip of our missionary choir in the American zone, in Augsberg we met the Ukrainian writer, V. Rusalski, who is now deceased. He knew nothing about our movement, but after obtaining a

Ukrainian Christian tract, he became interested and searched for our choir. We became acquainted with him at that time.

In our camp we also met Yurii Klen, a famous Ukrainian poet. He, as a Protestant, was interested in our work, and was very favourably receptive to our performances.

Candidates for baptism in Berlin, 1944

Unfortunately there was a very small amount of Ukrainian Christian literature and we could not fill even one-half of the needs. Some of the leading brothers in the Ukrainian camps turned to Czechoslovakia and to the USA. They soon received literature but it was in Russian. Although this literature was truly beneficial with deep spiritual content and Ukrainian believers read it gladly, it was not possible to distribute it to people who were not familiar or did nor know evangelical truth. Our brothers across the border could not at all fathom this common truth, that every nation must carry the Word of God in their own language.

THE UKRAINIAN EVANGELICAL-BAPTIST CHURCH

After the conferences in Lubeck and Hanover, the delegates and spiritual workers who ministered in the wide field among the refugees all went their separate ways to their camps, to their congregations and groups beginning with Hamburg in northern Germany all the way to Fussen in the distant south. Life continued the same as it was before the conference –daily life, work, various worries and concerns. Many Polish from our camp became tired and exhausted by refugee life and departed to Poland. They did not want to leave without doing some damage, leaving some kind of mark of their being in Germany. Looting, rioting and drunken behaviour began in our village and spread to other villages. Later they began to set German homes in Frille on fire. UNRRA, as well as the English military authority, had a great deal of trouble with those Polish rioters who were leaving for Poland and simply waved their hands at everything and loudly said: "for me it's all the same!" To slow down these fires, the camp authority set up a regular guard during the night. On a designated night each resident of Frille took their turn walking the dark streets of the village and guarding the buildings.

Summer passed and a wonderful German autumn began. Long, twisting rows of cranes were flying above our Frille. We followed them with longing glances and thought how we would also like to fly somewhere like that. But that time had not yet arrived and for now we had to wait patiently.

The winter of 1947 was marked by large snowstorms and severe frosts. It was cold in our homes. We were given only small amounts of firewood and so we sat all day, fully dressed as if we were leaving on a trip. We walked through deep snow to the nearby forest and gathered dry brushwood and branches, because it was forbidden to cut down any wood. Therefore, this winter was very memorable for many of us. But thank God, as well as our brothers and sister from across the ocean, for the parcels, because at least we were not hungry that winter.

Spiritual ministry continued in all the camps, without decreasing in fervour. However, in several places, that what had happened in Lubeck did not disappear without having an effect. In some of the camps, within our large family of refugees, friction arose between Ukrainians and Slavic people. The consequences of this were that on January 15-16, 1947, a group of Ukrainian preachers gathered for their own meeting in Munich and officially organized the Ukrainian Evangelical-Baptist Church. An executive was elected under the leadership of Brother S. Nischik and the Ukrainian Evangelical-Baptist church began its work, separate from the Slavic Union. It had its field of ministry and its own congregations.

To write about the formation of the Ukrainian Evangelical-Baptist Church, and its later work, is the most difficult page in all my memoirs. The difficulty was not because the Ukrainian Evangelical-Baptist Church tarnished itself with some kind of unchristian behaviour, or that the leading brothers violated some evangelical principle. It was difficult because later a wide variety of rumours were spread about the Ukrainian Evangelical-Baptist Church, which were far from the truth. And therefore, I am afraid that I would stray far from what had actually happened regarding this matter. I would like to sincerely say that which I most clearly remembered, what I personally saw, what I had experienced and suffered through and to say this from a clear heart and conscience.

Until my departure from Frille to Canada, I continued to be a member of the Slavic congregation in Frille. My personal conviction was that if we, that is, Ukrainians, Russians, Polish and Belarusians, were together during the difficult times of the war, then we can still live together. If we endured hunger, hid from bombs, helped one another as brothers in Christ, as is fitting for the children of God, then why could we not live in the same way now after God preserved our lives and sent us freedom? It was not only I who thought in this way, but also the majority of Christian refugees from all nations. God helped us so much during the course of the war. We began living as one family in the camps; our closeness was so tight and so deep, that to think that someone might somehow divide us filled our hearts with worry and horror.

Missionary workers of the Ukr. Ev.-Baptist Church in Germany

But not everyone thought that way. There were many brothers, especially in the Slavic Union, and even within the committee, who could not in any way understand why Ukrainians required their own language. For example, they had nothing against the Polish when they demanded their own language during the services. They had nothing against the Latvians or Estonians, but they did not understand this same desire by Ukrainian believers. Perhaps there were some reckless actions by several Ukrainian brothers, but the main reason why the Ukrainians decided to carry out their ministry independently was that after the conference in Lubeck, several of the older brothers from the Slavic Union began ignoring the Ukrainian preachers. They regarded any love by Ukrainians for their language or for their nation as a sin. This attitude led the Ukrainian preachers to feel that they were redundant within the Slavic Union. They were offended and began to look for ways to work independently. Another significant reason was that Ukrainians wanted to appear before the American authorities as a separate, clearly defined nation, and they also wanted to present the Ukrainian spiritual ministry among their people in the same way.

I remember that during the time when the Ukrainian Evangelical-Baptist Church was organized, at Christmas or Easter, the Ukrainian press, would print a Christmas or Easter message from the hierarchy of the Ukrainian Orthodox Church. Alongside there would be printed a similar message which was signed by the head of the Ukrainian Evangelical-Baptist Church. Several Ukrainian preachers attached a great deal of significance to that, rejoicing that both were considered as equals, but actually there was no great benefit for our ministry. We were especially treated as equals at those times when we were visited by many visitors from abroad, when we were considered to be among those Ukrainian organizations which were not headed up by Catholic priests. But ultimately, children of God should not go about and forcefully demand that the world should "recognize" us because when it "recognizes" us, then we would become equal with it and slowly our fall would come.

After the Ukrainian Evangelical-Baptist Church was organized, there was some friction among the refugee believers, but nothing terrible or tragic ever developed anywhere. In general there was a sound mind, faith and brotherly love among us. For example, there were many informed Ukrainians in our large congregation in Frille. The congregation called itself Slavic, but its sympathies were on the side of the Ukrainian Evangelical-Baptist Church. We could have easily created a "dissatisfied" group and divided the church, but such a thought never even entered the mind of anyone of us. God gave us His grace; we lived in brotherly unity with all believers until our very departure across the border. The same situation was also true in other camps, especially those in the English zone.

After the Ukrainian Evangelical-Baptist Church began, it also started its own publication on whose pages Slavic workers could also publish their work. For example, when brother W. Husaruk, the head of the Slavic Union returned from the All-World Baptist Congress, which took place in Denmark, he published his long and wonderful report and his impressions of the Congress on the pages of *Doroha Prawdy*.

There were sincere Christians on both sides who sought agreement, fellowship, love and unity. But because there were also those who hated the Ukrainian language without any reason, it was not possible to bring their Ukrainian brothers to any true agreement and unity.

God, like a good Father, loved all of us the same. He continued to bless the work of the Slavic Union; He also blessed the work of the Ukrainian

Evangelical-Baptist Church. There were quite a few congregations in the American zone, which belonged to the Ukrainian Evangelical-Baptist Church. The majority of the Ukrainian preachers were in the American zone where the entire Ukrainian evangelical ministry was concentrated.

The Ukrainian Evangelical-Baptist Church in Germany held a very large number of wonderful celebrations, especially baptisms, which took place several times in Korbach, Aschaffenburg, Bathorn, Munich, Pforzheom and other German places. The German believers allowed our people to use their churches. The Ukrainian word and song resounded in these places in Germany, where it had never been heard before. Quite a large number of new people were converted to the Lord. The Ukrainian Evangelical movement had its adherents among the Ukrainian intelligentsia as well as the common people. In the American zone, professor T. Hrebinka turned to the Lord. He was a professor at a Ukrainian university. Rev. H. Domashovetz baptized him in 1947.

Fellowship meal during the conference of the
Ukrainian Evangelical-Baptist Church in Munich

The Ukrainian Evangelical-Baptist Church in Germany had several large spiritual-growth conferences as well as conferences to resolve business matters. I had the privilege of attending one such conference. It took place July 12-14, 1947 in the city of Munich. The summer days were beautiful as a whole group of us set out from Frille. First of all, it was a pleasure to see unforgettable Munich where we had once travelled with our choir. Secondly, it was a pleasure to meet with many brothers and sisters and especially to be present at a Ukrainian conference, to see its work, and to experience its spirit. It took place in a large camp where a large number of people gathered. There were 57 delegates registered at this conference and over 150 guests were present.

The conference selected the leaders for its ministry and made action plans. Everything that we observed and experienced at the conference lifted our spirits. No one there offended or attacked their brothers from the Slavic Union, no one there was involved in any kind of politics, but only considered the question of how to best carry out the spiritual ministry within their nation.

The conference was a time of spiritual renewal. We listened to a whole series of deep messages from our preachers and enjoyed the singing of our wonderful songs.

Young people from the Ukrainian Evangelical-Baptist Church at their conference in the city of Munich

Germany – this is a country, which in the past, was noted for its high culture, its civilization and progress. One can see large museums and various historical monuments in every German city. Many of those memorials are now destroyed but a large number are still undamaged. Therefore, travelling around Germany, we did not pass any opportunity to observe these memorials. We visited many museums, the largest European zoos, and ancient cathedrals on hills and on islands. When the Ukrainian Evangelical-Baptist conference ended, our youth group from Frille decided to go to the Chiemsee Palace[196] that was famous throughout all of Germany. It was not far from Munich. The youth from the American zone joined us and we went as a large group.

Chiemsee Palace was on a large island. Surrounding the island was a clear and deep lake. The island looked like a large green hat in the lake. There were many trees on the island, especially oak trees, which concealed a king's palace.

A boat brought us to the island. Together, with many other tourists, we disembarked on the shore and walked along a path through a dense forest. Soon we saw a clearing, surrounded by trees that resembled a wreath, and in that clearing stood a wonderful king's palace. Large cement steps, which were somewhat cracked because of their age, led up to the palace. In front of the steps was a wide veranda, and still farther there were flowerbeds with beautiful roses and a pool with clear water. Around this pool stood various figures carved from white marble. They were mainly of women who were holding bouquets of flowers and large harps. Diverging from the fountain were narrow, cement paths going out in different directions and disappearing into green bushes of lilacs and cherry trees. Once various kings and queens walked on those same paths, the finest artists from Europe once came here. The most famous poets and writers wrote their timeless compositions and various monuments of them remain. And now we were walking along those same paths and listening to the wistful whispering of the ancient oaks.

We went inside the palace, taking our shoes off at the entrance. We saw large rooms, we saw such beauty that was impossible to describe in words. There were many paintings, many sculptures made of gold and marble, figures of birds and animals. Every room, every corridor and even the smallest corner were covered with flowered carpets upon which we walked in soft slippers. Our eyes shifted back and forth, becoming disoriented and it was not clear what we were looking at. The guide continued explaining everything. This was the bedroom of the king, this was a room for guests, this was the library, and this was the

---

196 The castle called Herrenchiemsee is located on Chiemsee Island near Munich

last chair upon which the king sat. From here the king went through the bushes to the nearby lake and ... drowned himself. That was the end of the king. Even now, people are afraid to swim in that lake because they say that it is dominated by evil spirits.

We crossed to a second island in a boat where we explored an old Catholic church, which was overgrown on all sides with wild hops. It was always dark inside the church. Only a faint red light flickered faintly lighting up frightening dark figures of Roman popes and other "saints". The church was built several hundred years ago when severe Catholic terror raged in Germany and in all of Europe. We were told that the victims of the "holy" Inquisition suffered in the rooms beneath this church. There, their hands were cut off, tongues were cut off, blood vessels were pulled out... and we, looking around the church, sensed within ourselves, as if some unseen evil force still lived there. The walls were dark, and the icons on them were even darker. We could not hear any sound anywhere, nothing even rustled. Everywhere there was only depressing silence like inside a grave. We were told that the king[197] from Chiemsee palace came to this church in a boat, which was rowed by oarsmen who were using oars that were gilded with gold. The bishop would meet him at the shore and respectfully lead him into the church. The king would make confession, take communion and then he would shoot at his prisoners in the hunting field... we looked at all this and sighed deeply. Lord, what evil times there used to be! Thousands of people were lost then in horrible sufferings at the hands of "Saint" Loyola[198] and now thousands of people were lost by ungodly regimes. But what was the difference between those executioners? There wasn't any. The only difference was that the present-day executioners are condemned by the world, but in various churches many naïve people still pray to those other murderers. They kiss their frightening portraits unaware of the fact that the suffering of innocents in present-day Osviciem or Dachau cannot compare to the suffering caused by the terrible Catholic Inquisition. But the greatest tragedy was that their suffering was carried out "in the name of Christ".

---

197 King Ludwig II (Mad King Ludwig)
198 St. Ignatius of Loyala, founder of the Jesuits

We left that church, we left Chiemsee Palace and sailed to the shore across the beautiful shining lake on which were growing a variety of yellow and white flowers. From the small station we returned to Munich and then to Frille.

The final large conference of the Ukrainian Evangelical-Baptist Church took place from June 12-14, 1949 in the city of Munich. Many guests from all over Germany still attended this conference but many Ukrainian believers were missing because they were already across the ocean. This conference had an atmosphere of a farewell conference because many of our people already had affidavits and were waiting to leave. I believe that the vice-president of the Ukrainian Evangelical-Baptist Church, brother M. Tesluk, left from the conference directly to the airport and from there he went to the USA. Those who remained continued the conference. There was also a large young people's service with the participation of F.K. Shatz, a representative of the World Baptist Alliance.

The Ukrainian Evangelical-Baptist Church began a wonderful spiritual ministry and carried it out with much success. But this was also the time when emigration across the ocean was beginning; therefore, under those circumstances the work slowed down. After brother Stepan Nischik departed to Canada, brother D. Marichuk became the leader of the Ukrainian Evangelical-Baptist Church; when he left, other brothers occupied this position, but the ministry never stopped. Even after a large majority left Germany, other people took over the work of the Ukrainian Evangelical-Baptist Church within the camps of Germany. There was even a magazine, *Holos Prawdy*[199] which was being published by brother S. Tymciw, who at one time was the head of Ukrainian Evangelical-Baptist Church in Germany until he came to Canada in 1962.

---

199 Voice of Truth

Brother D. Marichuk,
later leader of the Ukr. Ev.-Baptist Church

All the members of the Slavic Union and the Ukrainian Evangelical-Baptist Church contributed their energies and whatever resources they had and the ministry among the refugees in Germany continued, although it was significantly reduced. The exception was the Bible School where students continued to study. There were courses for future preachers, occasional courses for Sunday School teachers, for women and for young people. Especially beneficial were courses in choir directing which our directors led. We were all aware that this knowledge was no longer essential in Germany, because emigration was not far away and we had no visions for the success of our work here. At the same time we also knew that our path was leading us across the ocean where every bit of knowledge would be needed among us. We were not mistaken in this, because many of those individuals who received the appropriate preparation in Germany, are today working among our people in all the world.

The young people of the Ukrainian Evangelical-Baptist Church in Munich at Christmas 1947

Our large congregation in Ludensheid, and later in Frille, experienced many happy celebrations and uplifting moments during its time in Germany, but it was in God's will to also send sadness. A time of great sadness happened on May 14th, 1948 when our young brother, Andronik Melnyk, a fervent member of our congregation and dedicated student at the Bible School in Frille, unexpectedly became sick and died.

Brother Andronik Melnyk was a committed worker in the evangelical field while he was still in Poland, but especially in Volyn. During the war he ended up in Warsaw where he got married and helped in the ministry there. When we, as a large group from Warsaw, left Poland, brother Melnyk and his wife were with us. We worked together in different German factories, we hungered together and together we endured our difficult, unrelenting destiny. Later we were together in one camp and in one congregation. Brother A. Melnyk had a sincere Christian heart, lived in complete harmony and love with everyone and never offended anyone. When he unexpectedly became ill and died, leaving his loving wife, our whole congregation was enveloped in deep grief. The believers attended the funeral in large numbers and buried him in the city of Munich, not far from our camp. His funeral was a time of great sadness, but at the same time it was filled with hope in the life to come. If we remain faithful to the Lord, as brother Andronik was faithful, then we shall meet him again with the Lord.

**Brother Andronik Melnyk,
a student at the Bible School in Frille
Passed away on April 14th, 1948**

Andronik Melnyk died when I was already in Canada. We were friends from pre-war times; therefore the news about his death was very distressing for me.

EMIGRATION

As everything in the world comes to some kind of an end and every situation and problem is resolved in some way, so also our life in the German refugee camps came to an end. Each one of us continuously dreamed about departing, each one was planning something, carrying out different activities and making efforts, but it was not yet the time because we were all still in our places. Then suddenly the news spread throughout the camp that emigration will begin shortly. We strained our hearing and our attention. Was it truly so? And if so, then who will go first and where?

The news came to us from the American zone that lists were already being prepared in many camps for anyone wishing to leave for any place. Several brothers from our camp went to investigate if this was true. Yes it was true. Look at how wonderful the Americans were! Not like the English!

Evangelical-Baptist congregation of Lintorf.
Leader –brother Ivan Pidhoretsky

It was discovered that there were already many from the American zone who were ready to go to South America as long as they could get their names on an emigration list as soon as possible. But just before the emigration, various formalities made the transfer from one camp to another more difficult and so we all had to remain where we were. This again revealed the character and inclination of many of us. When the elder brethren from the Slavic Union executive had invited those who were preachers to go out to other camps for spiritual ministry, not very many individuals were found who were willing to go. But when the matter was to travel across the ocean, then there were many were ready to leave a large congregation and a significant fellowship of believers in Frille just to end up on an emigration list and depart to who knows where. None of us fully understood emigration in its full light; none of us knew what awaited us in England, Canada, America or in Australia. We never considered then that we would be bitterly longing for our fellowship. We were all rushing to get across the ocean, to put an end to this abnormal life and the daily waiting for the unknown.

I remember that the first enrollment to go to England took place in our camp. Our leading brother announced this during the service and the following day many went to the office to sign up. Several Polish government officials were sitting there and compiling long lists. Without asking any questions, they wrote down the names of everyone who came as long as the people had a desire to go. I, as well as many of the brothers and sisters, also added our names to the list. As soon as we left the office some kind of fear and uncertainty gripped our souls. We had a desire to go but it was a pity to leave such a large congregation. Our hearts had come to a crossroad.

**Members of the congregation in Frille
who were the first to register for the departure to England.**
From left to right: M. Podworniak, I. Barchuk.
S. Yankowsky, S. Nischik, S. Bychkowski and I. Tarasiuk

On Sunday, as usual, our large choir sang under the leadership of brother S. Bychkowski. All the singers looked at our director with sadness as if they were seeing him for the last time, because he had also signed up to depart for England. The brethren preached the word, intimating that the time was not far away when we would no longer be together, as many of the ladies wiped tears from their eyes. The impression was forming that we were no longer one congregation; that those who were the first to register to go to England did not belong to this congregation any longer. They were already on their way to leave and soon they would no longer be here. I can remember that service even now. I can still see in my mind the sad faces of my dear brothers and sisters of our large family. During that time each one of us felt some kind of pain within our soul, some unexpressed apprehension, because truly we all acutely realized that our time of separation was not too distant. We would be scattered all over the world and with many we would never meet again. And that is what later happened. Nobody at that time knew that brother F. Sitarz would go to Brazil where he would die before his time, that brother N. Nowichewsky would also die prematurely somewhere near New York, brother Skorobahaty would die in distant Australia. Although we did not know this fully, but in our hearts we felt that this would happen.

After some time it was announced that all prepared lists to go to England were cancelled. Only single young men and women would be allowed to go. Families would have to wait, remain in their places and await further orders. We, who were family people, sadly lowered our heads as the single people began to prepare for their trip.

Outside the weather was sunny and beautiful. Many of our people gathered beside the Lutheran church in Frille. Today there would be a farewell service for the first of our emigrants who were leaving to England. Everyone was in a despondent mood, with sad faces. It had begun ... The ice had broken and the flow of water was gaining strength. Nobody could stop it now. What we had waited for such a *long-long* time had happened. The emigration had begun and our farewell services had begun.

The large church filled up with people because believers had come from Frille, from Weitersheim and Ladhe. Brother F. Lewchuk, the pastor of our congregation, went behind the pulpit. He spoke a word to those who would be leaving us today and going into the faraway world. He reminded them about what is the most important thing, that they are children of God and that is what they should be in the places where they were going. His voice broke off in the middle of his message and he could not speak farther. Throughout the pews could be heard the soft crying of the women. The choir majestically broke into a thunderous song beneath the high vault of the church. It resounded not only inside the church, but also in our hearts, filling them with deep longing and pain. The song, *Moya meta daleko za rikoyu*[200], was sung for the first time in Frille and later sung at all the farewell services.

---

200 "My destination is far across the river". Words by M. Podworniak, music, by S. Bychkowski. *Ridna Pisnya*, No. 88

The following morning, before the dew had yet dried from the trees, we were all hurrying to the wide crossroad in Frille, where the office of our camp was located. Large open military vehicles were already standing there and beside them were the single young men and women, our first emigrants to England. We surrounded them in a tight circle. All the brethren from the church committee were there as well as the women with their children. They all came to say farewell and to look for a final time at one another. Who knows if we will ever meet again? The world is so wide and spacious with so many places to drift apart and lose one another.

Choir directors' courses in Schwarzenborn under the leadership of brothers S. Bychkowski and Ivan Polischuk.

The secretary came out of the office, read out all the names and the truck engines started. Our brothers and sisters climbed up into the open vehicles as we handed them their luggage. We gave them our hands and our warm hearts. We looked again for a final time into their tear-stained faces, we touched their hands one more time and the vehicles began to move.

"Have a blessed trip! Go with God! ... Write. Don't forget! ...Go with God! ...

Somebody began the song, "Shall We Gather at the River." We sang the first stanza and the chorus but by then our departing emigrants could no longer hear us because the vehicles had picked up speed, turned a curve and disappeared behind the bushes.

"Have a blessed trip!"

I returned to my place of lodging and for some reason it now seemed very large and empty. A table stood in the corner where we worked together on the magazine, *Doroha Prawdy*. But now there was not even one sheet of paper on it and it was not evident with whom I will now be working since many of my co-workers had already left. Feeling sad, I went to Lahde to pick up my mail. The path, which went close to a narrow stream, was trampled down like cement. Clumps of willows were growing beside the stream and beyond the willows stretched long German fields with carrots and onions. Some kind of yearning filled my heart, an unspoken longing for something and for some reason I was deeply aware of being in a distant foreign land. Others were leaving, and someday I also will depart; but not to my home but into another more distant foreign land. Who knows if there I would see such a beautiful sky as in my homeland, if I would hear the song of the quail and the nightingale? In general, will I experience with my whole being that which I had left behind at home?

On Sunday there was again a large service, but many places in the church were already empty. We received a bulletin from the Slavic Union, as well as from the UEBC and we noted that in many congregations farewell services were taking place. Everywhere they were singing *Moya meta daleko ze rikoyu* as believers were gradually departing into emigration. The same thing was happening in both the English and American zones. Some were going to England, others to Australia, still others to Canada, to the United States of America, to Brazil, Argentina, Venezuela ... Our large refugee family was splintering, dispersing into the whole world. And not one of us spoke even once about our past life and completed journey, although there was much to remember. We will all carry in the storehouse of our hearts that which we had experienced and suffered, whether it was bitter or sweet. The bitter, of course, will be forgotten, erased by new impressions and experiences, but the sweet will remain in the soul.

Although emigration was in full swing, the ministry in the camps did not slow down. Those who were left behind sensed their responsibility to continue the work and they carried out this responsibility conscientiously and sincerely.

Several transition camps were created in the English zone for those who were departing to go across the ocean. Occasionally our believers were in these camps where they sometimes lived for weeks awaiting the completion of their documents. They took advantage of their stay in these camps to preach the Gospel. The leadership of the camps was more than willing to allow our brethren to use some kind of a hall where evangelical services could take place. The people within these camps, who did not have anything to do, gladly came to the services. In the end there were quite a few of the listeners who still heard the preaching on German soil and were converted to the Lord.

Life for our congregation in Frille continued at its normal pace. Regular services continued, although there were fewer members now. Many already had their affidavits and sat on their suitcases and waited. An abundant shower of affidavits came from America. Many brothers worked in this matter, especially brothers N. Lukianchuk, the late brother I. Neprash, the late brother W. Shibanow and many others. The affidavits for the Ukrainians came from the Ukrainian Missionary Society in Canada and the USA. A large migration had begun, our large "exodus from Babylon".

An affidavit from Canada was lying at the very bottom of my suitcase. But I still had not received an order to go to a transition camp therefore I sat patiently and waited. I knew that the order would come but it was not evident when. I published the next issue of our sparse refugee magazine, I distributed it and there was my notification. Get ready to leave immediately for a transition camp near Hanover; I believe it was to Diepholz. This was the autumn of 1947, and this happened so suddenly that I became disorganized and was even unable to say goodbye to everybody.

First members of the congregation in Frille leaving to England

Our large cargo truck drove past Ladhe. I still saw the post office building for the final time where I would come almost every day for letters and newspapers. I saw the large railroad station, the shining Weser River with its thick spruce forest on the opposite side. For some reason I felt sorry for these places where I had spent such a long time. Many times I was hungry here, many times my soul was crushed by my life in a foreign land, but all this was forgotten. Only pleasant memories remained in my heart: the fellowship enjoyed with fellow believers, memories of the different trips, and memories of my personal family life. With those precious acquisitions I could now continue further. Three years ago I was going into a foreign land all alone, like a single blade of grass in a field but now I was not alone. I already had my own family. I was now going as one who was familiar with such travel – without a plan and without any clear purpose. The awareness that our abnormal camp lifestyle was finally coming to an end filled my soul with satisfaction but a second realization that we were going farther and farther from my homeland, filled my soul with inconsolable sadness.

The transition camp was located in some small wooden barracks which were overfilled with various people who were all waiting for their exit papers to be completed.

We were assigned to a small room where there were several wooden bunk beds on which emigrants like us were sleeping. They slept during the night and they slept during the day, because there was nothing else to do and sleeping made the time go faster. Brother S. Nischik was the last person to visit us in this camp. In the camp we became acquainted with many German Mennonites who were also going to Canada.

Ukrainian Evangelical-Baptist Church Conference in Munich (June 10-13, 1948)

From there we were transferred to a larger Polish transition camp near Hamburg. It was cold outside and the first snow mixed with rain was falling. The camp near Hamburg was large, surrounded with a high wall. At the gate stood a uniformed Polish soldier and above him two flags were flapping in the wind: an English and a Polish one.

Our vehicle entered a wide courtyard. A Polish officer showed us to a large red building and told us to occupy it. People rushed to claim empty rooms, looking for a good location. However, before I had gathered together my suitcases and small child, the rooms were already occupied. There only remained for us a large empty hall beside the entrance without a bed or a table. One window was broken and wind and snow were blowing through it. The door into the corridor was half-broken and did not close.

Evening came. We closed the broken window with some rags and sat silently on the dirty floor. Suddenly a Polish soldier entered the room and unscrewed the only small electric bulb. I went up to him.

"Please sir, we need to have light, we have a small child with us. Could the gentleman leave the light bulb?"

"This is my light bulb. There is an order here that everyone must have their own light bulb."

"That is fine, but will the gentleman come here and we will buy it."

The soldier thought about something and then grumbled:

"Five marks."

I gave him five German marks and he left.

The light bulb stayed with us, hardly blinking above the window but we were happy with that because at least we could see one another. Our small son cried all the time; he wanted to eat, but there wasn't any place where we could warm up some milk for him.

After a moment a second soldier arrived, bringing with him an old chair, which he placed underneath our electric light.

"Sir, what are you doing? That is our light bulb. We just bought it," I said.

The soldier paused.

"Whom did you buy it from?"

"I don't know, from some soldier."

"Sir, don't pretend to be an idiot. You could not buy it because it's my light bulb." He began to unscrew the light bulb.

Somehow I was able to persuade him, gave him some coffee and the light remained in its corner.

The soldier left and we began to wonder if perhaps a third owner of that poor light bulb would appear. It was not clear where we had arrived and what we had to do in our helpless situation. I was ready to go out and look for someone in charge, but my wife was afraid to be left alone in the large semi-dark room. Somewhere on the other side of the wall drunken voices could be heard and the irregular strumming of a guitar. We could go together with the child, but it was frightening to leave our belongings. We sat like that until morning. Nobody else came for the light bulb.

In the morning I went to the camp office and explained our situation to the Polish officer. He transferred us to a different building and gave us a separate room. In the room there was an old table, a chair with three legs, and a metal bed, which was leaning against the wall. Although, there was only a rusty spring without a mattress on the bed, it nevertheless was a bed and it was possible to lay the child down.

In the morning we were given some black German *ersatz*-coffee from the kitchen, a small loaf of bread and some soup made from split barley. I brought all of this to our room. We drank the coffee, but could not eat the soup. It was so disgusting, that in all my time in Germany, during the time of Hitler and the war, I had never tasted such a soup.

We stayed in that harsh transition camp beside Hanover for about two or three weeks. We considered that this was truly "purgatory" before we made our way across the ocean. We were hungry for all those days, enduring the worst needs and longings. Our son became sick and was taken to a hospital; my wife left to take care of the child. I remained by myself in the camp, counting long and endless days. The believers in Frille learned of our situation and sent brother Andronik Melnyk (he died after our departure) who brought us not only words of comfort, but also brought us money and food. I will never forget that generous act by my dear friends.

My wife and son returned from the hospital and we awaited our further destiny. In the camp we became acquainted with a young Polish man. He was from near Przemysl and he became our constant guest. He dressed in a long military overcoat with the collar always turned up. He was a totally illiterate person who worried a great deal about how he would present himself before the Canadian consulate, which required that every emigrant would be able to read. Wasyl, that was his name, came to me every day and I taught him to read. Unfortunately nothing developed from our studying, because all the letters that he learned on one day, Wasyl had already forgotten by the following day. However, later he somehow remembered the letters but when it was necessary to combine the letters into a word, Wasyl was unable to help himself. The time was getting short and we had to hurry.

Mother's Day celebration at the Ukr. Ev.-Baptist congregation in Cologne-Milheim. Leader – Brother H. Domashovetz

One morning Wasyl ran to me, very happy and satisfied. As he stepped through the doorway he loudly announced to the entire room:

"*Paneh, paneh*[201], I have news! Everything is going to be fine."

I could not understand anything but later Wasyl explained that he had gone to the office and requested a translator from the Canadian consulate so that somehow she would help him. She gave him the following advice: he would not have to know how to read but he could memorize several sentences and be able to recite them from memory. If the consul gave him something to read during the exam then he could look at the book and recite what he knew. The consul did not understand anything in Polish anyway.

Wasyl happily walked about my room and spoke with satisfaction:

"*Paneh*, when that happens, then it will be wonderful! And in Canada, we will see. Perhaps I will still learn to read. But nevertheless, it might not matter. I have already survived thirty-two years without that..."

---

201 Polish for "sir, sir"

The following day Wasyl brought a first-grade Polish reader and we began "to study". I read slowly and Wasyl repeated after me: *Wiosna slonko grzeje i skowroneki spiewaja.*[202]

**Baptism at the Ukr. Ev.-Baptist Church in Kornberg.
Leader – brother O. Harbuziuk**

In three days Wasyl learned to recite and wherever he went he whispered, *wiosna slonko grzeje...* He said that he would wake up in the night and repeat the same words, because this was the only thing that would save him from a difficult situation. There was no longer any time to really learn how to read because in several days we might be called to the consulate.

Later when we came to the consulate, Wasyl was standing in line behind us. He was pale and kept repeating all the time, *wiosna slonko grzeje...* We were the first to be called and then we were let out through a different door and returned to our accommodation. We were delighted beyond measure ... on our documents there was the stamp of the Canadian consul and his long-drawn-out signature. We were accepted for departure. We had in our hands the required documents and a visa. We prayed in our small room and thanked God.

---

202 The spring sun is warming and the larks are singing

After a few minutes Wasyl ran into the room. His face was all red and his eyes were full of tears. He threw himself at me and almost kissed me.

"*Paneh*, everything is good! Thank God! The translator gave me a book and when I began to read everyone just looked at me... They would not even allow me to finish speaking. But it certainly was very difficult and sweat was pouring down..."

The following day we left the camp, but Wasyl was left behind to wait for the next transport. He accompanied us past the gate and all the time he was looking down at the ground if perhaps there might be a cigarette butt lying anywhere. He liked to smoke and if he did not have any tobacco, he smoked whatever leaves he could find as long as there was smoke. When I asked him to quit that evil, Wasyl looked at me regretfully as if I wanted to take away from him that which was most precious to him. Then sadly he would say:

"*Paneh*, my greatest happiness—is to smoke! When I get to Canada, then I don't want anything except to have this smoke!"

I was sad about my unexpected acquaintance; he had a good heart. He had endured difficult times as a German prisoner, but he was a bigger prisoner to tobacco. In the short time that we knew each other, I could not rescue him from that terrible mire.

It was night. We were traveling by train, seated in warm cars and eagerly looking out through the windows, hoping to see at least something. But outside the window it was night and a light rain was drizzling on the dark windowpanes. We were told that soon we would be crossing the Holland border and then we will be travelling through Holland. A multitude of thoughts arose. There were good and gentle young men from Holland who were working with us in Rüdersdorf. If they had known that we would be passing through their land, perhaps they would have come and met us. Somewhere here in Holland there lived a well-known evangelical leader, de Geer, the author of an influential book "The Final Judgment of Nations" which was published in Russian before the war. However nobody was aware that we were here and so we silently passed through.

Our train halted its progress. We saw a small nice-looking station where there were friendly Dutch pre-border guards, who were standing there waiting for us. We went through an inspection of our documents and a casual inspection of our carry-on luggage and again we took our places on the train. We were moving and again we were looking through the windows trying to see at least a small patch of Dutch territory. Night overtook us as our eyes continued to search without success for something. Before dawn, when it became light, I was able to actually see several windmills, which were waving their wings as if they were trying to fly away somewhere.

At a Dutch port we were given a good breakfast. The room was spacious and bright. It had been a long time since we saw before us on a table white bread, butter, a fork and a napkin. We had forgotten that these items still existed somewhere in the world. We deeply sensed that we were also Europeans and not *auslanders*[203]. In the hall there were many tables covered with white tablecloths, many flowers, leafy green palms and many different people who were speaking various languages. But we could not hear our language as we sat there like mice underneath a broom...

We were not allowed to explore the wonderful Dutch port as we immediately begin embarking on a ship. All the time I had this feeling that we were not really going to Canada but this was all *otak sobi*[204]. At each new inspection it felt as if they would find something missing in the documents, something would happen and we would be told to return to Germany. And then it would be a great calamity and a great loss.

When we got onboard the ship my doubts began to disperse. Perhaps we would actually sail. It is almost impossible to believe that God blessed us unworthy people with such a great enormous grace.

In the morning the weather was fair and the glistening ocean appeared endlessly smooth. We stood on the ramp for a final time look at the Dutch shore. Our ship jerked and swayed. The people on the shore began waving their hands, their hats, and kerchiefs. Although all these people were foreign to us, but we felt that they were also saying farewell to us and wishing us a safe journey.

---

203 foreigners or outsiders
204 that's how it is

Refugee believers leaving from Ingolstadt to Canada

The ship drew away from the shore. Flocks of white sea birds circled above us with mournful cries. We stood in the doorway of our cabin and I thought:

"Thus far the Lord has helped us."[205]

We crossed La Manche[206] and along the way we became so sick that we were almost unconscious. We could barely disembark in England and if we were not holding onto each other, we would have fallen to the ground.

Some very large buses were waiting and took us to London. There was a very thick fog and we were unable to see anything, and because of that not a single image of England was stored in my memory. We were only thinking about the fact that somewhere here were many of our believers who had recently left Germany. They were not aware that we were here otherwise; they certainly would have come. Somewhere here was I. Tarasiuk, P. Ulaniuk, L. Pidhoretsky and others for whom recently we had a farewell

---
205 1 Samuel 7:12
206 English Channel

service in Frille and for whom we had sung *Moya meta daleko za rikoyu*. Now we are also travelling towards that goal about which we had dreamed and for which we had strived.

The only thing we saw in London were the tall double-decker buses which drove on the left side of the road and it seemed to us that a catastrophe could happen at any moment.

From London we travelled by bus through a thick oak forest and then across a field, where there was a large herd of sheep grazing. Occasionally we saw ruined buildings beside the road and we were told that these were ruins resulting from German airstrikes.

We later stopped beside a forest and drank some strong tea with milk. I walked in the forest and *thought-thought* about England. This nation was the cradle of Protestantism, here the Baptist and International Bible Society was located, here lived the great preacher C. Spurgeon, here worked George Müller, here occurred a great spiritual revival. The entire Christian world is indebted much to England.

In the morning we were already at the English port of Southampton. We waited in an enormous hall and then we went through a final inspection of our documents as my heart beat rapidly for a final time. What if they find something missing in the documents? What next?

Through the clear windows of the hall we could see a large ship and after a short time we were led to it. Here, one more time, they inspected our visa, and once again we were needlessly agitated and fearful.

And then we were inside the warm ship's room. We exhaled slightly and had no words to say anything. We longed only to be silent and think once more about all that we would be leaving behind us, to remember the paths we had walked and with humble hearts to thank God for everything. How good and merciful He was to us. He brought us through the fire and the storm and never left us.

******

There was deep night over the ocean, but above us there was bright sky where millions of stars twinkled. How wonderful it is that there is a heaven above the earth and in those times when it is dark here we can lift our eyes up high! To the light…to the stars…

We had already sailed from the shore, but its lights were visible for a long distance. With every moment they were becoming fainter and fainter, drowning in the deep ocean.

I stood on the deck of the ship, leaning on the cold railing and for some reason I felt sad about the life I had gone through. It was sad and tumultuous because it all happened during these challenging times. I thought of my far away home, my mother, my brothers and all the believers. I thought of Warsaw, the war, Germany ... These were memories of my whole life until now.

The ship swayed gently. Faraway from the shore, which we had left, the last glimmer of light flickered. Wistful and worried, I looked at it as I had never looked at anything in my life. With every minute and every second it became fainter...

I stood with my head hung low, wiped my teary eyes and fervently prayed:

"Lord, send your light and your blessing on this our, one more long road!..."

APPENDICES

APPENDIX 1

Матусю рідненька, ти бачиш, весна
У квіті своїм наступила!
Мені на чужину квітки принесла,
І згадки в душі відродила.

Пригадую зараз минулу весну, —
З тобою тополі саджала;
"Нехай виростають і втіху несуть", -
Мені ти, матусю, казала.

Пташок щебетання і свято весни
Я й тут, на чужині, зустріла:
Привітно всміхається сонце згори,
І квітка в траві засиніла.

Блакитні і ніжні фіялки зірву.
На спогад про весну залишу,
Згадаю при цьому твою я журбу,
І хати рідненької тишу...

Зів'януть фіялки, і згублять свій цвіт,
Їх хочу я все ж заховати.
Щоб в кращім майбутнім, як змінить світ
Цю весну ще раз пригадати.

Рідненька матусю, прийми мій привіт!
Хай лине, мов пташка, весною!

Бажала б весняний я пишний розквіт
Ще раз поділити з тобою...

Від щирого серця бажаю тобі
Тепер, коли все воскресає,--
Хай серце твоє у теплі весняним
Надію на краще плекає.

--Л. Лазарева

APPENDIX 2

Не расскажет ручей говорливый
Никому моей тайны святой;
По полям и лесам молчаливым
Пробежит он холодной струей

Не расскажет, что воды слыхали
Моей тайны великой души
Когда тело мое погружалось
При крещеньи в полночной тиши.

Я от мира сего отрекался,
Обет Богу в крещеньи давал
Жить по Слову Его обещался,
Я душою в Христе — ликовал!

В час полночный, при лунном сияньи,
Совершался священный обет
При блаженном, святом упованьи
Получил я от Бога ответ.

И молитве священной внимая,
Что неслася от вод к небесам
Миром душу мою наполняя
Благодать Бог мне в серце послал.

Тот поток был свидетель безмолвный
Моей тайны великой, святой,
Когда чистые, светлые воды
Над моею прошли головой

Не забыть мне ручей одинокий,
Когда сяду на берег весной
На тот берег зеленый, прекрасный,
Где завет заключил Бог со мной